Building an
Information Security
Awareness Program

Building an Information Security Awareness Program

MARK B. DESMAN

CRC Press
Taylor & Francis Group
Boca Raton London New York

CRC Press is an imprint of the
Taylor & Francis Group, an **informa** business

AN AUERBACH BOOK

CRC Press
Taylor & Francis Group
6000 Broken Sound Parkway NW, Suite 300
Boca Raton, FL 33487-2742

First issued in hardback 2017

ISBN-13: 978-0-8493-0116-2 (pbk)
ISBN-13: 978-1-138-43698-5 (hbk)

Library of Congress Card Number 2001037869

Library of Congress Cataloging-in-Publication Data
Desman, Mark B.
Building an information security awareness program / Mark B. Desman.
p. cm.
Includes index.
ISBN 0-8493-0116-5 (alk. paper)
1. Computer security. 2. Data protection. I. Title.
QA76.9.A25 D47 2001
005.8—dc21   2001037869
CIP

Visit the Taylor & Francis Web site at
http://www.taylorandfrancis.com

and the CRC Press Web site at
http://www.crcpress.com

Dedication

To Candy, who always wanted me to write this book.
I wish you could be here to share it.

Table of Contents

Introduction

So, you have just been named information security officer for the corporation. Please allow me to be the first to congratulate you on your good fortune and the company's wisdom in selecting you for the position. They have made an excellent choice and you have shown that you can do the job. The only thing left to do is to define the job and reconvince the people who hired you that the function actually requires their interest, cooperation, and yes, even funding.

What you are embarking on is the most frustrating role in current information systems (IS) staffing. You will be expected to do big things with minimal staff, low budget, and only grudging compliance by those all the way up to your own overall department. You will be asked to change habits as old as the company and protect against on-going and on-growing threats with single decisive strokes and little interest in evolving your solutions as the enemy evolves. You will be subjected to auditors' inquiries and "tsk, tsks" when they discover issues that you know exist, but cannot make the time or come up with the money to resolve. (Later on in this book, we will talk about making the auditors your allies and turning their findings into advantages.) You will be summoned by senior management — either directly or through the command chain — when one of them has finally heard or read about a threat you have been losing sleep over for the past 15 months. They will immediately demand to know what you are doing about it and how soon a remedy can be in place. Then, having demonstrated their concern, they will quietly return to the paneled offices and, most likely, will never bring up the subject again, congratulating themselves on the discovery and how they mobilized the organization for remedy, retaliation, mitigation, and so on (choose the word you like best) against the threat.

On top of having more work than you can do, needing more tools than you can afford, and stemming the tide of issues that would daunt even the Little Dutch Boy of legend, you will have helpful friends, colleagues, and even entry-level personnel contacting you about hoax viruses that they are sure you have never seen before. With any kind of luck, they'll come directly to you and get an explanation before they e-mail the civilized world with their words of warning.

It is the aim of this book to arm you against the alien forces (both internal and external) and show you ways to leverage even the most difficult situation to your advantage. To be sure, not all the information given will be applicable in all situations, but applied correctly, it will aid you in becoming more efficient in your work and in getting others to carry the banner as well.

In the past 15 years, American business has discovered the potential for disaster that loss, damage, or compromise of their owned or held information represents. The issue has lived for at least double that time, but having someone responsible for protecting said information has only surfaced since about the late '70s.

Yeah, I know, information security as an IS discipline has been around since the early '70s. We have had formal organizations and position descriptions for as long as many of us have been in the industry. During the formative years, the position actually was the red herring that IS management trotted out for the auditors. "Sure, we have someone working on that," was the standard comment. "Hey (insert name here)," come on over and meet our external auditors." You met them, told them of your grand schemes, and they went away, happy that this company was forward-thinking enough to have not just identified a position, but staffed it. Never mind that info security was another duty added onto what you were actually getting paid for, they did have someone assigned to the work.

Sure, there was someone assigned, but he or she operated with no budget, no scheduled time to address security issues, and few or no tools with which to approach the problem area. But, as stated earlier, "We have someone working on that."

"Working on it" meant going to the Computer Security Institute (CSI) annual conference, when annual dues were less than the cost of a book today, joining a few hundred colleagues, eagerly discussing what was coming along in the industry — release 1.2 of IBM's RACF, the new kid on the block; ACF2 and the dangers of magnets, power surges, and outsiders somehow getting to an online terminal bolted to the mainframe in question. A few good ideas were presented and some exchanged, and you could get in touch with a handful of vendors who presented clunky, resource-chewing remedies for your professional nightmares. Then, each of us went home, our heads still filled with the good ideas we had picked up at the conference, and walked directly back into reality. Production had to be run, no one wanted to be bothered with changing passwords, and your function, viewed as pure overhead, went back to "Working on it."

Only when the Foreign Corrupt Practices Act of 1977 was translated for business by their lawyers, and the top echelon of the company learned that they could be held responsible for loss or damage of information assets, did their interest rise to the level needed. Funny how the prospect of a few years in a publicly owned establishment, protected from the rabble by 15-foot chain link fences festooned with crowns of razor ribbon, caught their attention.

My 20-odd years in the industry really do demonstrate more than the excellent tolerance for frustration that I possess. That period of time has gone from your biggest concern being that the I/O clerk shuts the window after accepting the card deck from the programmer, to finding ways to secure a network that might go through several technologies, time zones, and even countries. Rather than have information centered in monolithic mainframes with hardwired terminals attached to them, we have both wired and wireless intelligent devices all over the world (actually, as well as figuratively) that communicate with our systems via private, shared, and even public communications media. The information no longer resides in a single room that can be secured, guarded, and isolated from all and sundry. Today, we have servers in computer centers, offices, and closets, with the ability to move entire files across communications lines among them and the end users with utter alacrity. Now, we have to watch the integrity of our data, not only in multiple locations, but also in an environment that changes before our eyes.

As has always been the case, talking to the nuts and bolts systems specialists about security is preaching to the choir. These are the folks who recognized the need and developed the position into which you have just been plunked. They chafe at the idea of being slowed by log-in processes, password change schedules, endless backups, and recovery exercises, but they — grudgingly at times — understand the need.

The user community, on the other hand, may range from sophisticated power users to clerks who approach a terminal or PC with trepidation and outright fear. Like it or not, information handling is a desktop issue now, rather than being limited to the computer room. Even that senior executive, the one who used to refer to "those computer people" and profess his ignorance of what miracles they wrought, now generates his own reports at his desk rather than through production control. Do not try to blow smoke at him now, he has taken control. If his knowledge of things computer based is even fractionally as poor as he states, his office has just become ground zero for risk. He will print those reports as certainly as he has learned to run them on his own and he will leave them secure in his office, available to no one but the janitors who come in at night, the recyclers who join them, and any vendor, competitor, or other individual who might happen to be in that office that day or night. But, he knows it is secure, it's in the boss's office.

Recall that I mentioned how information was in constant motion today and could pop up in locations undisciplined by international borders or natural limitations? And, along that rocky trail reside the end users of our information. Today, they may be company employees, vendors, contractors, subsidiary employees, customers, or just interested bystanders. No longer do we have control of terminal location, security precautions at remote locations, or the nature and moral sense of whoever might be perusing what is on the screen or coming off the DeskJet.

As mentioned, the proliferation of information has created an environment where the caretakers of the data themselves may well turn into the biggest threat against it. They will often respond as though the convenience in accessing it has removed some of the impetus on protecting it. If it is that readily available, they reason, it must not be that big a deal to leave lying around. Unwittingly, they will walk away from a highly privileged terminal without logging off, they will dump a sensitive report that has already served their purpose into the most convenient waste receptacle — usually the trash can under their respective desks — without a second thought, to go forward from there to seed the dumpster divers' greatest dreams.

Another area of concern, taking into consideration the examples noted above, is the action of those lower in the organization or even those performing menial services under contract. These are often the least privileged (in terms of systems access) people in the plant — clerks, janitors, and service people — yet to perform their duties, they have unlimited access to every area of the physical building or buildings. Perhaps your competitors need not pay a sophisticated industrial spy to thoroughly destroy your competitive advantage. They may be able to do it for minimum wage and a few hundred extra.

The rank and file will do as they have always done, find the shortest route to completing their assigned tasks. To be sure, there will be budding superstars among them, but do not count on them as aids in times of need. The majority will bypass security measures if it makes their work easier and will be off to lunch at exactly the right time, without concern for putting away the report they were working on or logging off or locking their terminal. And for the most part, if they get off at 5:00 PM and you want to talk to them at 5:00:15, you will have missed them by 12 seconds. No way the same shut-down elements will be discussed on their own time.

As can be seen from this brief description of the environment you are moving into, the world is not a bright and shiny place. I have been intentionally hard on the people you will come into contact with daily, as their worst characteristics are the ones that figure to cause you the most brain damage. Most of them are intelligent, dedicated, and absolutely honest. What they do not realize is the consequence of their actions. They do not realize it, because no one has taken the time nor put forth the effort to show them. That, in a nutshell, is the reason for this book.

As I mentioned earlier, I have been in this business since the days of the IBM 360 mainframes and have continued as we evolved through more sophisticated communications technology and have gravitated to more powerful, decentralized systems. Today, we have servers with many times the memory of the old mainframes that, within the constraints of single or multi-CPU architecture, are capable of churning out what was once considered mainframe levels of cycles. To be sure, the mainframes have grown in capacity while shrinking their footprints, but the capabilities of desktop or rack-sized boxes have grown exponentially. Now, the information is no longer attached to the network, it is on the network. The network itself has gone from hardwiring within a single building to worldwide capabilities that may hop from private lines to VPNs to satellite transmission with absolute ease, rarely leaving a trail as to its route.

To get an idea as to how things have changed and in how short a time, I will offer this little anecdote.

Some years ago, during my time with a large, international credit card organization, we built a new state of the art processing center in a major southwestern city. This place was as advanced as any in the country for the time — 1971 — and tours were proudly given. One of my duties was to take groups of data processors from other local companies through the data center to show off our technological advances. The centerpiece of the tour was the brand, spanking new IBM 370-168 that had onboard no less than 6 meg of "core memory." Imagine that in terms of today's processing. Imagine trying to get anything done with only 6 meg of memory in your desktop machine!

Today, of course, computer center tours are a thing of the past. What with environments ever changing and communications lines abounding, having additional folks walking through would be incredibly dangerous. A slight trip, brushing against on/off switches could cause considerable damage.

I point out these dramatic changes for a good reason. Remember the I/O window I referenced earlier? That was the big exposure in 1971. To keep it from being left open, you talked to the clerk. Today, that clerk does not exist. Instead, information comes and goes through myriad lines to innumerable destinations. The single choke point is a thing of the past. How, then, do we "talk" to all of the people who have replaced that single clerk?

One of the worthwhile accompaniments to the communications boom we now live with is the ability to use that same medium to get information to parties along the network. E-mail, broadcasts, Web-based news media, all are tools that we, as information security practitioners, can leverage.

In addition, the rapid expansion in size of companies through growth, mergers, and the introduction of new business lines has created the mega corporation and the need to get information to a lot of people in a lot of places, fast. What we are going to discuss is leveraging that capacity to get our work done.

Most companies today have media relations, publication, and even Web-publishing departments. In general, they are not IS departments but are run by corporate administration. These are the departments that have set up and maintain the channels of communication that we want to leverage (there's that word, again) to spread the gospel according to you!

This book is designed to convey all of the things I have learned in 23 years in this field. It is not a how-to book on information security nor a primer on tools or techniques for protecting information assets. What it does is put forth an orderly methodology for the development, implementation, and evaluation of a program that ensures that all persons entrusted with or exposed to your company's information are aware of the value of the information, their responsibility in protecting it, and the means by which they can do so. It involves establishing a presence that makes your means of communication a two-way street, one in which you receive information from those whom you are training. There is no magic bullet here: all of the techniques described require hard work and constant tuning for best performance.

Earlier I introduced the term *leveraging*, the technique we will most often use to describe taking advantage of other tools in place, causing new tools to be created, or hanging your message on the back of other communication. We will discuss the formation of teams to deal with specific types of threats and using their existence and performance to advance the cause of awareness.

Most of all, we will discuss the means to get the rank and file onboard, to realize the need for their compliance with information security measures, and the advantage they gain from "getting with the program."

The layout of the book is such that one can follow it end to end in establishing and augmenting a program or go to a specific chapter to gain insight into a single facet of the overall program. In all cases, we will try to provide a means for measuring its effectiveness. Finally, we will discuss the means necessary to make the auditors willing co-conspirators in the implementation of your program. I speak not only of the internal audit staff, but the third-party auditors, as well. If you are in the financial trades, the measures noted work with examiners, the Federal Home Loan Bank Board (FHLB), the Federal Reserve, or the Comptroller of the Currency. Each will provide you with the keys to getting your program off the ground. All you have to know is how to gain their cooperation and complicity.

Note: Although this passage suggests subterfuge at its worst, it is in no way that. The reviewers, be they internal or external auditors or regulatory agencies, will be looking for specific weakness in your schema of protection. Using that information in expanding your program is your task. If they can get their concerns met, then they have accomplished their goals. If you can get the required funding or resources to address their concerns, you win, as well. Hardly cause for concern.

I have arranged the chapters in the book in a continuum of how I would go about establishing a program were I starting from scratch within an organization for which I worked, either as an employee or a contractor. In most cases, the reader will have some subset of these provisions already in place. Perhaps they are functioning well, or perhaps they could use a tuneup. Hopefully, we will present the subject matter in a manner that will (A) allow for an evaluation as to how the measures are working or (B) offer some hints that might enhance their functionality.

The book is presented in four sections, with a subset of chapters within them. It begins with the very basis of a program and moves on into more and more complex issues. Specifically, the sections are:

Section 1: Getting Started

In this section we discuss getting the lay of the land. Somebody saw an issue, which is why you have been put into this position. Did they just decide that everyone else has an information security officer, so they should too, or was there recognition of a potential weakness in protecting corporate information assets? If they recognize the need, they have most certainly made some effort, no matter how basic, to install a program. Section 1 discusses how to find out what has been done, who is responsible for its inception, and the likelihood of its expansion into a viable program. It also discusses how to find out who the movers within the organization are. Sometimes it is easy to tell from their titles. Other times, it is not so clear. Once this is ascertained, there has to be participative buy-in by those same leaders. We will look at the ways to gain their trust and support.

Finally, in Section 1, we will look at ways to get the message out. No need to reinvent the wheel if there are vehicles already in place. For instance, no matter how you plan on putting your documentation together, there are no doubt company standards as to how the final product should look and what people should be in place to make sure that it happens. These folks will not only give you a product that is acceptable to the company, but will be a tremendous source of assistance throughout the process — a perfect example of leveraging other department capabilities toward accomplishing your goals.

Section 2: Establishing a Baseline

Somewhere, often in dusty loose-leaf binders on forgotten shelves, is a set of company policies, procedures, guidelines, and directives. They may be woefully out of date, but they are there somewhere. We are going to ferret them out and see what parts we can use. We are then going to set about making them both current and useful (these are *not* interchangeable terms!). We will get the documentation in place, get it blessed by the powers that be, and get it to the general audience, the people who need to know.

This section will, at times, wander from the limited discipline of information security. This is with cause, as the techniques that are most effective are effective in a number of other areas as well. However, there is much to be gained by using the techniques covered, as they will shorten the path to your ultimate goal.

Section 3: Communications

In every company there is someone who knows the whys and wherefores of every action the company has taken. That person will be sought out by any and all who desire to know anything about the past. For whatever reason, this human archive can lead you to it. Cultivate this person, but understand why he or she is so rare. For whatever reason, the greater part of the population of the organization is not aware of all of these things. We will seek to make them aware of all that is in our purview. We will explore means of communication that are available, discuss how to generate new ones, and review a number of means to get your message heard.

Section 4: Evaluation

This might be the toughest one of all. Now that we have gotten the message out, how do we verify that it has been received? We can do a lot of the work ourselves, but there are others charged with doing just that. We will discuss verifiable ways to test our program's effectiveness and whether or not it is reaching the masses.

In structure, this book allows you to go from end to end to develop the tools to build a working and effective program. No guarantees here — just the foundation upon which to build. By the same token, if you have begun building your program, you can go to a specific chapter for some hoped-for insight as to how you can do that specific thing better.

Whichever your need, we hope we can provide some direction.

What I would be looking at in the overall perusal of this book is whether the steps that you already have in place have the foundation mechanisms to support them as well. Procedures, for instance, are of little value without underlying policy. It would pay to review steps that precede the measures upon which you have already embarked, to see if they can assist you in moving forward.

Are the measures outlined the only way to go? Of course not. However, they do provide a baseline from which variance can be controlled and evaluated. In fact, I urge you to strike out on your own and hope that some of what you read leads you to just such actions.

No matter what your specific need, I hope that this book aids you in attaining those goals. That being the case, I will have succeeded in what I set out to do.

You will find that a great deal of this book is based upon a philosophy that I have held for many years, that: information security is not a technical issue, but a people issue. We simply use technical tools to resolve the problems we encounter. If we cannot speak and be understood, we will never reach our desired goals. As with the philosophy of democracy, if we do not gain the right to govern from those being governed, we will not. If we do not gain the cooperation of the rest of the company, nothing we do will come to fruition.

The objective of any awareness program is to draft a plan that defines exactly how corporate information assets are defined, who uses them, and what steps must be taken to protect them. To make it work, it must get across to every person that comes into contact with those assets. That, is the subject of this book.

Each individual in the organization may be a threat to the sanctity of company information. On the other hand, each can also be an ally in the struggle to make certain that the information is safe. Once they know the value of the assets to the company and then, by extension, to themselves, they can act as eyes and ears to you. What we will take the next few hundred pages to explain is how to construct the message and then, how to communicate it. Some of what you read may be old hat to you, but read on as a lot more may be new and useful.

My hope is to give you information you can work with in building your program. Not all suggestions will work in all environments and not all information will be spanking new. However if something said sparks an idea for you, then I have accomplished my mission.

Learn and grow, but most of all, enjoy!

Section 1

Getting Started

Some of you reading this section might decide that you have picked up the wrong book by accident. Little is said in the section about the information security awareness program. Rather, it spends most of its time in discussing the ways to build the foundation upon which the program will ultimately be built.

Learning about the environment within which you will operate is, to say the least, an extremely important aspect of getting your program up and running and, ultimately, keeping it there. To do so involves establishing relationships; understanding the things that do and do not work within the organization; and making certain that you are able to create or modify standards, policies, and procedures to fit into the company culture while ensuring their accuracy, completeness, and viability.

In sequential fashion, we will discover the company's current situation and how we can leverage the resources in place to build our program. We first will take a close look at the management team in place and try to ascertain whose assistance we need to make this project a success. You might be surprised to find out that all may not be exactly as it seems. Next we will move on to finding out how the corporate culture works. Generally, the public image of the culture is a contrived, overall, semi-official idea of how things operate within the organization and what the basic values are. Sometimes it even approaches accuracy. Our task is to identify this culture as it exists in practice.

Getting management to buy into your ideas is less an information security issue than one of getting projects in general approved. There are certain tricks of the game that make approval for a project more likely. We will explore some of these tricks.

Ultimately, we will finish building our foundation by poring through the corporate structure to find the communications vehicles that currently exist, establish a means of getting our input into those that would best serve our needs, and even get our own publication and/or Web presence approved.

In short, we will be attempting to put our four sections into place, built of solid materials and on solid ground. Later, as we get into the specifics of building the program, we will come back to those principals again and again. We need not reinvent the wheel each time; we will find that the original still rolls fine, despite the road we place it on.

Chapter 1

What Am I Getting Into?

The assumption here is, of course, that you are embarking on the creation of a program for a company with whom you have little or no experience. Or, if you have had experience, it has been in another area.

Your task — and by now, you have already accepted it — is to design, create, expand, implement, and maintain an information security awareness program. You are starting at ground zero. Nothing has preceded you and heaven alone knows what may follow. You are on your own, kid. Now what do you do?

Building any type of program can be pretty scary, particularly when you have only a slight idea of what must be done. To be sure, you are an accomplished professional; you have all of the tools. But, sometimes applying those tools in a new environment can be pretty daunting.

First and foremost, a starting point must be defined. The question is not so much where to start as what to do first. This may sound like a conflict in terms, but in reality it is not.

By means of explanation, I offer the following: Getting started usually implies that a piece of work must be accomplished. You begin with a blank sheet and stop when it reaches a predefined status that has been labeled — often arbitrarily — "completed." That is all well and good when you are treading upon virgin ground.

Perhaps we need to take a different view of our particular task. It would be unbelievably arrogant to think that we are the first to ever entertain the idea of building a program, or at least of installing controls and access limitations and tracking. I can assure you, if you are the first to embark on such an undertaking in your organization in this day and age, you are with a company that is either very young or possesses a level of luck that would have me wanting it next to me at the tables in Las Vegas.

If, then, someone has indeed preceded you part of the way, you need to locate all relevant documentation or the processes that it represents and verify their viability in the contemporary environment.

Fine, you say, but where do you start looking? We can offer a few excellent suggestions. First, when you joined the organization, did you receive new employee orientation? Did you learn how to get into the computer systems you most certainly would be working with? Did someone go over the log-in process, the standards — formal or otherwise — for building a password, the time span of a password life? Did anyone say what you could and could not do with your account? All of these actions indicate some type of formal information security considerations.

So, the first step is to find out who prepared the new employee orientation program and who is currently maintaining it. Somewhere, that individual or department got or is getting the guidelines to create the model they are dispensing. In most cases, the trail will begin in the personnel department. (If it is called "human resources," it will have a far larger staff, with more managers and a more twisted route to the information you are seeking.) Assuming that situation, you may have difficulty in locating the individual in charge. If all else fails, get to the individual that ran the orientation session that you attended. That person will have some idea where the information initiated.

Usually, you will then be looking at a documentation department that is responsible for all written communications from HR to the masses. At their best, they take ideas and create sound policies and procedures by translating ideas into English. At their worst, they create meaningless drivel on their own, feeling that the departments whose actions will be governed by said policies and procedures could not offer anything pertinent to the process. Generally, their sources of information are dated and of little use. Even if you discover the latter is true, you will at least have identified that what exists is of little value and will have to be replaced from the ground up.

Under normal circumstances, information systems is the first company group to recognize the value of information and the need to protect it and understand the tools needed to do it right. It should be your next stop.

When you first started, you were no doubt granted a log-on identification (ID) and a password, and probably some direction on how to change the password to begin work. In a similar vein, there are probably access needs for a number of applications or platforms within the company and some means of securing such access. While you may not find a neat set of procedures on how this occurs and why, someone knows what steps must be taken for a new hire to access the systems he or she needs in order to function.

Make either mental or written notes as to what access you have and what others might exist around the company, so that at some later date, you can search for any documentation that might be available. This documentation will not only indicate who must be contacted to get an ID in place, but what the password parameters are and the life span of each. Perhaps they are still only defaults, but that is a significant place to start. Whatever is there is known to someone, and that knowledge, and its later dissemination to the troops, will be a significant step in creating awareness.

Under what we have come to know as *normal circumstances*, you most likely will be reporting to someone in the IS structure. This is totally the wrong place for you to be effective, but that is an issue for another book. By now, you should have met a substantial proportion of at least the management of the department. After all, you are the savior that is going to protect them from the auditors.

From the interactions noted above, it should be fairly easy to find out what security measures are being used. You may be surprised that some very good tools have been developed and that a number of the security provisions available in operating systems and third party-software have been implemented. You will also find it necessary to talk to who implemented the security provisions to find out why it was done and how they work. Rarely do programmers bother documenting their reasons for invoking certain aspects of a software package, the time they did it, and their plans for maintaining it. As a rule, you will find that they also administer said security measures on an ad hoc basis.

Before you take another step, outline how these embedded mysteries — the reasons why things are as they are — are used, where they came from, and what issues they answer. This might be one of the more tedious tasks you face, as you will never be a high priority for these folks and a lot of information has been lost in the past. Your outline should include:

- Where does the security tool resides?
- Is it a software option or custom code?
- Who wrote or invoked it?
- What event or situation caused it to be applied and used as it is?
- Who is the end user to whom protection is applied or access is denied?
- What is the process for including resources under this protective umbrella?
- Is it documented?
- What weaknesses do you, as a practiced professional, see?
- How is the best way to formalize its use?
- What needs to be done to get the process published and accepted, first by management, then by the general user community?

You will find that the majority of what is already in place will be found as you resolve these issues. As mentioned, the majority of it will be held by the programmers/systems administrators who are responsible for the resources protected. They will often have synthesized the tool and are totally responsible for its application.

It has become *de rigeur* in most contemporary IS organizations to have a documentation group within the organization. These folks have been charged not only with the task of creating documentation, but also with setting the standards as to how it will be done. Treat them with great care, as they have the power and a set of standards for copy that might or might not be most effective for what you want to do, but will most certainly be cast in concrete. Later on in the game, when you wish to create policies, procedures, guidelines, and so on, you will most likely have to bring your efforts to their door to be translated into whatever standard format they are currently championing. For the most part, it pays to let them rework your efforts into their form, but review them brutally, as often they will lose the spirit of your meaning in their focused effort to fit your art into their receptacle.

Kidding aside, you will find that the documentation group has ownership of most of what has been written in the past and what is currently being worked on. Once you have made contact within the department, carefully review everything they have done and **ask to see the original copy.** You may be surprised to find that a lot more has been written than what they have translated. As mentioned, things do get lost when reformatted by someone who has little knowledge of the subject about which they are writing. In some instances, they may well have totally omitted something in the false belief that it was covered elsewhere. Issues like e-mail regulation may easily get lost in Internet-related policies and procedures.

Remember: look at the source as well as the finished product. There may well be differences of consequence.

In a number of cases, there will have been a de facto information security officer — someone who had the responsibility according to the provisions of his or her actual job description. Typically, there will be a lot of started projects but few finished ones. All too often, the incumbent has embarked on a project with all good intentions, only to be pulled away by his or her day job or a shift in priorities. In this part-time capacity, there is little clout for the person with the responsibility to identify the issue and have free rein to resolve it.

Your task will be to review those abandoned projects, prioritize them, and if it makes sense, reenergize them. You have a luxury, however, that this individual did not have. You can act on your prioritization. While others may make a case for the continuation of a pet project, they can no longer dictate what will be done, what will be stopped, and when the deliverable will be due.

Now, do not take this as a license to rule unencumbered. As with any IS organization, your time is spoken for by the user community and the results affect them directly. However, they will view you as the expert in this particular milieu, particularly after you can demonstrate solid successes in a few areas. Those are the "slam dunks" or "low hanging fruit," and we will visit them shortly.

Another place to investigate is the company-sponsored communications media. These may include Web pages, online documentation, published company manuals, and newsletters. Any means the company has to communicate with its legions is a potential repository for formalized policies, procedures, and guidelines.

Once you have gotten this far, the second round of finding out who is responsible takes place. Again, you need to find out who wrote the documentation, what the impetus was for doing so, and on whose behalf it was published. From the answers to these questions, we hope to understand corporate reasoning on matters of information protection.

First, review said documentation for adequacy — not superlative, but adequate — something that can stay in place in its current form and perform a function. This will move that particular item far down your priority list.

If this media was the product of a formal documentation department, that is the next place to review. First, get to know the staff here. They may prove invaluable in the future as you spawn reams of notes that have to be converted into clear and concise policies and procedures. Second, get a clear view of what they are doing in the area of information security and what the driving force behind them is.

You may at this time find yourself retracing you steps back to the areas previously discussed. This is fine, as it closes the circle. You have a beginning and an end to the trail on which you embarked.

As time goes by — including some heavy coverage in a later chapter — you will find the internal auditors to be friends and allies. Discussion with them, with the knowledge you have accumulated in the previous steps, should solidify the reasons and sources behind what you have so far unearthed. Better yet, they can give you insight into why much of what has been done was forced to completion. Old reports and discussion are all ways to find out what has been done and what is waiting in the wings. Once you have those covered, you can begin looking for bigger fish to fry.

So, ground zero is beginning to look a bit better, isn't it? There are some things already there, maybe forgotten or fallen into disuse, but still there.

One of the things you have no doubt discovered by this point is that you cannot go it alone. Your search, no matter its beginning, has led you to people, usually those that have been around awhile. Keep track of these folks, as the relationships you forge now will bear continuous fruit as you move forward.

Earlier, I mentioned the internal auditors and their outside counterparts. These might take the form of third-party auditors — a major third-party accounting firm, for instance — or bank examiners or other regulatory agencies. They have measured your organization in the past and will do so again in the future. Normally, they examine and report their findings in relation to industry recognized standards or those adopted by the particular agency they represent. While their reports make incredibly tedious reading, they do specifically address weaknesses they have found in terms of the standards they audit against.

The best places to obtain copies of audits previously undertaken are from departmental management or from you own internal audit department. These documents, taken far enough back, will trace the history of a recognized issue, the steps taken to rectify that issue, and the individuals assigned to enact that rectification. Again, we have traced paperwork to an individual.

In many cases, the issues will remain unchanged or marginally corrected through a series of audits. Responding to an audit finding is time consuming and is usually assigned to someone who has too much to do in the first place. Often, the respondent's initial efforts — if indeed, there are initial efforts — will be quick-fix type actions, glossing over what might be a deeper problem. A true solution and steps to prevent the condition from reemerging are not often found in the initial response to the audit. Indeed, in many cases, the respondent will declare that the issue is not what it seems or that the company has decided to assume the risk for the continued existence of the issue raised.

By reviewing the original reports and the corresponding response documentation, you will often discover issues that have been treated as just mentioned. A sad truth about auditors is not so much that they vary so widely in technical expertise as they do in incentive to do a complete job. Most are conscientious, well trained, and competent. However, the energy expended and the time allotted to complete the project often dilute the depth of their efforts. Read and learn, seeing the findings that have mitigating controls that were not noted or responses that were either not complete or actually attacked the symptoms of the problem.

Enough, now, for the search for documentation. Let us move onward to the issues toward which this book is directed: information security awareness. Awareness is just what is stated, a knowledge of conditions and their impact on a well-protected environment. Employees, no matter how conscientious, will not behave in a prudent manner with regard to information assets just because you want them to; they must be told the what and why of the protective scheme.

With even minimal luck, someone in the organization has used some medium of communication to make the rank and file aware of the value of information, threats that are current or ongoing, and expectations of behavior in their daily work, This might vary from a few words spoken at new employee orientation to columns in the company paper or more electronically based communications.

If there is anything said at orientation, find out what it is. Later we will talk about how to take those few words and convert them into full classes for new hires. But, this is down the road a bit. For now, we want to find out what they are doing, so that we can fill in the blanks with our later work.

Another, rather remote potential location for such a program that the company has in place or has attempted to put in place is a parent company's policies and procedures. In cases where subsidiaries are remote (either geographically or in terms of communications), there are often measures in place that simply do not make it to the field.

In a previous life, I worked in Arizona for a New York-based company. To say there was a communications gap is an understatement. We rarely even spoke the same language. I must admit some amusement at their shock at finding out that the parking lot at the Western center was paved and that rattlesnakes were not a major deterrent to going out for lunch! Not only was the physical environment different, but so too was the litany of issues each of us faced. Something as simple as the work ethic and length of the workday were at odds with one another.

Still, the direction for operations came from there, forcing a review of what was expected and the application of the parts of such edicts that were applicable at the second location.

Your job (and it is no longer your option to choose to do it; you have already accepted) is to find out all of the provision they have put in place, not just for the company in toto, but for the home office and other subsidiary locations. In some cases, there will be provisions in place that simply will not apply to a remote location, such as having all applications servers or mainframes located at the home office. What is in place for the protection and usage guidelines will not have a counterpart at your location. These have to be weeded out of what is present and, in some cases, will have to be replaced with more pertinent rules. Only review can reveal that. We will talk a bit about the replacement process later on.

As you learn your way around the company — assuming that you, too, are a new hire — you may well discover other work that has been done along these lines in different locations. I have, in my past, found security provisions written into applications code that were inserted by the programmer for purposes of securing the function but have never been turned on. In fact, in many cases, the individual who wrote the code is no longer around and, because this bit of programming is not doing anything at this time, is ignored on updates and regular maintenance. If the creator is gone, you may never discover it. If the creator is still around, that person is no doubt still chafing over the calculated ignoring of that neat little piece of code. When you get down to talking to programmers or project managers, you will turn up just such items. Remember that the program you are embarking on is designed to create awareness and that neat little security feature may come to light as a result of the open discussion of security needs and provisions.

What we have talked about up to this point is hardly rocket science. It is a simple search of every manual, file, or document you can lay your hands on that might have some verbiage with regard to information security hidden within it. We have attempted to see the problems and find out what someone else might have done to repair or modify the problem. Anything you find that can be reintroduced with little or no modification will make your job that much easier. And, the review will have made you that much more aware as to where the real problems lie.

Summary

As you no doubt have figured out by this time, there is more work than any one person can do. As you grow within the job and additional staff is added, you will find that the problems have grown right along with you and extra people will encounter extra problems. Still, if we did this right, we should have gained a leg up on the issues to be faced. If nothing else, we now have plenty to do over the next several months.

Let's review the recommendations made:

- Find out what is already in place in terms of processes. To be sure, they may be de facto, done that way since everyone in the company was on a first name basis, but they are a baseline and can be documented with or without modifications. You may well want to change or recommend changes to these processes, but at least you now have a place to start.
- Verify what policies and procedures already exist in the organization and where they reside. As noted, these may be in the form of formal documents (some of which will no doubt predate the Dead Sea Scrolls and have about as much impact in the current environment) or are simply "the way we've always done it." The former will of course have to be brought into the 21st century but are at least a place to start. The latter will have to be formally documented, a subject into which I do not intend to delve too deeply into at this time, and put into a location that allows it to be advertised and circulated to all employees, contractors, and other users of company computing resources.

- In some instances, what procedures do exist are within the areas that control the resources in question. These might be buried in desk instructions or online procedures that have no distribution beyond the department. Still, if their provisions effect activities outside of that department, they too, must see the cold light of day.

- Check with human resources folks as to what input they had or still have in the presentation of information security information to new hires. They might have something or someone within their organization who has created this information or may be in liaison with someone somewhere else who has fed them this information.

- If there are areas within the company that specialize in documentation, check closely with them. They may have raw input that has never been formalized into information security policies and procedures or may have produced such documentation somewhere in the past. Whether or not it is still in circulation or has fallen into disuse and disrepair, it may still provide material for a more responsive effort. If these folk have gotten the basic information from elsewhere; perhaps they can identify the elsewhere and put names to it. Again, a valid place to start.

- Check with the internal auditors. They will not only have copies available for every audit they did back to the time of the American Revolution, but will most certainly have copies of audits done by third-party auditors, bank examiners, state or federal officials, or any other regulatory agencies whose standards your company has to meet. To be sure, the latter only involve certain types of companies, but I think you may be surprised at the extent of those types. Financial institutions will deal with the state or local regulators as well as appropriate national agencies (Federal Home Loan Bank Board, the Federal Reserve, the Comptroller of the Currency, etc.), but public utilities, publicly held companies, and others have to meet minimum standards set forth by those regulations to continue operation. It is best to find out which ones early on in the game.

Each of these audits elicited a response from some party within the organization. Along with the reports, copies of these responses should also be available. They might well point you at some processes that have been put in place in response to audit findings or, worst case, identify the persons who did not fully (if at all) respond to the findings. Again, a place to look, if only to find out the thinking that precluded a fully responsive action.

Our objective is to put an awareness program in place that encompasses the entire organization without regard to job functions or relative position. To do so, a common ground must be established. Finding out what the company has been doing to this point is the logical place to start. The time spent in digging out what has been done, what has been dutifully ignored, and who had responsibility for doing either will serve you well in getting your program under way.

The next barrier we face is finding out whom we have to convince to make it all happen. We will talk about that in the next chapter and beyond.

Chapter 2

Learning the Players:
Where the Power Resides

Alan Krull is one of my very favorite speakers on the subject of information security. He is one of the old guard, IBM Blue, through and through. What I have found to be some of his more endearing traits are his knowledge of the field and a wonderful sense of humor. Years ago, he recognized that the most wonderful plans in the world have no chance if you cannot sell the idea to the big boys in the company. With virtually no knowledge, they will make decisions that can render your program impotent.

Alan's reference to this person or persons has always been "The Big Gorilla," a term he liberated from the time-honored joke: "Where does a 600 pound gorilla sleep? Anywhere he wants!" He quickly realized that the individual with the power has no impetus to adopt what you suggest unless you have made a pretty compelling case for it. He will "sleep wherever he wants" and you are not about to toss him out.

I do not think the parallel here is particularly sophisticated in terms of what we are trying to accomplish. If you cannot convince the folks in charge that what you are trying to do will benefit them, they will not budge.

Alan always had a picture of his "Big Gorilla" that he flashed up oh the screen. The picture was of a teeth-clenching, bull-necked Neanderthal-looking character who looked like his favorite snack might be information security officers!

Although this little gimmick was always worth a good laugh, it demonstrated his point superbly. If you do not get it past the big guy, it is not going to happen.

The difference between Alan's presentation and the world we live in is the identity of the gorilla. His was easy to recognize, ours might not be quite so apparent. Let me explain a bit.

Most of us today are working in large companies, most of which have not yet recognized that information security should report well up in the overall management echelons (shameless plug for getting the ISO more and better exposure!) Unfortunately, there are all too often a number of middle to upper managers between us and the recognizable big gorilla. These lesser gorillas can be just as big, when they block our paths to the big fellow himself. Once a petty potentate has sidetracked an idea, it often languishes and dies without someone to carry it forward. We must, then, calculate our strategy to make sure that this cannot happen. We are facing a plethora of gorillas, and they're all bigger than we are.

One of the recent (last 15 to 20 years) incantations of the corporate design is that of the internal "culture," some kind of idealistic mumbo jumbo that means that we are all supposed to look, think, and act in a certain way. Like so many new wave management philosophies, there are certain weaknesses that are quickly visible to one who has not bought completely into it.

First, the creativity of individual approaches to problem solving becomes sublimated beneath a philosophy of sameness. The outstanding individual has a tendency to stand out, something not always rewarded in a culture of sameness.

Second, at its worst, this concept becomes an overriding concern in hiring. We have ceased to look and how well individuals might perform the tasks related to the jobs for which they are applying and view them through a cultural eye, looking first at how well they fit the corporate picture. What is lost in this mix is the fact that everyone there at this time came from different corporate "cultures" and brought a piece of that with them. They constructed the culture that exists and are now endeavoring to keep anyone else from making the same leap. Interesting, is it not?

A second contemporary feel-good approach is that of consensus to act. This is a scenario in which someone gets a good idea, calls a meeting, and introduces the barest of hints as to what the overall concept is. By interaction, others get to contribute their views. Often these are good, but as often, the meeting leader is waiting for someone to suggest what he had conceptualized already. This continues ad nauseum.

Generally, this artful dancing will be revisited for several meeting with the originator adding details as they fit — assuming that another party has not stumbled over them in the process. Finally, after many meetings and untold fruitful hours lost, the group arrives at the originator's idea. Sometimes the group interaction has added something; more often, we are right back at the original concept. The difference? We still have a great idea, but now everyone that has been involved in the meetings to this point, thinks that it was their idea!

I did not intend this chapter to be a commentary on management styles nor the philosophical foundations of the well (or not so well) run company. My only aim here was to demonstrate that huge differences exist in how companies view things. It behooves us to fully understand just where the chips are stacked at our current place of employment before forging forward with a "good idea." The road to obscurity is littered with the broken bodies of great thinkers who were less than great executors. Learn the lay of the land, my friend, or join that sad group.

Business organizations are governments unto themselves. They control every aspect of day to day life within their walls and vest the power of accomplishment carefully. If you do not comply with the corporate concept of a "team player," success could be fleeting or nonexistent. Unless you enjoy gazing upon the burning wreckage of your wonderful plans and projected victories, you had best get with the program.

I am not suggesting here that you sell out completely to a philosophy that is alien to your style and personality. What I am saying is, you must learn how the structure works and use the channels available to initiate your projects and to bring then to the attention of those that can make them reality.

Most business magazine articles play big on the term *power*, alternating its use among noun ("where the power resides," as though they were discussing an entity), adjective ("power struggle," "power structure, etc.") or a verb ("to power one's way to the top," etc.). While all of these applications demonstrate the flexibility of the term, they really all reference the same thing: the how and where things can get done.

In day to day practice, it is important to identify the means to move forward and use it to your advantage. Often, that takes little beyond reviewing the corporate organization charts. They neatly reflect the formal reporting structure of the company and, to a greater or lesser extent, identify the pecking order. I use the term *lesser* because there is as often an unofficial ranking system as there is the formal one. What is more important is to know that some of the individuals that wield significant clout may not even appear on the page. They are somewhere within the organization and have earned the trust of the power structure on specific aspects of company operation.

These people may have chosen to remain in line functions rather than move up the corporate ladder, may have realized that their skill set or comfort level remained within the technical, manufacturing, research, financial, or other line functions of the company. Still, they have earned the trust of the higher ups who will come to them for advice and confirmation of factual matters before acting. Think of a simple approval loop, one requiring the signature of someone in senior management, and how often you have heard that the appearance of the signature of someone substantially lower on the internal totem pole is the only criterion the senior manager uses for signing off. What now would have happened if that knowledgeable lower level signature had not appeared? There is no question that the approval would have been denied.

Due to the immutable fact that you are probably an army of one at this point in building your program, it behooves you to get a good look at the overall corporate structure and see where these guardians of rational behavior reside. Overall, it is really not that difficult a task. In your own area, be it information systems or financial, there are certain parties who will always be pointed out as being particularly expert at one or more aspects of the business. Not only can your colleagues point you to them, management above you can identify each and every one. They are the acknowledged experts, usually with reputations forged by many years of service within the company. For what it is worth, relative newcomers are rarely accorded this respect.

As you move through areas of concern and begin making notes on the things you want to address first as you get your program off the ground, you will naturally run across this particular class of elder statesmen or stateswomen. Listen closely, they have already come up with the formula for success and can be valuable allies when the time comes to request funding or other resources. Work with them as much as possible to make certain that your proposals have the structure and hit the hot buttons in order to get the attention and approvals you need. Their wisdom will often get you into the same tree with the big gorilla when it counts the most.

Another interesting phenomenon that appears in the management, particularly in a large company, is that of the unofficial reporting structure. This used to be known as the "Good Old Boys Club," but its makeup, if not its nature, has changed over the past many years. Now, it is not the country club connection that creates these unofficial strata. Today, depending on the region, it might be mutual activities, social connections, or some other means of drawing people together. There is an unspoken — probably mostly unnoticed — tendency to assume that those who share the same interests somehow share the same qualities.

An interesting sidelight occurs in some organizations that have grown quite large in relatively low population zones. Often, you will find that the powers that be have the same scholastic background — the "old school ties" that are so often noted. Of course, the courses of study that drew one into the game will lead management back to that same institution for others in the same curriculum. At times, it might even be shared athletic adventures that are the connecting point.

A similar situation occurs in start-up organizations that are offshoots of other companies. In recent years, many companies have sprung up that either complement or work on a subset of work done by a previous employer. Simply stated, people leave a successful company, take their knowledge with them, and either compete with the original employer or provide a symbiotic service to the segment of the industry addressed by that previous employer. Specialized computer companies are started by engineers from established computer companies. Special tools are designed and marketed by former employees of the company that produces the technology that those tools enhance.

Should this offshoot become successful, and particularly if it becomes successful at the expense of the original employer, others will want to follow in the footsteps of their former colleagues. Conversely, the owners of the start-up will greedily take the best and brightest from the older shop because they are comfortable working with former colleagues and take a perverse delight in robbing the company of their best people.

No matter the cause of the breakaway, people that have worked together through a few jobs will have closeness not easily broken into. As with all of us, we are more comfortable with a known quantity. Our problem in a situation like this is to use the techniques listed to find out how the strength is distributed and make certain to enlist the aid of one or more members of this inner circle.

What with today's workers working longer in a career than in the past, there begin to be lines drawn along age lines as well. Now, we all appreciate that there are regulations against any form of either discrimination or advantage based on age, but the natural tendency is to associate with those with whom we are more comfortable. Contemporaries, so to speak.

We have dwelt on the different dynamics that make up company manage-ment and control. In the final analysis, how things got to be the way they are is of little interest beyond finding the common bond that could lead you through the maze of management that leads to the promised land — the adoption and implementation of your program.

Obviously, if we are going to market a product, we try to present something that the marketplace is seeking. This is not so different in the business environment where we attempt to provide solutions to recognized problems or present evidence of issues that were perhaps not recognized in the past. But, how do we go about finding out what the burning issues are? I offer the following as a good starting point: The people that hired you or put you in your current position no doubt noticed a need. Somehow or somewhere, they recognized an exposure that they could not themselves fix. You, then, were the answer to their concerns. Why not find out first hand what the concerns are?

Coming into a new environment is always pretty scary in and of itself. Coming in to do a job, the parameters of which are not yet known, is even scarier. In truth, that is exactly the position you now find yourself in. You are expected to do something, the exact nature of which you do not really know. Here is a novel approach. Why not ask?

In the previous portion of this chapter, we discussed the nature of corporate organization, politics, and the probability of finding power in out-of-the way locations. We even went into the various relationships involved and the many ways they are built and maintained. Now, by carefully examining all of the information that we have gathered, let us explore the ways to find out where the bones are buried and what it will take to exhume them.

I usually begin this exercise by doing exactly what I described. Find out who is running the place, who they count on for good counsel, and any other relationships that could prove useful in getting your arms around your new job.

You probably got some insight into the problems that the company is facing during the interview process. Each interviewer's description of the position indicated what had to be done. This is an excellent place to start.

Make half-hour appointments with each of the persons who interviewed you, including those in your direct reporting line. Select your questions to find out exactly where the respective individual's head might be. If the interviewer remembers some of what transpired during the process (assuming that you do), review some of the items that were discussed then. Even if you do not recall much from that, you can build questions that will keep your knowledge and the company's needs in the forefront of the conversation.

Some questions that I have used in the past are:

- If I reported to you, what would be the most important thing you would like me to start working on?
- Where do you see the company's greatest weakness in information security?
- What audit findings have you worked on in the past? Was there a resolution, or did you feel that the issue did not warrant being addressed?

■ In terms of the last issue, do you feel that the resolution completely addressed the problem? If not, what remains undone?

■ How do you view the future with regards to information security? Where do you see the next challenge?

■ What negative experience — to your knowledge — has the company had with regard to information security breaches (viruses, hacking, trade secret theft, etc.)?

■ Are you familiar with any information security policies and procedures that are current and in place? Where are they kept and maintained? (This should corroborate and perhaps enhance your own search for such documentation and processes in place.)

■ Do you feel that the company is committed to bettering the security around its information assets?

■ Where do you see resistance to new steps being taken?

■ What is your opinion of our internal audit department? (Be prepared for a philosophical discussion on this one. IS managers do not always have the highest regard for auditors. I have heard it said that they are totally unnecessary, as the only function they perform is to justify their own existence by continually finding things wrong. The responder went so far as to say that they would incrementally add in issues they had recognized earlier in order to create new audits for the following season. Needless to say, I did not revisit that subject with this individual!)

■ Where do you feel that this new function can make the most impact in the shortest time?

■ Do you feel that the average employee is aware of the need for information security?

■ Do you feel that that same average employee has knowledge of his or her own role in protecting the company's information assets?

■ What do you think others at your level are concerned about?

■ What should they be concerned about?

I am quite certain that these few questions have given rise to others in your mind to be asked of your own management as you move forward with your program.

One of the things you will notice is that you will begin building categories that all of your interviewees can agree on. If it is an IS group, you will hear a great many concerns about viruses, hacking attempts, and network intrusion in general. These concerns translate into your marching orders for the next few months or years. Accomplishing something that resolves a lot of people's concerns builds both credibility for you and a track record of success. You will be able to trade on those successes later, when support is needed from a lot of different places.

Unfortunately, one thing you will very likely not hear is the matter of employee awareness. As this book is about that subject, I made sure to address my last two sample questions to exactly that point. It is quite past time to begin making the point that everyone that enters the company is directly responsible for the safekeeping of corporate information and the processing thereof. If management has yet to figure that out, take advantage of this face time to make sure that it is firmly implanted in the front of their individual and collective minds. This is first done through the search we spoke of in Chapter 1 and carried on through the interview process.

We know that building a strong employee awareness program is an absolute necessity and by this means, we begin marketing it. And make no mistake: it is a marketing project from day one. First, we have to convince our direct management that incoming employees need to have knowledge of the potential threats to corporate information, the negative monetary effect of security breaches, and what they can do to prevent them. This is as much a sales job to them — at the appropriate time — as it was with their supervisors. By the time we reach the end of this book, we will have discussed many means to succeed at that.

Summary

This chapter has been a review of the things we can do to get to know who we are working with, who our allies are, and who can be counted on for support in putting a program in place. As has been demonstrated, involvement may be anything from ardent support through lip service all the way down to outright hostility toward the program.

What I have tried to do here is to show you how to tell the white hats from the black hats and to work out what to do with the ones that refuse to even wear a hat.

Briefly:

- Find out who the power people are and who the power brokers are. Some are in nominal positions of authority whereas others' strength comes from their knowledge and the vesting of authority by those above them. The latter make wonderful allies and dangerous enemies. Do everything you can to curry their favor and enlist their assistance.
- Corporate organizational charts are not the only way to find out where the decisions are made. Look for the unofficial depth chart, the place where social interaction may give persons strength in the decision-making process far beyond their station in the organization.
- Beware of biases that might exist, often the result of failing to be a part of an outside-of-work activity or carryovers from earlier history. Most typical of these are the old school chums and co-workers from a previous life.
- When an inner circle is identified, find a means to enlist the cooperation of one or more of its members. You might find that addressing one of their pet concerns is a good entry point to gaining their cooperation.
- If biases are encountered, make certain that you maintain awareness of how they work. Informed is protected.

- Make a point of interviewing as many managers as possible whose areas of responsibility will be impacted by your work. Find out what they think is important and where they see the threats to the environment arising.
- Use anything you have learned from your process and procedure search in this interview so that you can ascertain the depth of interest held by the individuals.
- Verify the attitudes and responses to audit comments that have appeared in the past. If the individual you are interviewing had responsibility for any of the responses, find out what they were, what was done, and probable long-term effects of the response.
- Broach the subject of employee awareness in each of the interviews and get some feel for how well they feel that new employees are made aware of, and how well current employees are kept aware of, the need for security measures and their responsibility for them.
- Look for areas of common concern among the interviewees. These are usually the places you want to first concentrate your efforts. Success on one or more of these gets a lot of allies lined up for future undertakings.

What this chapter has been is a lesson in office politics. While most of us in the technical world find this arena somewhat unappealing, the hard, cold fact is that it will exist no matter where you go. The nature of it will pull you in, whether or not you do it voluntarily. Our objective here is to help you learn to play the game or to put yourself in a position so as not to be negatively impacted by the game as played by others. As certainly as politics makes the rules, using it to gather consensus and support works to your best interests.

Perhaps this coverage has extended past purely operational concerns in building the information security awareness program, but it has made specific points about learning the environment within which you must function. As you move into more advanced projects around your area of responsibility, what you can learn from this chapter is what buttons to push to get the cooperation and, in many cases, financing you need to continue growing the function.

At the same time, you must guard against staying on — or worse, getting pushed to — the outside. Not only will you not be able to perform your own responsibilities, but also you will not be able to grow beyond them. Information security will become a background operation that will, at best, go back to being the "someone working on it" that was described earlier.

Play if you will, but watch and understand the playing field you must.

Chapter 3

Just How Cultured Are You?

I have a friend who was recently offered an opportunity for employment with a very nice organization in rural Florida. Now, my friend is a lovely person, with the milk of human kindness fairly pouring from her every pore. However, although she has lived for many years in the West, she still maintains important vestiges of her New York City upbringing. Certainly, her accent is not that of a born and bred citizen of the Isle of Manhattan — she has spent far too many years among the softer speaking Westerners that surround her. Still, there are certain unmistakable traces of The Big Apple remaining in her everyday speech.

For whatever reason, New Yorkers, despite having made the Miami/Fort Lauderdale area into the sixth borough of New York City, are not real popular in the more rustic districts. Perhaps it is the more hurried speech, perhaps the apparent impatience, perhaps even the style of dress that brings out the standoffishness among the locals.

If, then, she goes into an interview without thoughtfully masking that trait, she might well jeopardize her chances for the position. Simply, the culture of the rural or suburban South is not comfortable with the value system they recognize as New York, and sounding like you might be from there will create a negative response.

Whether or not she gets the job is not really important here. What the situation illustrates is that when an element deemed foreign by the indigenous folks is introduced, there is a certain discomfort felt. Unfortunately, people tend to distance themselves from what they find uncomfortable. In this case, it could cost her the job.

This situation parallels what each of us encounters when entering a new workplace with ideas that are different from those of the organization. In our case, all of our ideas are pretty new, as the need for our field of expertise has only recently been addressed. Perhaps we could stand a warning as I gave her about losing the New York accent before plunging headlong into the new responsibility.

In today's business world, many, if not all, companies have struggled to identify themselves by standards of behavior, workplace conduct, and community presence. Fortunately for all, the latter item has more come to represent the company more often than others. Through scholarships, fellowships, bequests, and funding of community or scholastically based programs that are a large part of that community image, the entire community benefits.

As was mentioned earlier on in this review, other aspects of corporate culture can be a bit more artificial than any of us would like. The internal machinations of building that culture more often than not grow into more of a debilitating force than a positive one. Where once there was an open seeking of new ideas and approaches to problem solving, there becomes a ritualistic drive to keep a single (or linked multiple) approach to locating, approaching, and resolving an issue, and that defies the ability to think outside the box (heavens, I've just uttered the politically expedient term for freedom of thought!). Rather than searching for new ideas, people, and solutions, we begin searching only for those things that fit the model we have constructed. As with most things, that model tends to dissolve in the light of newer technologies and discoveries, or its perpetrator does so.

As an example of the company that puts culture before substance: I once interviewed with a relatively young and very successful company. As with any interview, I wore a suit and had my shoes polished to a bright shine. When I walked in, I found that casual attire was the standard there. Not really surprising, what with the current trend toward casual office wear. However, these people, few having been with them a full decade, clung to that aspect of culture to the extent of making rather insulting comments about my attire. Although I dismissed them with a reference to how "you only have one chance to make a first impression" and that I rather envied the comfort of what they were wearing, it was apparent that they had decided that anyone who would wear a suit wouldn't fit into their culture. I often wonder how many of them were in a more formal environment when they came to that company and, in their effort to create a culture, had simply forgotten where they came from. In this case, experience and expertise took a back seat to Dockers over blue serge.

So much for the high-minded discussion on what goes on with companies today. I am sure you recognize some of the symptoms I have listed as part of an organization with which you have become involved. More likely, there are more than one.

Just an interesting sidelight: As we have become more sophisticated and our world of endeavor has enlarged, the one company town ideal has disappeared into a hazy past. Even those "company towns" and their patron businesses have either been bought up by a larger conglomerate or have ceased to operate under the pressures of other such mega businesses.

What I find interesting is that today's companies often see themselves as villages unto themselves. Their benefit programs are designed in a manner so as to not only provide for employees, but to create a dependency on such benefits. Junior only goes to college if he gets one of the ABC Corp. scholarships, the new soccer field has been furnished (usually with much fanfare) by ABC, and ABC has just put another million dollars into the metallurgy program at the local college.

All of the above are good and wonderful things, to be sure. My aim is just to demonstrate the nature of the large company and some of the things you may well have to take into account when trying to establish your program.

As I mentioned earlier, and will stress throughout this book, the internal auditors are most often your most reliable resource in getting a clear picture of what is wrong, what is needed to correct it, and through whom the correction must be routed. As discussed before, those not recruited as allies too often become obstacles.

Let us then take a look at the culture of the organization for which we are trying to build an awareness program. What has worked here in the past, what might work in the future, and what we can count on to minimize the time needed to get a program off the ground? To be effective, any program must make certain that there are processes in place and that the rank and file are aware of them. This can be accomplished in a number of ways, but while we will discuss most of them, chances are that some will work better than others in a given set of circumstances. And despite our rather circuitous route to them, that is what we are addressing in this chapter.

What Works?

First and foremost I always try to identify the institutional sacred cows. In many companies, lax security in certain areas is construed to demonstrate the organizational trust in the employees at large. Most often, they understand the risks but are willing to absorb them in the name of creating loyalty. Mention them, if you see some issues that might not have been previously addressed, but do not harp on issues that will not likely change.

Whether this is an evolving company or one that has been around for decades, it has certain vehicles for transmitting information that are generally accepted on both ends of the organization charts. The bosses like them and the masses have become used to using them. Whether it is a bulletin board system or a Web-based newsletter, there are certain trusted and expected sources for information that all parties keep regular tabs on.

Note: While we recognize the value of the informal network, normally referenced in terms of a vinous plant used to produce the fruit from which wine is made, its operation and depth of validity, along with the rather skeptical acceptance by management, are so undependable so as not to warrant close coverage here. But beware, what you are doing could well become a subject well covered in this arena!

One of the first places I look is into the robustness of the internal educational system that the organization supports. In more technically based companies, there is usually a robust training program, often offering multiday courses in specific areas of manufacturing, information systems, and course materials directed at the business line of the company.

In a less technical organization, or one that is fortunate enough to be centered in an area of multiple businesses in the same sector (for example, Silicon Valley), there are often third-party educational companies that will deliver canned courses or produce specialized classes to meet the needs of individual customers. These people also produce computer based training (CBT) aids, video courses, and other forms of self-paced training.

Based on the availability of the latter and the commitment of the company to education, the training department may be nothing more than a clerk or two that act as schedulers for third-party training or librarians for the CBT, video, and audio classes.

I have gone to the level of detail I have to demonstrate the need to find out just how your company approaches this function. It stands to reason that if you are going to prepare presentation materials, you will have to utilize the preferred vehicle for that organization. Class work is the single best means to convey information in a structured manner and to deliver it with absolute consistency. If that can work in your particular location, then we need to find out how to get it underway and operational.

Once you have ascertained the method of delivery within the company (assuming that there is one), you need to understand the means to get on the road to getting it done. Now, we will not go into the detail of creating class subject matter here — that is a subject for a later chapter — but we will discuss how to locate the right resources and make the right moves to get it approved.

First, talk to who is in charge of training. This might be a department manager or the clerk we mentioned earlier. They know where they get their input and they know the means used to initiate a request to create (or buy) training. Follow their lead to the point of inception, whether it is a written request to your manager or a discussion with someone in human resources. Let us get it approved and on the way; we'll talk about building it later.

Of course, now we have the question as to where the newly planned training is to go. Does the company have a formal orientation program? Is it possible to fit your new learning experience into it? If so, how will it be delivered? If there is no such program — come in the front door, put down your lunchbox, and get to work — how do we get the message across?

At this point, you begin to see some of the need to get familiar with the corporate culture. If there is no formal orientation program, chances are that the idea of a sit-down class will never fly. Had you paid attention at the beginning, you would not have embarked on this course of action.

How then, does the organization communicate its basic tenets and rules? Do they pass you a manual on your way in the door? Do they have a curriculum of required courses to be taken during the first several months of your employment? Do they follow the newest technology and pass information along through Web-developed training aids? We will, by the way, discuss this exciting new way of creating awareness later in this book.

My point here is to make it clear that we need to use the vehicles that are in use and are trusted within the organization. Only by getting on board with what is currently in place can we begin to spread the word.

Note: This is not to say that what is in place now is the best means of communication nor that you must adopt and live with it during your tenure. However, you must start somewhere, and the accepted vehicle is the only way to do that. As you become more familiar with the company and gain credibility through your work, you can begin to introduce other vehicles. If you have done your homework as outlined in Chapter 2 of this section, you will have support from much-needed sources when the time comes.

Let us now assume that you have discovered that new employee orientation is short, concise, and most likely inadequate and that you cannot find a place in which to wedge a bit of instruction on how to protect the company's most valuable asset. That means that you, as a conscientious and aware information security professional, must find an alternate means of getting your message across. Let us look at some options.

In general, but certainly not always, a company that treads lightly on introducing new staff members to the environment through formal presentation distributes huge volumes of paper policies, standards, and procedures. These will be interspersed with directions to the cafeteria, information on the 401(k) program for which the new hire will not be eligible for a year, and a map of the entire facility and parking lots. Comment will be made as to how this should be read at your earliest convenience, but no means for verifying that reading will ever be apparent. Manuals will become the first and later, dustiest, additions to the credenza or bookshelf.

Sounds pretty dreadful, doesn't it? To get your message across, you are going to have to create something of a similar nature, or it just is not going to get seen. I will tell you here: design and write it as you will not find another means to get the word out to people as yet unspoiled by the environment as it exists. The secret is to make sure that they read *that* item, even if they ignore the rest. We will discuss ways to do that in a future chapter.

As you make yourself comfortable in your new professional home, take note as to what you see and hear around the buildings. Are there bulletin boards in the break rooms (are there break rooms)? Is there a place to post informative documents near the entryways, the cafeteria, and any point that is passed daily by a majority of the staff? If they do exist, what type of information appears there? Is there any discussion about what is on the boards? Do they change frequently? An unchanging bulletin board is wallpaper: everyone knows it's there, but probably no one can describe the pattern. Check to see if there is any regulation as to what goes on the boards and when it comes down. You do not need pertinent information buried among ads for cars that were sold six months ago, recipes, and requests for car pooling!

Finally and foremost, when it comes to bulletin boards: Does this medium contain informative company information, or is it used only for the aforementioned ads, localized (that area) commentary, who had a baby, and the evacuation map? If there is no pertinent information there right now, your addition will fade into the same wallpaper as was mentioned earlier.

Check that, and whether or not posters in other locations are a company norm. Do not even build it if you already know that they *will not* come.

How does the e-mail system work in the company? Is there a broadcast capability? If it does exist, what are the criteria for its use? Where does one have to go in order to get access to that broadcast or general circulation mail group?

How about the previously mentioned Web presence of the company? Is there an internal information Web page? Do the majority of staff members have access to it? If they do, and you can get your message posted there, you will reach that wide audience you need.

A word about Web presence and development: Learning to code in HTML is a quick and effective way to get a message across. Work with your Web developers (assuming this presence exists) to get your words out to the masses quickly and effectively. You may or may not be called upon to create the page or bulletin yourself, but the training will give you a good understanding as to what is possible and to do your own maintenance in the future.

Another extremely important means of communication is the company newsletter or paper. Most companies of size have them in varying forms and degrees of sophistication. As a rule of thumb, these papers are not often as responsive as they could easily be. Copy usually comes from a small and overworked group of editors who are often called upon to edit a contribution from a technician that covers subjects they have little or no background in.

The front page is usually covered with pictures of senior management in their latest foray into community service or turning over a silver spade in a groundbreaking ceremony for a new facility. The materials aimed at the great majority of employees is usually limited to the service awards listings on page six.

Somewhere in this is where you must put in your valuable two cents' worth. To do so effectively, you must cultivate the editorial staff and assist them in getting your materials in. Again this is just a suggestion on a way to proceed. We will go into great detail later on.

Another way to get ideas across is the old handout/sticker methodology. The idea here is that if you put something in someone's hand, it will help him or her to write. The truth is that unless they are attuned to that type of message delivery, all a pen with a message represents is something to take notes with. The red, slashed across circle — the "not allowed" symbol — with the "No Hackers," or "No Viruses" message wears out pretty quickly.

Before you try handing out pens, pencils, stickers, or pins, find out what the history of such promotions is within the company. If they love it like candy, go ahead and stay with the tradition. On the other (more likely) hand, do not waste your limited budget on gadgets that will more likely turn into kids' playthings than be effective.

Every company has a way of doing things. Whether or not they make complete sense in the contemporary world is probably immaterial, as that is the vehicle you must ride to success. At some time, "the way they've always done it" made sense, and it probably does now, too. By the same token, the original effectiveness has no doubt been a bit diluted, as well.

Whatever you do, it will have to meet the comfort level of the company at large. If you can use a mechanism already in place, so much the better. If you can see a better way yet of doing it, be cautious in attempting to utilize it. Feel around and find out if change of this nature is welcomed as progress, or viewed as an outsider rocking the boat. You might find that what management is willing to do by way of change will not rest as lightly with the folks on the production floor. It pays to see what they feel comfortable with as well.

I would be remiss in not mentioning a previous life in Vermont, where progress is viewed much the same as progressive gangrene. To make it more interesting, the company had installations in a number of other areas of New England that were on the cutting edge of technology. Try, if you will, to prepare a set of procedures that will be equally effective for those on that cutting edge and those who still view the pre-Pentium 286 PC as something to be feared and mistrusted!

Make sure that your audience is either relatively close in their understanding of company procedures or that you dumb down anything you do to the least common denominator.

Summary

Let's recap what we have covered in this chapter:

- Whatever means you choose to get the message across, make certain that it does not initially stray too far from the company standard of the time. This way, although the information will be recognized as new, the means of delivery will be both familiar and comfortable.
- As often mentioned and to be mentioned even more: use the internal auditors to get a feel for how the company approaches specific issues and the means to communicate. Their interests are the same as yours, but from a reviewing standpoint. If you are acting on their concerns, they will support you. And remember, they have the collective ear of the board of directors.
- Watch out for the sacred cows. If you see something beyond what you are able to get a justification for, make a note to handle it later. Never fly in the face of tradition as a newcomer. Try to build allies wherever possible.
- Explore the new employee orientation processes used by the company. Generally they will range between nice, but leaving something to be desired, to nonexistent. Security is not an on-the-job-training technique, so try to get something into the orientation process. Get to them before they can make the first mistake.
- Look for internal publications, whether they are paper or electronic. If there is space available in a periodical, try to get your message in there. If there is a vehicle such as e-mail or a Web page, get something on that.
- Make certain that you can speak knowledgeably to the folks that run this informative media. Try to know something about writing (no one that cannot write gets into this profession, do they?) HTML or whatever other medium is available. Be helpful, so that your contribution is value added. Good copy requires little editing and is most welcome.

- Verify the means of communications that seem to be successful in the organization. Putting up full-color posters, then leaving them there for six months is rarely effective beyond the first week. In those cases where folks do not expect to see informative information there, the effectiveness is lessened to a greater extent.
- Direct your efforts at the comfort level of the majority of your audience. Programmers generally understand English (despite their protests to the opposite), but clerks and assemblers rarely understand highly technical copy.
- Do not try to change the world overnight. Use what is in place now. Improve on it a bit if you can. If you see something that could be done better, mention it to appropriate persons. If that mention does not bear fruit, try a small implementation later, after your credibility has been established. The new sheriff in town does not always get the respect he deserves, simply by being perceived as being heavy handed.

In short, deliver the first parts of your message through known methods and in a form that all can understand. Once that trust is in place and you have gathered support for your efforts, then attempt to use what seem to you to be more appropriate means of communications. By the way, do not be surprised if experience demonstrates that certain vehicles of communication work pretty well and do not require updating or change.

Use the best methods and materials available to you. Find them by discussion and by observing as you go. In the long run, it will make improvement evolutionary, rather than revolutionary, and will be accepted much more freely by your audience. What we will discuss later is how to make sure that your message is clear, concise, and timely. Once you have established your credibility as the source for information on the subject, the word will be much easier to spread.

Above all, speak to the masses because if they cannot understand it, it will not be accepted. And if they view you as pedantic or overbearing, they will not accept your message even if it makes sense later. Remember: always write to the least common denominator. The more sophisticated will get the message, but the inverse is rarely true.

Wherever you settle, you will find an order in place. That order is the culture of the company. Whether they trumpet it as the end-all or simply operate within parameters that have worked their way into place over decades, every company has some type of culture, something that makes them unique in corporate values or operations. Find and honor it.

Chapter 4

Getting the Heavyweights Behind You

I once came up with a great idea to combat staff apathy toward virus attacks. It seemed like once we discovered and eradicated a virus, or so we thought, it would break out again somewhere in the plant. We had the necessary filters in place, we had updated our virus profiles on our antivirus product, but it just kept cropping up again and again. For whatever reason, the many copies of an attachment bearing with it some form of the address book raiding malicious code that had entered the environment before we got our defenses up were still out there. No matter, you say, people know not to open them, right. Not even close to right!

As individuals who had not been present at the original outbreak began returning to the office, they began opening the mail that had accumulated in their absence. These might have been folks on vacation, shift workers, or someone out of the plant or out of touch for some reason, and they either did not know or care about the threat from the infection. Despite signs on the doors — paper, hastily put there when the infection was discovered — that they had to walk right by to get to their workplace, they signed on to their computers and checked their mail. Of course, when they found one or more of the auto-forwarded virus-bearing notes, they opened it at once. Now, on the inside of the defensive perimeter, the virus again spread as before.

Of course, these new outbreaks infected machines that were as dormant at the time as was the infecting machine just moments before. They too, became delayed reaction bombs when someone who had managed to miss the notes, e-mails, and other forms of communication that had been called into action, logged on, and started the same ugly routine again. Even more frustrating were the users that repeated the same mistake a second and, yes, even more times! Nothing could get through to these people.

Information security and a number of other departments within the organization were kept busy for months after the initial outbreak just picking up after these individuals.

How then, I thought, could we get the message of a virus infection across to the masses quickly and with a degree of urgency that they would remember even after the warning signal disappeared from their immediate field of vision. The answer came to me as a revelation that was destined to alter the course of the planets.

I had seen a number of electronic message boards in a storage area some weeks before, they were large enough to be easily seen and read from many yards away, flexible in that a message could be displayed and controlled from a central point some distance away and that controlled all such signs on its own network. Heck, the message flowed by, could be made to flash, blink, and even make alarming noises simply by entering the desired effect into the remote console. We had plenty to cover all of the exits; they could be weatherproofed if we wanted to mount them outdoors. The answer could not have been easier had it been manufactured for just the purpose we intended. There were even spares, as the project for which they had been purchased had been cancelled. Providence had, for once, smiled on us.

I set to work getting the wheels turning to get these signs installed at every entrance on a multibuilding campus. We needed the building services folks to take care of hanging them. We needed the electricians to wire them. We needed the network people to wire them into the building network system. And, we even needed a designer type to make sure that the presence of these flashing message carriers did not damage the esthetics of the lobbies in which they were to be installed.

The plan was that as soon as a virus was recognized our network and its means of transmittal identified, we could flash news of it and how to avoid infection on these great new blinking, flashing, flowing, and beeping sign-boards almost immediately. By using the sound effects available, we could virtually guarantee that people would notice the warning a lot better than the feverishly prepared paper warning signs we had been using to that point.

The plan was fleshed out by coming up with things to use the boards for when a virus had not become rampant within our walls. They could announce activities, stock prices, and news of the world and of our more cloistered business environment. The difference would be the flashing and sounds when we were announcing a virus and warning how to deal with it. Heck, even the esthetics lady had no problem with it.

What I had not counted on when planning this communications coup was the opinions of those far from the problem and our plans for a solution. It seemed that the aforementioned esthetic lady had a short line reporting chain to the top guy in the company. When this little project came up in her weekly report, his thumb dove quickly toward the earth's crust, effectively canceling the project on the spot.

What I had failed to take into account was the feelings of management on this particular item. Although the sign boards were paid for and gathering dust in a storeroom, the boss felt that they could be better used elsewhere.

Besides, he was concerned for the sanctity of the lobbies, which, I found, were a compelling interest of his.

Two years later, we were still hanging paper signs and the lighted boards were still, in the majority, gathering dust. And, oh yes, we still suffer satellite outbreaks of new viruses long after the protective measures are in place.

I appreciate that the preceding story was long and detailed, but it perfectly illustrated the central theme of this chapter and how not to go about doing it. An excellent plan was aborted because I failed to get management buy in before charging headlong into it. If they do not like it, they will not approve it. If they do not know about it, they are just as likely to deny it.

Every organization has one or more approval loops required to get a major project off the ground. There are usually matters of finance, then of resources, and finally the projected payback. I know, that sounds pretty simplistic, but no matter how many documents you have to fill out to get into the hopper to get your project going, ultimately, those are the questions to be answered.

We have spent a good deal of time discussing the means to find out both the official reporting structure and the substratum version. We should, by this time, have a pretty good feel for what exists, what we can build off of, and what is a total vacuum. We took pains to find out whether we are in the jeans and sneakers mode or a more formal suit and tie group — the culture of the organization itself. In other words, by now, we should be able to traverse the approval process with a degree of certainty and as few missteps as possible.

From hereon out in this chapter, I will keep referring to a nebulous "project," one we understand to be the first formal coming of the effort toward building the information security awareness program to which this book is dedicated. Although I will only rarely reference back to that nature of the project, that is what we are addressing. However, what ensues is a template for embarking on and completing all of the other areas to which you will be addressing your time in the future. Just like the programming code that all programmers know, use the good routines wherever you can — reusable code — and do not reinvent the wheel. Such is the world of project management. Use good bricks, build a strong foundation.

Therefore, one of your first chores will be to learn what steps must be taken to have a project approved and to gain upper management agreement to it. For the most part, your efforts will be one-person forays with the occasional luxury of help from other areas. When the latter condition is met, when you have to divert others from their normal duties, it is imperative that it be done with the full understanding and agreement of their management.

I call to your attention the interviews with management that you conducted when you first arrived. By now, you have digested their comments down into a number of areas of concern that all interviewees seemed to be aware of. If, then, the proposed first project addresses one or more of their voiced concerns, how difficult do you think it will be to gain their agreement to proceed?

Once you have identified areas of concern that will require the concerted efforts of more than one person, it is wise to go to your immediate management with an outline of what you want to do, how much it will likely cost, and what the benefits to the company will be. If you are fortunate enough to have the project directed at resolving an open audit issue, the approval will be much easier to come by. To this point, management has most likely wrestled with responses to audit with little luck. Simply, there is rarely time to address it and almost never the personnel. Your assignment as information security officer makes you particularly suited to this task. You may have to convince management, but I doubt it, as you are probably the first person to ever volunteer to do an audit response.

Now, working with your manager, examine the cost outlay that will be associated with the proposed activity. Work together to identify the other areas that will be impacted by the proposed change. Whether the participation is to be as workers (coding, wiring, keying, etc.) or as recipients of the service provided, there will be consequences with respect to current day-to-day operations. To gain their approval and cooperation, you must demonstrate that the success of this particular project will benefit all who participate.

Once approval has been gained from middle management — not including those higher up who might need to bless the effort to gain necessary funding — a presentation must be prepared to bring the project to the attention of higher management, at least to the level needed for approval of funding.

Now, preparing a presentation of this type may fall in a number of categories. In some companies, a slick, project overview document with necessary management summaries, graphs, and schematics as needed to define the finer points of what is to be accomplished and a budget page are the preferred method of presentation. For the most part, you will be trying to convince the "Big Gorilla" of the need to support the project. Ask around and find out exactly what particular information should be presented in greater detail, what can be left out, and where the bottom line usually resides. That might mean straight financials, a demonstration as to how the successful completion of the project will meet a recognized need.

A second way in which this type of approval process is likely to run is the audience with the "Man" (The Woman or The Gorilla may also be options here). In this scenario, you are generally given a brief period of time in which to go over what you are trying to accomplish, how you propose to do it, the overall cost to the company, and the benefits that it will elicit. Is this order of important points starting to sound familiar?

Chances are that your audience will not be very familiar with the subject matter, so be prepared to give a quick overview as to what instigated your interest in this project, what it will provide for the company, and the cost-versus-benefit equation. Do not worry too much about financial details at this point, unless some monetary impetus is what spawned the project in the first place — "We face the possibility of losing more than $400, 000,000 over the next three years if we don't do this!" Somehow, that always gets their attention.

Be ready for questions and have the answers readily available. You might be surprised to find that this particular individual asks virtually the same questions in any such discussion. The people you spoke with that helped you get this far probably can tip you off on these well in advance of the meeting. Have your responses to those and related questions at the ready and you will not be caught off guard.

Make your presentation fit into the time allotted and have a brief but compelling summary to close. Then, be ready for the questions mentioned or others that might spring up. Remember, the person to whom you are talking is in control of the time and can run over if more input is needed. Make certain that you have it.

A third, and by far the most appealing, means of introducing a project is a general meeting of interested parties. This can usually be done in a conference room that has the luxury of supporting presentation visuals, whether they are overhead slides or a more sophisticated PowerPoint or other presentation package computer-based demo. Try to avoid on-screen demos unless you have a projector available. Gathering people around a PC screen is not terribly effective in getting the message across.

Again, your presentation should be in terms of presenting the issue, presenting your solution, and demonstrating how that end will be met. Because of the size of the venue and the additional people present, it is usually a good idea to involve others that have been involved since the inception of the project. They may be analysts that helped identify the problem, programmers who have worked out how they intend to prepare the needed program products, or end users who feel that they need this resolution to their issue. If the proposed change is the addition of third-party hardware, software, or other devices, this might be a good time to let them take part of the show. Warn them up front that this forum is to demonstrate the advantages of the projected changes and that the time for selling is over (or yet to begin!).

Again, finish in plenty of time for questions and answers.

I have gone into a lot of detail here to demonstrate the "right" way to present a proposal, something you might well have done innumerable times in the past. However, the underlying issue here is to sell your program at the same time. You are establishing credibility while introducing a new idea to the company. If you do so in a professional manner, made certain that all details are in place, you have set the groundwork for a second, third, and all future projects.

Now, let us go into a proposal to begin building an information security awareness program. Using the skills and techniques listed above, we are much more likely to get what we want.

First and foremost, it is necessary to be able to relate the germ of your idea to a third party that we must assume is neither knowledgeable nor interested in what you have to say. The person will, as a rule, be your superior and be higher than you in the pecking order. If responsible for putting you in your position, that person will be supportive of your actions. This might be the last time you have that luxury, so plan on learning from this meeting.

Make your presentation brief and with sufficient background to define the reasons supporting the project. Whatever else you do or say, make it quantifiable; there must be a bottom line easily recognized and clearly defined as the request goes higher in the company.

The best types of background to use are things that have happened to the company or weaknesses you have noted that could cause grief in the future. If you cite a security exposure within your organization, make sure to back it up with a historical event where that exposure or one very much like it was exploited elsewhere. If you choose to reference these items, make certain that they pose no embarrassment to the party to whom you are presenting. No one likes to be made to look bad, and getting help from people who see your project as showing them up is not likely. Leave plenty of time for questions and make sure you have the answers available. If your audience comes up with something so far off the wall that you have neither foreseen nor prepared a response for it, beg off with a promise to get the data. Provide the requested data as soon as possible after leaving the office. A quick response here underlines your enthusiasm for the project and is a reassurance to your hoped-for backer.

Note that to this point, we have talked about general projects, albeit in the field of information security. We have not truly addressed anything as awareness program related. That is not without reason, as my message is that the development of an awareness program must be viewed as a working project and not as a one-time dog and pony show, as the industry likes to call it. It takes careful review of circumstances within which you live, areas of need that must be filled in before there is anything of which to make people aware. Solid policies and procedures are needed for a framework for the program and a series of well-thought-out steps must be outlined.

These are the steps that must be described and justified before you can ask your boss to carry the program forward or pave the way for you to do so.

Assuming that you have followed these suggestions to the letter and your superior is as excited about the project as you are, it will be up to your superior to define the next step. Depending on your position in the organization, there might be a similar presentation to a higher up or a presentation to a select group of individuals. Now is the time to brush up on your Visio and prepare a compelling case for that presentation.

The invitees to a soiree of this nature should include management from all departments to which you may go for help. For example, if there is a training department, their cooperation will be invaluable. Similarly, a publications group, the documentation folks, and whatever other support you feel you will need should be represented.

A word of caution at this point: Earlier, I described a number of cultural characteristics that companies tend to portray. They might want you to present a fantastic idea, tell how you intend to go about implementing it, and ask for status reports along the way. Go forth, and do good unto the world.

Unfortunately, there is another side to that coin. You might well walk out of the room as alone as when you walked in. You have the authority to go on with your pet project, but keep a wary eye out for the effects of apathy. To counteract that effect, make certain that the work you have undertaken is fully documented and status reports are issued on a regular basis. If the forum of a department or management meeting is a regular occurrence, make sure to have a report ready for each one. If that vehicle is not available to you, make sure that you publish those results on a regular basis. "Regular" here would mean monthly, but definitely not any longer between the reports. Send it to your boss and copy as many of the attendees of your original presentation meeting as possible.

I also mentioned the trend toward "consensus management" that is modish in many circles today. This might mean holding your first meeting, outlining what it is you intend to do, and requesting feedback from the attendees. If you carefully present the right materials — defining a problem and a direction (rather than specifics) for solution — you can usually draw out some input. If it lags, drop a bit more information and see who picks it up. In general, these meetings should not last longer than an hour and the minutes can be made up in a short time. Make sure that plenty of action items come out of it and that you claim as many as possible for yourself. That way, you can steer the way the action items are described and carry them out in that direction. Later, hold another meeting, picking up where the first left off, but including the results of the action items. Again, take as many of the items as possible from the second meeting as well and continue moving toward your goal.

Repeat as necessary. By the time the pre-implementation meeting takes place, everyone in the room will think it was their idea.

Now, I know what I have just related seems pretty duplicitous and, in truth, it is. What I am trying to identify is a means to work within a system that inadvertently quashes individual effort. I suspect that consensus management will be replaced with some other faddish management style or will evolve into a rubber stamp operation where you bring the fruits of your labor to a committee who will approve it, decline it, or send you away to fill additional requirements. Oddly, this can be quite an effective way to do business with experts in specific fields, undertaking and resolving issues that require their specific skills and training. By getting approval to proceed, reporting back as work progresses, and getting additional approvals as needed, you can carry the project through to its legitimate conclusion. The last meeting should have a project known to a management team with mileposts created along the way approved for implementation based on a clear understanding of what business need the finished product meets and how it will be accomplished.

The ultimate objective of all of this preparing and presenting is the implementation of a well-rounded information security awareness program. It will entail publications, hands-on education, "gimmicks" to grab attention, embedded warning, and whatever else you can dredge up that will assist the overall company staff of the importance of company information, the means needed to protect it, and their responsibility in doing so.

Summary

You have been brought into the organization with the specific responsibility to build safeguards for the corporation's information assets. To do that, you must put into place a series of safeguards by working through the information systems team to identify the weaknesses and put them in place. Most important, you must inform the company employees of what you are doing, what they must do, and how they must do it.

To get all of the above in place, agreement from the corporate power structure is an absolute necessity. As with any other project, you must begin with an identifiable segment of what must be done, document what purpose it will serve, what burning need it will address, what value it provides to the company, how much more will be saved than the project will cost, and what the final advantage will be.

Depending on the environment within which you work, you will have to identify the issue — in this case, embarking on the building and implementation of your awareness program — and get it in front of those parties who are needed to assist, approve, and finance the undertaking.

It is imperative that you become familiar with the process within the specific organization and use it to your advantage. Whether a series of meetings with an ascending chain of management or permission to present your idea to a general or select group for approval, you have to tailor your presentation for the environment.

Certain things need to be demonstrated to get the project off the ground. Basic ingredients — no matter which forum you are forced to operate within — are:

- State the nature and size of the project.
- Identify the business need it will meet.
- Point out the potential impact of not going forward with the project. Cite real facts from other organizations.
- State the probable costs.
- Using examples from other installations, cite the potential losses if the plan is not implemented.
    Note: If you are working in a regulated industry, make a point of referencing all points covered in regulations that this measure will meet. If there were audit findings with regards to it, lay them out on the table.
- Show how you intend to reach the ultimate goal.
- Allow sufficient time for questions and answers, but do your homework first. Make sure that you have answers at hand for probable questions. If someone comes up with something for which you have not prepared, make it clear that you will have to research it and will get back to them. Make every effort to set a new world's record in getting that information back. Enthusiasm is catching, so spread it as far as you can.

Assuming the natural path of this type of presentation throughout the company, you will receive approval to continue with your program development or be sent back to the drawing board to find another way to present it. Should the latter happen, make certain to carefully record and address those areas of concern. A second trip through the system is always looked at a bit more askance than was the original. Later ones have little chance of getting wholehearted approval.

Sort out the things that can be accomplished most quickly and set about putting them in place. There is no magic wand for this one; try to focus on your own strengths and address the areas within which your greatest expertise lies. Success builds on success, so get the slam dunks first. The success of each step increases the credibility of what follows.

Will this always work? Probably not. However, we have established a means to get serious consideration for whatever projects we need to embark on. Even a refusal for cause is a learning experience. You will go back, you will fix the situation, and hopefully, you will add what you learned in breaching the shortcoming noted to your overall toolbox.

Chapter 5

Getting the Word Out

Let us assume that what we have done to this point has been a smashing success and we are ready to begin the project to create and implement our information security awareness program. All we really need, then, is to spread the word and all will be well in the world. This should be a fairly simple task, after having found all the hidden previous work (if any), located the most amenable members of management, and begun to find out where the bones are buried.

That is all well and good, until the culture spectacle again rears its ugly head. Where in this fabricated icon of corporate culture do the tools for communication reside? Finding that out can be a task unto itself. There are always the usual suspects such as the company paper and the bulletin boards, but they, too, often have a lot of cautions and caveats attached. Let me give you an example I once had the "opportunity" to live through.

When I first started with the organization in question, my initial explorations were in the areas described earlier in this section. I tried to find out what had been done in the past and where the real seats of power were, so that I could get support for the programs I had hoped to get going, I conducted interviews with as many managers as I could find. Fortunately, my own manager was committed to the program and was of immeasurable help in identifying the interviewees and setting up the meetings. Where I came up short was in reviewing the media vehicles that were in place. Now, this organization had labor practices that took one back half a century, so keeping the troops aware of what was going on within the company was no particular priority. For the life of me, I could not find any form of regularly issued employee newsletter or paper. From all indications, a memo was issued when senior management had something to say to the troops, and there was an occasional overall update (about biennially), but that was about it.

For years I have used a system of bulletins to bring urgent issues to the corporate population in general. Sometimes the message was less than urgent, but by wording it so that it had the look and feel of urgency, it got attention where it was intended. This is, by the way, a cheap and effective way to make the general populace aware of something that needs to be brought to their attention quickly. Today, we need not even go to paper with it, assuming a corporatewide e-mail system.

At any rate, I published my first such bulletin not long after I arrived on site with the purpose of notifying everyone of my presence and charter. I used a few of the problems we faced daily as evidence of the need and of the need for companywide knowledge and actions toward mitigating those problems.

The bulletin had been "on the street" for no more than a few hours when I received a call from a petty potentate buried deep within the corporate structure downtown (some distance from the operations center) whose message was that he and his organization were the only point from which internal publications could emanate. His "organization" it turned out was one clerk/secretary and him. However, he did, indeed, have the responsibility for press releases, the annual report, and whatever modest publications were made internally. What my small bulletin actually did was increase the amount of good copy he had to publish by a significant percentage despite his protests. Still, he was not unaware of the potential benefit such input could be.

When talking to him, in the original phone conversation and afterward, I attempted to make that point. Here, I said, was a source of input that could improve what little inside publishing he was doing and it provided an immediate benefit to the company. While being aware of the ego that prompted his call as well as his obvious recognition by those higher up (annual reports have a way of doing that), I attempted to demonstrate the good I was doing for his program and the company.

Ultimately, I did get permission to keep using the medium, only having to pass it by him before publication. As I recall, a word or two was changed from time to time, but that was the extent of editing that my bulletins received. My point here is that I missed an important point before I sent out my first bulletin. The issue was minor, but it took a bit of stroking to get it righted.

For what it is worth, I always make a point of finding out if such a function exists within any organization for which I do work. Whether as a staff member or consultant, look for the little offices in the basement, they sometimes contain the folks you either are looking for, or should be.

The lesson here is to work through everyone you have met to find out what communication media exist and who has ultimate control over them. The preceding story is a perfect illustration of that potential and the possible upshot. I never kid myself that the gentleman with whom I spoke — while somewhat self important — could have caused a lot of problems had he not been reasonable.

Never gamble on anyone being reasonable, particularly when they feel that they are protecting their turf. Toes not stepped on are toes that need not be kissed at some later date.

If then, we are going to trace down the communications media that a company might already have in place, the best place to look is in the employee break areas or lunchrooms. Without fail, anything printed or published internally is going to wind up on the tables in there. It might not be a high-tech means for searching, but it is relatively effective. (Okay, use a binary search method-ology: start at one end of the cafeteria, and review the tables in one half of the room. Repeat for the other end.) In most cases, there is some type of special table or other point at which these things are distributed. There might even be what looks like a newspaper rack in which the corporate organs are displayed for picking up.

Another place to look is in the personnel department. For some reason beyond my ability to fathom, many companies publish slick and informative documents that are not distributed to the rank and file. Instead, and despite their content being of interest to the general populace, they go only to the local human resources office and are distributed on an ask only basis. Go figure.

Of course, one of the first places you would look is with the folks who are responsible for the periodic employee newsletter or paper. These folks can be definite allies for a number of reasons. First, they own the vehicle that most employees look to for news. Second, management looks to them as a vehicle to distribute their various pronouncements. Third, the combination of numbers one and two lays a mantle of credibility over the publication. Obviously, all three characteristics work to your advantage. When you wish to distribute something about, say, the importance of logging off when leaving your workplace, the assumption already held within the company is that if it is in the *ABC Company Chronicle*, it must be important and accurate.

Your first job is to get familiar with the structure of the paper. Are there regular writers who produce the majority of copy? Do certain departments have regular segments in each or most editions? Is it directed at management or the folks in the trenches?

The last question is not idly put forth. Perhaps one of the saddest things about too many company papers is their dedication to chronicling the activities of senior management. For some reason, a picture of the chairman of the board turning over the first spade of soil for the new public library downtown is deemed to be what Sally on the assembly line is dying to hear about. What they do not know is that Sally, if she read the article at all, will most likely be miffed that the company is dumping money into a library that she may never set foot in rather than adding the excess fund into her salary. Literally, a satisfier is turned into a dissatisfier right before your eyes.

Opinions aside, if the paper exists and already solicits copy, you are home free. It is a virtual fact that most such papers do not have enough full-time staff to fill a paper on a reasonably regular basis. Even if other departments do not provide regular articles, you, from now on, will. I can assure you that your contribution will be welcomed.

A word of caution on submitting articles for any such publication: Without fail, the editorial staff reserves the right to edit any submissions for content, grammar, or length to fit the space. Understand that you cannot change that. That is why they call them editors. What you can do, however, is to request the right to look at the edited copy before publication. You can justify the request easily, by pointing out the technical background that governs what you write. You may or may not like the results of these journalism majors' editing, but learn to live with it. In fact, learn from it. From what they do to your piece, you will be able to better judge the size of the article they seek and their potential taste in styles so that future submissions can be more in line with their image of the perfect item.

With today's tendency toward online publications and Web pages, there might well be an employee information medium that never makes it to paper until someone prints it off for their own use. These online newsletters are proliferating as this is being written. Often, a limited print publication is put out, with the majority of the staff expected to view it online. As with the purely paper version we discussed earlier, find out if it exists, find out if you can get information into it, and find out exactly how those in charge like it to look.

You can usually find out about the existence of such items through your co-workers when you originally come on board, and they will direct you to any other news media available around the company.

Company Web pages are all the rage today and are perfect for our purposes as information security professionals. They have a built-in circulation, going to every workstation in the company, and they are flexible, allowing for moment-to-moment updates if necessary and overnight update as a regular part of business. When you seek out the Web publishing folks who have responsibility for maintaining the online newsletter, make sure to fully understand how often they need your input and how long the item is likely to stay on the primary page. This is a powerful tool, so make sure to take full advantage of it.

Very often, the publishers of the Web-based news service are also the keepers of the company's entire internal Web presence. That is, in order to publish a Web page, you will need to work with them. This can be a great advantage, in that they have the ability to produce slick, finished products from your relatively humdrum input. There is nothing like plenty of flashing headers and lively background colors to get your message across.

At the same time you are reviewing the Web-publishing aspect of this medium, you might check with them as to what policies and procedures are already in place. If there is something that can assist in what you want to present or that you can update as time allows, these are good things to remember.

One of the truly great capabilities of the Hyper Text Markup Language (HTML) is the incredible flexibility to link among Web pages. While you might find something of value that someone else wrote, you can make it your own by having your Web page link to it.

While making these searches, it is good to remember that what you are looking for may reside within some type of document already in place under another name or subject. You may find rules, for instance, that govern the use of company computing equipment that could contain rules on the protection of information. They may or may not be fully applicable to what you are doing, or even reflect clear and contemporary thinking. Remember, incorrect or incomplete information in place has to be either updated to current accuracy or removed and replaced by more up-to-date considerations. **Inaccurate information, particularly that which conflicts with what you are putting in place, must be found and either brought into synch or removed completely.**

If your organization is a subsidiary of a larger company, you may well have to get in touch with the parent company's information security department to make certain that nothing you put into place is in conflict with overall corporate rules. What we are talking about here is media used to circulate information and that is what we hope to examine from the parent company. If they have regulations in place, what you produce must dovetail with them. While outside of the scope of this chapter, it may be a good idea to meet with them, find out what policies and procedures exist, and how they spread the word. If you can hitch your wagon to their tools, so much the better. Remember, though, to keep close contact with them so that you do not wind up working at cross purposes. This is not to say that ideas cannot come from you, as your work may well take you places that theirs does not. Make certain to share what you learn and what you plan to do with them, and urge them to do the same with you.

On the other end of the spectrum are subsidiaries that report to your parent company. If you are the information security officer for the parent, by normal reporting structure, the steps taken by counterparts in subsidiaries are secondary to yours. Unless the subsidiaries work in a field so disparate from the parent, virtually all of what they do should be reflective of your corporate standards. Make regular checks to be sure that this assumption is true. If they do not initiate communications, do so yourself to be sure that it is going on. Not only should you establish a link with them, but check on the data circulation means as well. If they have company papers, newsletters, Web pages, and so on, by all means use them to spread the gospel according to you. Be certain not to step on the toes of anyone in the subsidiaries, but make certain that they are taking the same line as you have set up for the corporation in general.

Another word of caution: Even if the subsidiary is in an entirely different line of business than the parent, they still maintain information that belongs to the company and has intrinsic value. If they are more consumer oriented, make sure that they properly protect customer as well as company information. If they are strictly a software house, make certain that source code and financial information are fully protected against exposure, loss, or damage and that they use whatever means they have in place to get that message across.

Multinationals have another level of issue beyond simply spreading the word. In such cases, you are concerning yourself with language differences and cultural differences (for real this time, not just a matter of corporate culture!). Also, be aware of the legal climate in the other countries in which your company has a presence. Things that can be done with alacrity here, in terms of policies and procedures, may be against the law in a second country.

Still, there should be a baseline security code that crosses international borders, and communicating it to the troops requires some means of circulation. Check on the means of communication that they have and the means required to get your words into them. To do this, you will have to count on translators for installations that are not located in places where English is commonly spoken. Establish a connection with the editorial staff of those papers and make sure that you are comfortable that a number of conditions are met. First, make certain that your message does not run counter to local or national laws (do not laugh on this one, as people around the world do not necessarily take an American view on everything). Second, make sure that the translator has a good understanding of the message you are trying to get across, as errors in knowledge of idioms, acronyms, or figures of speech can destroy the message (although often giving the recipients a number of good laughs). This can be true even in English-speaking countries where a napkin is table linen in America, but a baby diaper in Australia.

The best of all worlds in the latter instance is to have a central company organ prepared in all the languages of the countries of operation. That way, you can prepare your message once, run it through one set of lawyers who have international experience, and have it translated by a known source. Just be certain to understand what considerations went into any changes to your message for consumption in another country. Anything you can learn about restrictions in those foreign locations will be of use in the future or when composing corporate standards about things used in all locations. E-mail and its review by corporate entities are looked upon much differently in other parts of the world.

Another point worthy of examination here is that of nationalism. What with the trend to mergers and purchases of smaller companies, despite their geography, you may well find that your company has made a relatively recent acquisition of such a company. Like it or not, the most powerful nations in the world are not always looked upon with favor in Third World or lesser industrialized nations. Make yourself aware of the nationalistic feelings in the new location and tread with caution and respect for the differences in the new country.

By now, we have delved into every aspect of our parent company, its parent, and its subsidiaries or alternate locations. Our basic design was to identify what they use to disseminate information and what might be available that they do not use. We have even initiated searches in subsidiaries or alternate locations that might be in other parts of the world. Let us take a look at what we hope to have learned.

Ultimately, your search will not only reveal those places where you can find regular publications, but also those departments or functions whose cause in life is to produce policies and procedures in a regular and consistent manner. The latter are of great importance to you for a number of reasons. First, they are usually the owners of whatever policies and procedure that are now in place. They may or may not actually have procedures directed at information security, but they will have some form of information systems documentation that may well contain a lot of the policies and procedures that might be identified with that function. If they are adequate, they may be left alone or transferred to a dedicated section or new set of such documentation. If they are not — a more likely eventuality — you now know where they are and what they need to make them responsive to current needs. By working with the parties in these departments, you can not only get your message across, but can do so in a manner the company has already accepted. This keeps them from being questioned in too many quarters and makes them fit seamlessly into the procedures already in place.

The search we have described will provide any number of outlets for the information security message but should not be construed as complete. Even if you find complete policies and procedures departments and company newspapers in place and eager to get your input there, it does not ensure a smooth transition to getting your message distributed. Still keep the idea of bulletins in mind if the use of them is supported. Long ago I found that using this medium of approach is extremely effective for getting messages out quickly and effectively. Depending on the size of the company and the tools in place, they may come out as paper, Web page "flashes," or e-mails.

You may also find that publishing your own full set of policies and procedures will either continue with the corporate methodology or create a new one. If you are fortunate enough to have an online outlet already in place, your message may get out with a series of links. As time passes, your Web page will become the known source for information security knowledge and, therefore, the core element of your information security awareness program.

Summary

Every company has some means of spreading the word, whether it is about the company picnic, awards and service recognition, or news of economic conditions. It is up to us to find these means and take advantage of the circulation they have already accomplished. The homes of these publications may be in a media department, a department dedicated to putting out a company newspaper or letter, or a even a third-party operation that takes input from your personnel department to put out a slick periodic publication that is usually too infrequent and too hard to get copy into.

To be effective, you must make certain that all avenues of publication that currently exist are known and, where possible, are leveraged to spread your message.

A few things to consider in doing this:

- Tread lightly on toes. If there is someone responsible for a certain type of communication, make sure you know that person and work within the guidelines in place.
- Find out how the company currently gets information to the overall team. If there is a newsletter or paper, contact the publishers to find out what needs to be included. Generally, you will find that they are happy to get input that they do not have to write themselves.
- Take the time to find out the submission criteria for the paper involved. Try to keep submissions within length and form requirements as they stipulate.
- Look in obscure areas for other published documents. Some may well be found in the personnel department, but despite their being excellent sources of information, they do not seem to be in general circulation.

- If you are in a subsidiary, find out how the parent company spreads the word. If they have internal publications that drift down through the organization — to subsidiaries and branches — get a look at them and ascertain whether you can leverage them for your own use.
- While checking with a parent company, make certain that you are not building or publishing anything that is not in line with their established policies, standards, and procedures.
- If you are the parent company, find out if any work has been done in the subsidiaries and remote locations. Salvage and apply what fits, and try to spread it across the organization.
- Installations on foreign soil create their own types of problems. The obvious one is the language barrier; others might include ethnicity, the law of the land, and the overall relationship to not only the parent company, but to Americans (or whatever nationality your home office is) in general. If your ownership of the sub is fairly recent, you may have the additional task of bringing it up to your company standard.
- Check out any policies and procedures that the company has. If a specific department has control of such things, examine any technical or directive materials that might have snippets about information security. You might find it practical to update, move, or eliminate them.
- Look for the most contemporary of news distribution out there today, the Web. If your company has an internal Web presence, see where your message can fit in. Get assistance if you must in creating your own information security Web page and make it the residence of all of the policies and procedures involving the discipline. Adopt what you can, modify what you must, and create as needed to fill in the blank spaces.
- Take advantage of the versatility of the Web and have your page link available on the home Web page. Using that page to announce changes and urging employees to "go to" your web page via the provided links.

In short, use everything that is available to you before embarking on a new road. If there are communication vehicles, use them. If you can use bulletins in emergency situations, make sure that the publication thereof does not step on any toes. Every department head, no matter how small the department or what the driving force behind his or her management, is a potential ally. Approach them diplomatically, without threat or bombast. That is the best way to get the assistance you need to produce and manage a comprehensive and effective program.

Chapter 6

Using the Building Blocks Already in Place

In Section I, we have relentlessly attacked the archives, files, libraries, and document management tools the company had in place in search of usable documentation that pertained to information security standards, policies, procedures, and/or guidelines. Now, we are going to take what we found and figure out whether we can use them, all or in part, or whether we need to start over.

The first criterion for any type of document is whether or not it does what is intended. While this might seem an oversimplification, the annals of documentation writing are filled with paperwork or stored bits that do little beyond demonstrating the author's command of the language. Fine points are made that are covered elsewhere by major points, leading to needless redundancy. More about not grinding too fine later.

A lot of previously written material is going to have to be eliminated so as not to send an incorrect message. But, you ask, how does one decide whether or not the message is correct? I will give you a number of questions to ask with regard to any documentation found and its current location. Often, the message is clear and accurate, but resides where only librarians and chance sifters will ever find it.

As you read through the discovered media, try to keep these questions in mind:

- Does the material reflect the environment as it exists today? Carefully written procedures about the handling of 5 1/4 inch diskettes may be interesting, but cannot resolve any problems that exist today. (This assumption precludes organizations that reside in certain parts of the country where the handling of punch cards might still be pertinent.) Check with the keeper of the source and get rid of outdated material immediately.

Note: This question does, of course, refer only to entire segments of copy that can be excised as an entity. In many cases, as will be discussed, the copy can be updated (e.g., if the wording is right, replacing *diskette* with *CD* might just save you a lot of writing). Of course, the rest of the section must also be usable with minimal alteration.

- Is the material in a place easily reached by the rank and file? The best procedures in the world are not going to provide much guidance to any but the most privileged user if they are available only in a highly protected library or resource. Getting this documentation into a convenient and readily accessible location is the only chance to have it make an impact.

- Does the material refer to systems or processes currently in place? This may sound like a repetition of question 1, but it really covers an entirely different area. Often, a system is replaced in total, from the software through the hardware it was running on. While a similar, or even identical, function may have replaced it, the steps taken to secure the now defunct system may be useless. No one contests that the HR system must be protected from general viewing or alteration. However, maintaining information on the security provisions that were resident in the original system or the operating system it ran under is of absolutely no value.

- Is the information presented in a form approved for company policies and procedures? For some reason, a lot of grandfathered documentation is kept in a form that is either outdated or in a style developed by its author. You have spent a lot of time with the documentation folks by now; why not verify the form and content with their standards?

- Is the original author still around? Often documentation goes off in a lot of directions that, while useful to a greater or lesser degree, may not be easily analyzed in terms of the author's intent. Such copy, while marginally useful, may prove itself far too difficult to maintain in that form. If you cannot figure out what was meant and the author is not there to assist, get rid of it and replace it with something that meets the need while concurring with the established standard.

- Will the old documentation fit into the new standard? This includes the environment, the corporate philosophy, the apparent need, and the vehicles to be used to present it. Often, you will find that while a particular procedure makes sense and you will be able to use its content, the form in which it is presented is impossible to fit into the rest of the document. In this case, it is far better to paraphrase than to try to shoehorn it into place.

The questions above should be asked about every bit of information you have discovered in your earlier search. Hopefully, you will have discovered a huge quantity of information. But most often it has been prepared by a number of persons whose areas of responsibility varied widely. Much like the parable of the four blind men and the elephant each defining it in terms of what he can feel with his hands — one imagined a wall as he felt its sides; one a rope, as he grasped the tail; one a tree, as he hugged a leg; and one a snake, as he felt the trunk — each has prepared their offering in a manner reflective of their image of the problem. Your job, on the other hand, is to make certain that what you write conveys your message to the intended audience. Coding standards are not your problem; use of the products of such efforts is.

Now to set about slicing, dicing, and plugging the leftovers into what you have to write. **Remember, no part of what you will be doing to build your program is more important than the underlying policies and procedures.**

Your objectives in preparing policies and procedures is to present a clear picture as to how the company views its information assets, what each employee's responsibility is with regards to protecting those assets, and how to go about doing so. Not only will you be singing the corporate tune, but also you must include industry-recognized steps in the creation of the documentation in question.

This might be a good time for a little aside on your role as an educator.

Corporations have specific characteristics that make them individuals among their peers (note that I did not use the term "stand out among their peers"). A large part of that is the culture issue that I raised earlier. A huge percentage of culture is strictly feel-good stuff around how much the good corporate parent cares about their "offspring" (employees). "We want to demonstrate our trust and care for our team members" is the usual type of comment made in the company's slicks about the work environment.

Sadly, such "cultural" undertakings often lead to lax security in areas that cause the company the greatest exposure. If there is one statement that I grow weary of, it's "We are aware of the sensitivity of the situation, but have chosen not to protect the _____." (Insert word of your choice: server room, company vault, keys to the kingdom, etc.) Sometimes, if you are good enough and possess the persuasive powers of an evangelical preacher, you can get them to rethink the situation. The best way to approach it is to define the threat and the possible means for compromise by well-meaning but honest employees in day-to-day work.

Your job, as much as you have come to love it, too often includes protecting a stubborn company from itself. The above example demonstrates it clearly.

Note that we are starting to build a good definition of what has to be put in place to form your baseline. You have to pick and choose among the documents already in place for those you can use, those you can update or upgrade, and those that need to be discarded. Then, you have to identify what is needed to complete the suite of documentation needed to make the system work.

Let us then define the documents that are needed to make up the suite I mentioned:

First, there is the policy statement. This is a simple statement of the company's view on the securing of their information assets. It should be short — barely one page — concise and on a very high level. The more detail put in, the more exceptions will crop up.

The second item is the standards section. This tells what the company is striving for, on a detailed level. It tells what is to be used, how it is to be used, and what the final outcome of any action should be.

The procedures section tells how to go about attaining those standards, which are in themselves means to reach the goals outlined in the policy statement.

They will be step-by-step how-to information, designed to force compliance with the safety measures in place for corporate processing and information.

Finally, there is a guidelines document that I consider completely optional. Under normal circumstances, this section is used as a catchall for all of the other sections. It does not say you must, but rather that you ought to. If you put enough effort and thought into the other sections of the overall documentation, this section should be superfluous.

Let us revisit each of these sections and attempt to set clearer definitions for each.

The Policy Statement

This is the simplest and yet most often misunderstood section of the overall documentation. It is by definition a short, concise statement of the company's position on information security and contains a brief outline of who bears responsibility for maintaining that level of security.

Chances are that if you found any such document at all, it was a long, drawn-out treatise of many pages and few firm statements. One of the traps many fall into when preparing a policy statement is to try to be too inclusive, leading to too many conditions being addressed.

In actuality, the company's position can be summed up in a few statements: "XYZ Company considers information a company asset and expects it to be protected as would any other valuable asset of the company." The statement is simple, concise, and leaves absolutely nothing out in terms of what is to be protected. It triggers off of many volumes of other corporate wisdom and drivel about how the company feels about desks, machines, and widgets. There is no need to mention degrees of valuation as that, too, is covered in the same cold tomes noted earlier.

Another catchall statement that should be included in all policy documents is the statement of least privilege: "All persons shall have access to all information assets necessary to perform their work functions and none other." Assuming that your company does not have a problem with the statement (stranger things have happened), this simple sentence gives credence to your entire authorization function. It is the basis for access group structure and individual specialized authorization. Again, only a single sentence.

I will not go into a full policy statement here, but I have included a sample that can be adapted to virtually any type of company, whether finance, government, or manufacturer of the ubiquitous widgets.

A few things to remember when preparing the statement:

- Make it short: one page or so. People rarely read complicated documents completely, and this is one you want to be certain is read. Statements should be all-inclusive, with no exceptions or special cases. You can put caveats into the procedures later, but the objective here is to state the company's position and the end users' responsibilities.

■ Use statements like the principle of least privilege, one with which few corporate managers can find fault.

■ Define responsibility from senior management down to the spear carriers. Everyone has a piece of this thing and they had better know it.

■ Make it read like the Declaration of Independence. It is the keystone of your whole program so anything you find necessary to do should be defensible through it. By being extremely high ended, that is always possible.

■ Do not let the lawyers get their hands on it. Certainly, they are going to want to look at it and make some comments (that is what they get paid for), but resist letting them change the language to legalese. This document is for consumption by the entire company and you do not want anyone scratching their head trying to figure out what you are saying.

■ Find a way to multipublish the statement. This item should not only be in IS or even information security documents, but should also be in the new employees' handbook (more on this later). It is imperative that everyone sees and understands what is contained here. We will spend a lot of time on that later.

The Standards Section

This will be a much longer and more detailed document. It is highly unlikely that the world will be terribly excited about reading it and that is fine. First and foremost, this is the place where the whys and wherefores are spelled out.

For instance, a statement like "All production systems will be afforded protection that minimally requires the use of a user ID and password to gain access" is simple and straightforward, but it implies a number of other items. If we need to use a user ID to log on, what is the makeup of that ID? Does it relate to your name, the department you work in, or the specific site where you are located? If so, then a pattern should be established. If a password is required, how long must it be? What is the acceptable makeup of a password? All of these questions should be answered in the standards manual. This is the place where you can specify that all PCs have a virus protection package installed, and indeed, you can name the package.

In short, the standards document is where you set up what must be done and how it must be done. You can specify who may have access to specific assets and what steps they must take to get it. You can describe the steps that must be taken to ensure security, either with or without specifying products. In fact, you can outline the process needed to validate products for use simply by providing a list of criteria for testing and acceptance of the product.

Another item that can and should be included is a methodology for the validation of the ability to secure other software products that may be evaluated for purchase. Setting up standards as to how such products must perform in concert with the security measures in place and what provisions must be built into the product to ensure its security is a vital part of a standards document.

Later, we will explore the means necessary to make sure that this document is readily apparent to anyone entertaining the idea of bringing in new software. Of course, it goes without saying that development teams must adhere to the same standards in internal development of production program products. These, too, must be constructed in a manner so as to strengthen security rather than weaken it.

The standards document, then, gives you the opportunity to state how things should be. Later, when we get into procedures, we will demonstrate the way we attain that goal.

A quick aside: never get too involved in what other people call things. What we have defined as our four sections might not be the same as what someone else has labeled them. If anything called policies, procedures, standards, guidelines, operational instructions, or any of a hundred other names that someone has come up with appears on the radar screen, review it for content. In many cases, you will find items that, according to our definitions, belong elsewhere but can be used in preparation of our own documents.

In the time you spent with management during the interview process, you gained valuable insight into what they felt was important. Make sure that the standards manual includes all of them or reasons why they are not included.

The Procedures Section

This is where the rubber meets the road. Now that we have established company policy on information security and introduced standards for how things should be done and how they should look, we will prepare a much more detailed section on how to go about attaining those goals. To do so, there have to be clear, concise, and step-by-step instructions on how to go about doing so. That is your procedures manual.

In your travels throughout company documentation, you have encountered any number of manuals, files, and other items that purport to be procedures. They may be labeled "operating instructions," "desk procedures," "standard operating procedures," or as many other titles as you can name. Review them all for what can be used and make detailed notes on what cannot to make certain that the latter disappears when you publish.

These instructions may be companywide, local, or department oriented. In preparing procedures in that manner, there may be a huge variation in how they are stated and what is defined as a procedure by the entity. Some may be worthless, some dangerous, some pointless, and some (and I suspect a worthy percentage) of real value to you. Your efforts have to be in terms of deciding which is which, using a solid validating system. Directions you may wish to take are:

- Have a good laugh where warranted and discard what cannot be used. Make notes on what is counter to the task at hand and, once you have something to replace it with, tactfully suggest that the offending information be stricken.

- Verify that what is said is what the company wants said and can be used in further development of documentation.
- If the format is effective, entertain the idea of incorporating it or, even better, basing your continued work on it. There is no pride of authorship here; the task is to get the job done right and in good time.
- Make certain that the environment still supports what is in place.

All too often, each department has, in the absence of something corporatewide, created their own policies, procedures, standards, and guidelines. As noted, be careful not to exclude anything that references instructions as they may contain data that you want to see (whether you choose to include it or delete it).

Another issue often faced when researching "found" documentation is the type and quality of format and writing style. To be sure, a lot of it will be sufficiently flexible to be moved to another document with little effort or loss of content. On the other hand, you may be dealing with insider type information that includes a lot of acronyms and jargon that may not be recognizable to someone from outside of the immediate environment. If you can, adapt it. If not, it is best discarded. To do a complete job of reading such media, it is imperative to locate such insider terminology and correct or remove it. If it is not easily removed without loss of meaning, then it is extremely possible that the information is too focused for a general audience. Likewise if you fail to remove one of those references, it might well invalidate the entire statement. Unless the overall content is extremely pertinent, it is often not worth the time and investment of effort to try to salvage the copy. Paraphrase if possible, else, it may best be left out.

Another issue around locally written procedures is the nature of the author. While I enjoy a crossword puzzle as much as the next guy, I do not want to challenge my English skills while reading a company document. Too often, the writer is someone who was either assigned or jumped at the opportunity in order to demonstrate his or her vocabulary. Impressive, I am sure, but of limited value. Be careful how you go about declining to use such pedantic offerings as the writer may well be sitting across the desk from you. Knowing the ins and outs of a department, as reflected in such manuals, often leads to promotion. When you search for an author, do not be surprised to find him or her in a management position.

Again, I stress the importance of checking any documentation that refers to policies, procedures, standards, guidelines, and instructions. Very often, manuals will be put together with meanings far in excess of the definition I have given here. "Guidelines" may well translate to procedures in someone else's definition. Check it all.

Take advantage of the procedures section to give step-by-step instructions on how to meet the standards previously put forth. Do not be so proud of your skills that you do not use good work already completed. Good work lives well and can often make your job easier. If you came from a programming background, you know exactly what I mean.

The Guidelines Section

If you can afford to leave anything until a more convenient moment or to omit it altogether, this is probably it. The term *guidelines* is usually synonymous with *hints* on how to get things, do things, or build things. Rather than ironclad directives, guidelines suggest how to do a better job at whatever you are doing. It may include what companies might be able to provide certain commodities, in what languages coding may be done, settings or ranges thereof for equipment, or any number of different items.

For instance: if the corporate guideline is $15 for supper when on the road, it is unlikely that a $13.50 dinner check will be kicked back. Likewise, a $15.25 one is just as likely to be accepted. If lunch is allowed at $10 and breakfast at $7 and the total for the day did not exceed $32, you will not likely run into any problems. On other hand, if you were in New York City and expenses were figured on a Des Moines budget, you would be hard pressed to meet that schedule. However, in practice, adjustments would be made.

Before you ask what the price of supper in New York has to do with information security, remember that this is just an example of the flexibility of guidelines.

Now, we have a good working definition of guidelines (remember, it was only a couple of pages back?) and will adhere to it for all aspects of this section. But, is that definition as widely used elsewhere? I seriously doubt it.

When doing all of your reviewing of documentation, never overlook anything that sounds like it might contain some kind of instruction. (Is this starting to sound repetitive?) One person's guidelines may be another person's procedure, and in accordance with our definitions, may well be incorporated into a different section of the overall information security documentation. If a guideline states that all passwords will be six characters or more minimums, the statement transfers readily to our procedure section. Use it if it fits; do not concern yourself with the name of the volume it came from.

Assuming that you prepare guidelines, you can use this document for a repository for any helpful information you wish to pass along. If, for instance, the company has standardized on a number of antivirus products, list them. You are not making a direct statement of fact, but are providing useful information. By the same token, it is fine to list a number of products that can be used for any specific application. You can use this section to offer hints on selecting new hardware of software by listing the requirements that will have to be met to get them into your environment. There will not be hard and fast rules, but rather options that can be exercised to make new purchases to be added. Examples of this are the need for new software to be compatible with security measures now in place, for operating systems to be able to play well with what is already here.

In short, use the guidelines section to pass along useful information for users to apply when attempting to meet the more rigorous requirements of the standards and procedures sections already completed. Prepare a guidelines section if you have the chance and if you feel it is applicable to your particular environment. Do not get overly excited about having it in place with the first wave of documentation.

Summary

What we have covered thus far in this chapter is how to take advantage of any work already done toward meeting your goal of having good documentation in place as quickly as possible. We have discussed many of the hiding places where we often find valid information and have issued cautions against assuming that something is valid because it is labeled correctly.

Found documentation may often be valid, but there are a number of pitfalls to avoid:

- Watch out for narrowly focused information that may need so much updating to get it into form for a companywide distribution that it would be more effective to start over.
- Do not look just for documents labeled in a manner that fits our definitions. Many good ideas may be labeled differently or even have labels not in our limited vocabulary. Watch for valid information in "desk instructions," "departmental policies," or other similarly named documents. You will learn many of the hiding places as you go.
- Watch out for the aging factor. Too many procedures were written in times immemorial and put aside never to be seen again. Some of what you find will no doubt predate the Dead Sea Scrolls and will be as often and widely read. Make sure that such copy is relevant in today's environment.
- Make certain that what you adopt is readable and fits into the format you will be using. Much of what you find will have been written independent of any writing standards. Make a decision on whether to use or replace and stick by it.
- Try to remain within the definitions of the sections as given in this chapter. Keeping these areas apart will work for you in the long run.
- Fully understand the corporate standard for each of the sections of the documents you are preparing. Making the judgment calls as stated above will be much easier.
- Watch for insider jargon and acronyms. When you review for them, read carefully so as not to miss references to them.
- Be diplomatic when it comes to information already in place that is wrong or, worse, dangerous. It is usually necessary to tell a department, location, or other group that they will have to get rid of some of what they may view with extreme pride. Telling them to remove something that was prepared by someone still around (particularly if that person has since been promoted) is not often well taken.
- If you are going to tell people to drop their documentation, make sure you are offering something to replace it. Updated information is usually welcomed and makes the concept of giving up a treasured relic more palatable.

■ Do not make the mistake of writing for a Ph.D. thesis. Anything you put together must be easily readable by the rank and file. Curtail the desire to impress people with your vocabulary.

What we are attempting to prepare here is the foundation for our overall program. In turn, we are telling the people what the company stance is on information security and what their personal responsibilities are (the policy). We are stating, in detail, what must be done in support of that policy and spelling out each area in which it is applicable. We are literally building a recipe to maintain good security practices (the standards). We will then tell them, again in detail, how to go about meeting those standards and how to protect the company's information assets (the procedures).

As time allows, we may put together a book of hints on how to carry out the provisions of the first three documents. The book may contain overviews on how to meet the standards and how to carry out the procedures (the guidelines).

In putting together these documents, we will take advantage of everything available at the time our project began. Once we have evaluated these discoveries, we will use such sections as are applicable, even to the extent of rewriting what is valid to make it more universal and more in keeping with our current plan. We will take good ideas and will include them in an acceptable manner.

On the other hand, we will eschew documentation that is out of date, invalid, badly written, or counter to good security practices. We will make certain that the offending copy is removed completely, rather than let it continue to send out its misguided and, now, contradictory message.

Getting the policy statement prepared and out is our initial function. It can be prepared quickly, but at such a high level so as to be viewed much the same as motherhood and apple pie, and can, for all of those reasons, become immediately acceptable to corporate management. By introducing this first, we create a pattern of credibility that, I can assure you, will serve well in future endeavors.

From this basis, we will create the standards to detail what full compliance with the policy looks like. These will replace all of what went before (while liberally helping ourselves to their choicest parts) and be the reference point for what information security is to look like.

The procedures that follow will be step-by-step directions on how to go about meeting the provisions of the standards. Here, in particular, the language must be clear, concise, and readable to all who must comply with it. Most word-processing packages have utilities that can review copy for both readability and the grade level for which it is written. Aim for about the ninth grade level.

And, as the usual afterthought, put together a guidelines section only if you think it necessary. If you have quantities of information to share that do not seem to fit into the sections already defined, this is probably the best place for it.

Getting these documents out is the most important single step in putting an awareness program together. You are telling your audience what is expected, what is in place and what they are to do in support of it. We will talk about how to put it together in the next chapter.

Section 2

Establishing a Baseline

Up to this point, we have spent a lot of time just outlining how to go about getting ready to do the job and how to get it off the ground. All of the material we have covered is, in reality, applicable in any type of project initiation: find out what is there, find out who authored, controlled, or maintained it, find out what needs to be added, and find out what it will take to get changes going. Whether we are building an information security awareness program or a backyard fence, these are pretty much the baby steps in getting started. Checking the stability of your neighbor's last attempt is not much different from reviewing old documentation and processes.

In this section, we are going to begin the active building or improving upon the program we are trying to install. Rather than just reviewing and making notes, we are going to begin to build documentation, establish processes and get the program in front of our designed audience. We are going to make it a real thing.

Reviewed procedures will become updated procedures. Missing documentation will become tangible and directed, and processes will be put in place to not only make the environment more secure, but to continually remind the users of corporate information assets of the importance of safe information handling, and of their responsibility in doing so. The kicker we are going to add to the latter is to achieve their buy-in by the simplest means possible — by defining how it can benefit them.

Every book or article ever written makes a big issue about policies and procedures and this one is no different. However, we are going to give it added value by demonstrating how buy-in can be achieved by putting the policies and procedures in front of the crowd on a daily basis. We will not create reams of paper to be kept on shelves and forgotten, as are so many corporate dicta, but will try to place our documentation directly in the path of those who need it most.

To this point in time, the biggest barrier to adoption and use of information security documentation has been the relative vacuum within which it has resided. To be sure, some form of policies, procedures, standards, guidelines, and various other documentation has usually been prepared (often in a manner so rudimentary so as to be better described as *skeletal*) but relegated to internal IS document control systems that have linked them closely to the Dead Sea Scrolls in terms of availability.

Note: It might also be said that the referenced documentation matched the noted Scrolls in terms of currency, as well.

As we find, overhaul, and augment these relics or, if needed, replace them. We must find a way to make them items of use to the corporation. That will be covered, as well.

Preparing additional documentation will be treated at a high level, as it is not the aim of this book to teach how to prepare policies and procedures. Our focus will be on making certain that the right things are included and that they make sense to us, to the company, and to the end reader. There will be discussion on wording and on a few key phrases that can never be overused.

As you develop the process, you will need to make certain that end users are involved in it. They must not only be aware of the requirements, but be invested in them as well. How they go about gaining access and being allowed to use corporate information will be covered in this section.

We will put the marketing strategies — with regard to management — that we discussed in the last section to use here. Once we have put together valid documentation, we must get it blessed by management and circulated. The last issue, getting the news out, will be covered herein as well.

In order to make this section a bit more palatable, we have included pattern forms for a number of the documents suggested. They are extremely generic in style but will provide a solid baseline for building your own. Actually, most could be used with very little change.

We are now taking the first actual steps in building the program. From here on out, it is simply a matter of getting it across to the user community.

Chapter 7

Filling in the Blanks

Up to this point, we have mostly been discussing how to use what is in place and how to identify what needs to be added. In this chapter, we will look at some of the things that are likely to be missing or inadequate. Remember that we discussed how to identify those items that can be salvaged and those that would be better discarded and replaced. From here on out, we will dwell strictly on the replacements and how to make them quality endeavors. Part and parcel of that quality is to make them instruments of education and, therefore, contributors to the program we are trying to establish.

As mentioned, a policy statement, standards to identify good practices, and a procedures document are necessary components of the framework of a good program. In this chapter we will try to define the required elements to make these documents accurate, sturdy, and usable by all concerned parties.

A word of caution at this time: This is not a book on how to create policies and procedures; there are a number of excellent publications available that are devoted to just that subject. If such a book would interest you, I strongly recommend Tom Peltier's fine volume on the subject from CRC Press or Charles Cresson Wood's from Baseline Software (now a subsidiary of Pentasafe, Inc.). Both of these books have detailed instructions on how to go about writing your own documentation and offer prewritten policies and procedures that are all but "plug and play." They may be adopted as is or customized to meet your needs.

What I will do here is go over the components of each document (or, as we named them earlier, segments of the overall documentation), what to include, and a few failsafe items that should never be overlooked.

The policy statement is the shortest and, therefore, most critical of those segments. To that end — as promised — I have included a sample of a policy statement. Feel free to customize it to your organization's name and specific needs.

Standards are, on the other hand, quite detailed and require certain basic elements to make them responsive to the needs of good security. They should be tailored to the environment and cover all aspects of how things should be done to address good security. We will point out some of the things that should be covered.

The procedures segment is designed to inform the end user exactly how to comply with the standards. They will be step-by-step instructions covering each aspect of the standards, which in turn, will address the concerns of the policy statement. Is the common thread running through these items beginning to become apparent?

Before we get too deeply into this subject, a word of caution is needed: Whatever else you do, make sure not to go into this thing alone. You have worked hard to find the people responsible for what currently exists, now leverage their knowledge throughout your preparation of these important documents. They have already learned the ins and outs of what the company feels is important and they know exactly what subjects might have gotten their knuckles rapped.

As you progress in each section, make sure to keep in contact with whoever was responsible for anything in that area. If the area is untouched, ask several of them, to find out if there is a reason why it was untouched. Their input might send you off to talk to someone else, but you will find the time well worth your while, particularly if it keeps you from creating something that will have to be redone or eliminated altogether.

Present drafts to these folks and/or your documentation people as you progress. Their input can often make the producing of valid documentation a one-shot operation, rather than your having to rethink and rewrite as additional input comes in. Again, we are talking about leveraging resources.

To be effective, a policy statement has to be black and white; there can be no shades of gray. The directives state what the company wants in terms of the security of its information assets, and there are to be no degrees of compliance. To be sure, there must to be some exceptions to ironclad rules, but they belong in later segments, not here. Management runs the company and their approval of the policy indicates their agreement with its provisions. By the same token, if changes or exceptions are to be made, it will be done only with their agreement. We will talk about how to recognize and use that particular right of royalty. There are certain phrases that need to be inserted in a number of places that make the standards make sense. Again, more about that later.

The policy statement must be clear, concise, directed, and brief. The latter characteristic means about a page, give or take a few lines. This is one that everyone must read and the best guarantee for that is that it requires a minimal time investment to do so. Also, by attaining that level of brevity, the entire text may be included in publications normally thought of as for general consumption. As an instance, I point out the employee manual that every new hire at every company gets upon sign on. If the policy is only a page, it is only a page of the book, as well. Much more complete and easier sell than excerpting a longer document.

You will find that the hardest part of building a policy statement is keeping it short. Fight the tendency to try to cover too much within the confines of what should be a very high-level document. If it seems to want to extend too far, examine each component and see if more than one could be included under a larger heading. Do not worry about protecting machine-stored data under one item and paper data under another. They are both information assets and should be treated as such.

As the example in Exhibit 1 shows, the statement needs to be broken down into specific sections, each of which covers a particular aspect of its overall shape. Let us look at those sections a bit more closely and see what makes them functions as part of a terse, yet complete, whole.

- *The purpose section:* Simply describes why this document is being prepared and what it intends to accomplish. It need only be a few sentences, defining what it is you wish it to do. Just make certain that those sentences are clear, concise, and have no out clauses buried within them. Each should be absolutely definite.
- *The scope section:* Makes certain that the reader understands what areas the document covers. In general, that will be all information assets of the company. But in the case of subsidiaries or other related organizations, it might not. This is the place to define that. It often is not necessary to list the exceptions, as long as the statement of the scope describes completely what areas are involved.
- *The definitions section:* Makes certain to leave no word or term in the document less than fully understood by the reader. Will the words be the same in any document? Of course not, but the same terms might well crop up in a majority of such written policies. Have a third, or even a fourth, party go over it, to make sure that they understand what each word means. If there are questions, respond to them with additional definitions. If the number grows to ten or more, take a long hard look at your work. It may well be that you are writing over the heads of the expected audience.

If you key the philosophy of the document around the principle of least privilege, as I tend to do, this is the point at which to state it. As can be seen from the sample, it can be clearly stated in only a few words: in this case, a total of 26. If the name runs a bit longer than our fictional company, so be it. It is still only 25 words, exclusive of names like "International Consolidated Universal Automobile Parts, Supplies, and Other Assorted Gadgets and Gizmos." If by some misfortune of jobs seeking, you wind up working for an organization with a name like that, I strongly recommend that you make a parenthetical reference to a familiar name right in the purpose section. Use that reference from that point forward.

The policy statement itself will generally lend itself to a bullet format similar to the presentation in the sample. While I will not reiterate what is already in the sample, I strongly suggest that you use something very similar. Note that all of the statements are absolutes — there are no exceptions in any of the seven points — yet they cover all aspects of an ideal program. If you want to grant certain exceptions, deal with that in the standards soon to be written. We will present some foolproof wording for that when the time comes.

Exhibit 1   Information Security Policy Statement

ABC Corporation
Information Security Policy

Purpose
To identify ABC's information resources as corporate assets. To define the responsibilities of those through whose hands these resources pass. To state the corporate position on the handling, use, and disposition of these assets and the provisions for penalty for misuse of said assets.

Scope
This policy incorporates all information assets owned, used, or produced by ABC or its subsidiaries and its provisions cover all persons or organizations who may come into contact with them by means of responsibility, business contact, or coincidence.

Definitions
All information resources are hereby defined as ABC corporate assets. Assets are those items that are of monetary value to the corporation. It is stated that no assets — save staff members — are of greater value to the corporation than are the information assets. For purposes of this policy, assets used or produced by ABC are deemed to be owned by ABC

Principle of Least Privilege
All users of ABC information will be granted access to all of those information assets necessary for the performance of their duties and none beyond that.

Policy Statement
- Any use of ABC information assets must be done in compliance with ABC information security standards and procedures.
- Any use of ABC information assets may be monitored and recorded to ensure compliance with ABC information security standards and procedures.
- Information assets may be used for ABC business only, without exception.
- Access authority or entrusting with assets is granted to the individual and may be used only by that individual.
- All legal, licensing, or contractual requirements involved in the use of assets will be adhered to completely. Copying of licensed software outside of the provisions of that license is strictly forbidden.
- Information or software may be removed from ABC premises only with the authorization of the manager responsible for those assets.
- Failure to comply with the provisions of this Policy or the Information Security Standards and Procedures is grounds for disciplinary actions that may include termination and/or prosecution.

Responsibilities
- ABC senior management is responsible for the implementation and support of this policy.

Exhibit 1 Information Security Policy Statement (continued)

ABC Corporation
Information Security Policy

- Line management is responsible to support this policy and to ensure that respective staff members comply with the policy, as well as the standards and procedures.
- The manager or information security is responsible for preparing, maintaining and, updating these documents as necessary and for the discovery and implementation of restrictive, measuring, and monitoring measures to ensure compliance with said policies, standards, and procedures.
- Each employee, contractor, vendor, customer, or other party entrusted with access to ABC information assets is responsible for the maintenance of said assets in compliance with this policy, the standards and procedures, and other such documentation as management might see fit to implement.

While the seven points made cover the majority of most environments, I do not for a moment suggest that additional items cannot be added nor some of those present deleted. However, do not do so lightly as the "magnificent seven" can be located in almost any industry.

You may, within the responsibilities section, find that you need to slice a bit finer than is done in the sample. Perhaps responsibilities differ sufficiently among certain levels of staff to warrant that they be treated differently here. That I leave totally up to you.

I strongly suspect that this sample document could be easily moved into any corporation with changes made only to the extent of internalizing some of the language — for example, "team members" or "associates" instead of "employees," or the use of acronyms or shorter names ("Met" vs. "Metropolitan"). In any case, this should be a useful template.

As I mentioned earlier, we will not go too deeply into the standards and procedures sections here except to define what should go into them. The books I mentioned do a far better job in their content than I can do in a single chapter. What I will do is offer some suggestions.

First, you may find that combining the two sections into a standards and procedures manual may well be to your advantage. This is stated for several reasons:

First, by having a standard and following it up immediately with step-by-step instructions as to how to address it, the book is much more readable for many. Rather than prepare materials on the subject in two separate locations, the full complement of information on the material is in one location. If you choose to go that way, try to use a structure similar to the following model:

- ***Standard:*** *Passwords will be changed no less often than every 30 calendar days.* This statement is not only clear in its meaning, but discriminates between calendar and work days as well as suggesting that passwords can be changed more often than every 30 days. The statement is clear, concise, and contains the only outs you will need.

- ■ ***Procedure:*** *Passwords are to be changed only using (software product/utility) and can be accomplished by doing (1,2,3, etc.)* This states what you are to use and the steps needed to accomplish the password change (steps 1,2,3, etc.). The statement is neat, compact, and readily implementable.

There are specific items that should be covered in all such documents, whether separately or combined. Should you use the separate option, remember that the standard tells what, while the procedure tells how.

Try to include the following items in your document or documents as you so choose. In this instance, we will treat it as though both sections are combined. Under either set of circumstances, the content and order will be the same.

The Introduction

This is a statement of purpose as to what you are attempting to accomplish with the ensuing copy. It should prominently mention the policy that it is designed to enrich and support and make note of that intention. Make certain that whether or not you combine the two sections, the reader is well aware of the fact that he or she needs to understand what is contained.

Make a point of preparing this and ensuing chapters in plain English. While your command of the language might create awe and jealousy among your readers, it will not enhance their vocabularies quickly enough to make pedantic copy intelligible. Aim for the ninth grade level and use your word processor's grammar tools to make certain that the copy stays on that level. This is more than a suggestion; it is an imperative. Use the same caution in all sections.

Protection of Information

The objective of this section, and the reason for placing it first in the manual, is to make certain that a good understanding of what is to be protected and why is carried forward in the document. Here, you will describe what information is, making certain that people understand that it can be electronic, paper, microform, online, off-line, and mentally imaged. What you have access to, can pick up, or know all fall under the heading of information and where that pertains to the company, falls under the provisions of these standards and procedures.

Later, well after covering all of the other points of this document, we will discuss personal responsibility. That section is designed to take the provisions from this section, through the specifics covered throughout, and bring them together under the expectations of the company with regards to the handling of its proprietary information by those authorized to do so.

From here on out, sections can really be put in whatever order makes the most sense within your organization. The interviews you held way back in the first section of this book will come into play here, as you address the points you found most important to the interviewees. As with most things, the concerns of management are the concerns that should remain uppermost in your mind while writing.

For the sake of this book, I will place the sections in what I consider a logical order. However, conditions within your own company may well dictate an entirely different order of importance. Take what you can from the chapter descriptions and arrange them as you see fit. There is no such thing as a mistake here, as long as all subjects are covered. You may, however, find that you will need to add sections to cover issues of concern in your environment. In fact, you might well find that you want to divide these sections into smaller fragments for processing. Personal computing devices may or may not address the matter of PDAs, for instance, depending on the degree of detail you wish to relate. That being the case, and with the rapid evolution of the technology, a separate section can focus much more sharply on this area.

For now, I will continue with the sections as I see them.

Log-Ins

Not a large subject, in itself, but the place to talk about what a user ID should comprise, the company criteria for establishing one — initials, department numbers, etc. — and for what systems one is likely to be assigned. This is the perfect place to talk about the importance of not making it a public issue, despite its tendency to be formulaic for the company.

You also need to be talking about how one goes about logging in to the various systems at this point, as well. Go through the steps for each system (on the procedures side) and use this opportunity to make certain that your audience hears about the importance of logging *off*, as well as logging on. Remember, this is an awareness issue and should be presented at every opportunity.

Passwords

Again, a subject with a lot of angles, all of which can be used for teaching. This section should be used to state the company standards for length, minimum number and nature of characters (alpha, numeric, special), and frequency of change requirement. Go into detail as to how the change mechanism works and what the user must do. If steps have been taken to ensure security, such as the use of a hackers' dictionary to test selected passwords against, history files, make sure that the reader knows about them.

Basic truth of security: If the user knows that you think something is important, they are more likely to.

Another area to be covered is to make the reader aware of means they might use to keep their passwords complex and hard to break. Offer them the means to use right hand/left hand patterns, where some characters are typed in a row with one hand or the other and a second set is typed with the opposite hand. Use pronounceable nonsense — a meaningless string of numbers or letters (or combination thereof) that can be pronounced to make it easily memorable — like "GROWPF" or something similar. Or, talk about how often passwords are easily traceable to an individual by someone who knows them only casually — names of family, pets, schools, favorite teams, and so on — and how such knowledge is a hacker's favorite tool.

I often use anecdotes to sell a point whether speaking or writing. One of my favorites with regards to passwords is one my son coined at the age of 11. I had been — perhaps more than I realized — teaching him about information security from about the time he was five or six months old (can't start too soon!) and he had a pretty good idea of what good practices are by this time. A password he was using was "OHAYA," something I certainly did not recognize. When asked, he casually told me that he had "made" the word by taking the second letter of each word in "Go ahead, make my day!" Another gimmick for creating an unguessable password.

Stories like the above bring a concept home much better than do dry, dull rules and regulations. Our objective is to gain compliance, not to put people to sleep. There is no need to make a manual sound like a Will Rogers monologue, but never overlook the impact of anecdotes.

Terminals and the Network

In today's work environment, virtually everyone at a terminal is going to be attached to one or another network. This may be as sophisticated as a worldwide, multitopology net, in which multiple platforms talk to one another and the user community on different levels, or something as simple as a few PCs attached to a single server. Obviously, the lengths to which this section goes should be reflective of the level of service provided. Still, certain consistencies exist.

For one, the issue of logging on with a well-protected log-in and password will be the key to accessing any network. Make an issue of "well protected."

Remind people to log off of the net if they are not using it, whether or not they are using their PC offline. Network enabled terminals, casually left connected, are each an extreme exposure. In describing that, remind people that the computer knows only who logged on to the system, not who is sitting at the keyboard. Whatever is done, it sees as having been done by whomever logged on. Remind them of the consequences of untoward actions that are credited to them, despite their denials. Also make the point in terms of the company's exposure. Bad for you, bad for the organization.

Make clear the impact things done at a PC can have on a network. A virus, for instance, introduced at a workstation, can be transmitted across the network at the next log-on. Admittedly, we are crossing over to other sections here, but better to say it twice, than not at all.

Under standards, go into the reasons why access is allowed and that it is allowed for purposes of doing the company's work, only private use is a no-no.

This might be a good place to introduce another universal concept. This will work for you in any standards and procedures manual, for any function. **The phrase "Unless authorized by management" can be used in virtually any situation.** Its function is to simply say "Nothing is so concrete that it cannot be changed. However, it will, by golly, only be changed if the top dogs authorize it!" You can alter the wording in a number of ways, add "in writing" to the phrase, "your management" can be substituted for management, or it can become "senior management." In short, it states that there is an out, but it is not yours to select. Someone higher up is going to have to make the call and is going to have to be responsible for it. This phrase is the only delimiter you ever need to use and you can use it as sparingly or often as you deem necessary. It will, in most cases, save pages of writing with regard to exceptions or odd situations. Use it in your documentation as you would use a condiment at the table, sprinkled where needed.

For this section, try to limit yourself to the terminals/workstations and save talk about the network itself to the next section.

Corporate Networks

You may or may not choose to use this heading, depending on the level of sophistication of your network. If it is, indeed, far reaching, you may well want to devote some time to the facts surrounding topology, firewalls and security software, and the users' responsibilities. By all means, outline the fact that there are checks and balances, without going in to much detail.

Assuming that there is some type of server based archiving or storage capability, this is a good place to go into how it works and what the conditions are for its use. If there are server based tools, this is a good place to discuss them and the concept of licenses — use a package, release a package, so others may use the license.

If cryptography is a part of your system, this is a good place to touch on it. Go into detail in the section labeled "Cryptography."

The need for privacy can be stressed again in this location. Make the nature of networking clear to the reader: how one can never be sure of where other nodes might be or who might be on them at any given moment. I know that this terminal is in a restricted location, but are all of the others?

E-Mail

Now that we have established that there is interconnectability, the next step is to recognize the probable use of e-mail.

Now, in today's workplace, e-mail has at the same time become the greatest advance in interpersonal communications and the biggest posterior pain going. The conversations that used to take place over coffee at break time can now be conducted throughout the day from the privacy of one's workplace. Additionally, in the case of the Internet, we can now communicate worldwide with the same alacrity. We will hit the Internet much harder in the next section.

First, make it extremely clear in your standard that using e-mail for anything but work purposes is not allowed. Now, we all know that this type of provision usually has a built in "wink factor" — what we might turn a blind eye to under normal circumstances. However, it is imperative that the issue of nonbusiness use being disallowed is clear. You will find that that wink factor will vary widely from company to company, from department to department, and sadly, among individuals. We are not here to judge the wisdom of any of those aberrations, but to state clearly what is expected.

Another item, covered elsewhere, is the issue of e-mail borne viruses. Today, this is the most common method used to spread viruses and the techniques used in the Melissa virus distribution — using the host's own address book to spawn additional e-mails — is used in most new viruses discovered in the wild. Make a very large point of this item in discussion here. We can talk about the nature of viruses elsewhere.

This is not a bad place to discuss e-mail archiving and housekeeping. Too many servers are now clogged with messages that serve no purpose at all, but were never deleted.

The Internet

If we are going to discuss networks and e-mail, we certainly cannot leave out the Internet. Here is a medium that truly connects the world. Through this medium, e-mail circumnavigates the globe; information can be found in quantities that we often cannot understand, much less use, and advertising, shopping, and survey are as close as the screen.

When one is researching an item for business purposes, this is as good as research tools get. On the other hand, when one has idle time (the individual's assumption, not the company's), there are more things to explore than one could do in several lifetimes. Therein, Shakespeare stated, lies the rub.

Excess employee surfing has become one of the worst time wasters in corporate America today. There are a number of tools available to keep track of such goings on and they are often a good investment. How then, do we handle our own staff with regard to this siren song?

First, make a clear statement that use of the Internet, from company terminals, during business hours for anything but company work, is forbidden. Second, make Internet access an authorized activity. In short, you do not gain access without the express permission of your superior(s). Build a form for requesting access, be it paper or online, and make certain that no Internet access is granted without it.

Almost any network-monitoring software can detect what is being done from any terminal on the network. To identify the URLs that have been accessed from it is a relatively easy task. In addition, the software mentioned earlier that monitors Internet use, reduces even the minimal work that goes into that. Make a specific point in your procedures section that the ability to monitor Internet access is part of the suite of tools that IS has. That knowledge, coupled with the specifically stated bans on misuse, are all the threat you normally need. In the vast majority of cases, that will be sufficient to deter most potential abusers. In those cases where abuse is suspected (or reflected by the monitoring-specific packages) appropriate actions can be taken.

Remote Access

In many cases today, what with telecommuting becoming so popular, employees wish (or their superiors wish them to) to gain access to corporate systems from home. To grant this, a number of things must be put in place. Obviously, there needs to be some means to qualify a calling party before granting them access to the system or network. If they dial in, there are a number of things available to reasonably identify them. As this is not a book on hardware and software, I will go into no more detail. The company must decide what level of security they feel they need and provide it.

At a minimum, an employee's access should have to be approved by the manager who feels that such access is beneficial to the company. This authorization may result in the programming of communications devices to accept a call from a specific point — the issuance of tokens to meet the needs of token-based access authorization systems or even the issuance of communications hardware. In the latter case, the hardware should bear a signature that can be recognized on the receiving end — an electronic handshake, so to speak.

The steps that the user must take to gain such authorization should be the subject of the procedure, as should the expectations with regard to maintaining security. A means to make sure that management is aware of their responsibility in issuing such authorization should also be included.

Software Utilization

This is a subject with a few vital issues involved. Specifically:

- The issue of nonstandard and third-party purchased packages
- The issue of software licensing

By way of explanation: In a company of any size, there are usually well-accepted software products tested and in place to perform the tasks the company feels need to be done. Often, in more complex environments, these packages are specified due to their ability to interact effectively with other products in use. On the reverse side, there is always the issue of incompatibility that can cause systems crashes.

Your task, outside of this manual, is to make certain that some organ within the IS community is charged with reviewing software before it can be used on any company system. Without such a function, little you say in this document will be attainable.

Assuming that such a departmental task exists, your standard should read in a manner that expressly states that only software with the seal of approval from this department is acceptable for use on company systems. In addition, you must set forth a procedure that gives the end user options to request that program products that can be used to perform needed functions be reviewed by that organization. This would assume that one of two scenarios exists:

1. The user department has "discovered" a program product so utilitarian that to consider the company continuing to function without it is unthinkable. It must be submitted to the department in question for purposes of evaluation to accomplish the outlined tasks and reviewed against other similar products for a better solution.
2. A specific issue is recognized by the end user that, to their way of thinking, could be remedied by the addition of software to perform the functions associated with the issue. In this instance, the department would be charged with reviewing the objectives in question and locating software that accomplishes the necessary ends while fitting into the current operating environment.

In today's world, with processing on desktop units being so facile, there is often an issue around given individuals feeling that they can resolve such issues with a trip to the nearest Egghead or Comp USA outlet. While these are splendid sources for software, this practice must be specifically forbidden if the operational environment is to remain safe.

A final thought on the purchase and distribution of software: The same easy access to countless products either from retail sources or on the Internet has led to a somewhat cavalier attitude about licensing. For one, only certain individuals within any company have the right to make contracts on behalf of the company. Signing a license agreement on behalf of the organization or accepting a "click wrap" download are likewise against policy.

Worse yet is the practice of purchasing a copy of licensed software and proceeding to load it onto whatever systems are seen as needing it. Almost without exception, this practice is in violation of the licensing agreement. Your standard must specifically preclude the use of any software beyond the provisions of the license agreement.

Only the forbidding of the practice and reasonable auditing of what resides on systems can preclude drawing the interest of the Business Software Alliance (BSA) or the Software Publishers Association (SPA). An audit by either of these organizations and the finding of violations can lead to heavy fines and damages being assessed against the company.

Make a statement forbidding the practice of making additional copies of program products, loading them on machines not provided for in the agreement, or accepting any software via "click wrap" or any other means on behalf of the company. In addition, make certain that some level of audit is conducted regularly to make certain that no violations exist.

Viruses and Virus Detection

Today, viruses get more ink than any other aspect of information security. Malicious code like Melissa and IloveYou have smitten thousands of machines around the world and have brought huge networks to their knees. The old days of worrying about such programs hidden on diskettes inadvertently placed in a machine are gone, in favor of the simpler, e-mail carried viruses.

Much can be written about viruses and the steps that can be taken to track and destroy them. However, that is not our aim here. What we wish to do is set up a list of rules on how to prevent such items from coming on board and how to treat them once they are here.

Your standard should reflect the do's and don'ts of handling potential carriers of these programs. Also, you should specify an antivirus product that is to be selected as outlined under software utilization. It should be on every terminal on a network and some form of server-based product should be in place, as well.

In your procedures, you need to define what product is used, how to use it on your systems, and how to go about updating it on a regular basis. If your network is advanced enough to have push technology, you should be describing how the antivirus product gets updated so that its download is run interference free.

There also needs to be a segment on recognizing potential carriers and what to do about them. Provide information about how the virus is contracted and how the user with the infected system should respond.

Our initial aim is to make users smart enough to avoid infection, responsive enough to prevent its spread should their systems become infected, and technical enough to make sure that their antivirus measures are operating at current peak performance. It does not hurt to make sure that they have someone to call should their computers become infected.

Backup and Recovery

This section is designed to set forth standards on how to back up sensitive data so that it will not be lost due to any action, intentional or accidental. The standards should outline what is to be backed up and how often and where it should be stored. The company should also have a schedule for taking backup media off site.

The procedures aspect of this section should include information on doing backups, the best materials to use, and some information on the dependability of the various storage media. In addition, there need to be instructions on how to retrieve information stored elsewhere and how to troubleshoot the difficulty and ensure nonrepeat.

The next section will examine true business-resumption planning in more detail.

Contingency Planning

This section is more a follow-up to the preceding section than a stand-alone process. The reason for backup is to make certain that the information needed is available and in a usable form. The standards we will want to create here include the provision that every production system should have a complete contingency plan in place to ensure its ability to be reproduced in a minimum length of time and in a remote location. Along with information, we face the need to be able to replace machinery, communications, and location for this to work.

Because contingency planning is such a specialized field, we will not go into the nuts and bolts of it here. If you are interested in learning more, I suggest Auerbach's *Business Resumption Planning* written by Ed Devlin, Cole Emerson, Leo Wrobel, and yours truly. It contains information that will allow you to create a plan from the ground up for any size installation.

Physical Security

First and foremost: before beginning this section, check with corporate security to find out what provisions they have in place. While the measures you might suggest are no doubt effective, you do want to make certain that they are not in conflict with those set forth by that department. If, during your review, you find something that is dramatically out of line, discuss it with security personnel. An agreement is sure to be reached.

Your standards should set forth the measures that need to be taken to ensure the physical security of any and all parts of the network and its components. For instance, data centers, communications centers, or server farms should have minimum requirements listed in terms of construction, cooling, and entry portal locks. Alarms and fire and water detection/prevention should be specified as well.

When you get to terminals, the road gets a bit rockier in that they can occur in so many different locations. If, for instance, you are involved in multinational processing, some of your network will node in areas with problems much different than you face at home. Where possible, try to provide instruction for securing those sites with that in mind. You may have terminals in relatively open areas that cannot be readily locked away from public access. For example, a terminal in a bank lobby has access to the bank's mainframe or servers and so should be restricted closely as to what it can access. Home computers have much the same problem.

Your standards should include isolation and locking instructions, acceptable temperature ranges, and a statement as to the responsibility of the end user to make certain that it is secure from misuse, damage, or destruction.

In the procedures, give examples of how to accomplish the above.

Personal Computing Devices

More and more, corporate information is being loaded and stored on privately owned computer systems. In some cases this will simply be work taken home to be done on a personal computer, carried abroad on a laptop, or even downloaded to a personal digital assistant (PDA). At this writing, the latter is being beefed up to where desktop computers were a few years ago — and they are starting to look like mini mainframes — and can download vast quantities of information. Due to their portability and, therefore, attractiveness to thieves, they present many significant problems. The problem is growing daily.

Your standards must reflect absolutes as to who can download information, what they can download, and how they are to store it. All personal computers, for instance, must have up-to-date antivirus products in place before downloading company data. No laptop should contain sensitive information on the hard drive or the hard drive should be removable and be carried separate from the machine. It is estimated that one in four laptops will be stolen, so this is a very real threat. Let the machine go, but make sure there is no company information going with it.

Your procedures should outline how to go about getting permission to take information off the company site (another form: approval by management). It should also include information about using a removable hard drive and the care and protection of smaller, yet high-powered computing devices. Portability may be a boon for the traveler, but it is a nightmare for security.

Telephones

This might seem a bit of a stretch in terms of information security, but actually it does warrant our attention. The most important aspect is, of course, voice mail. This is both a blessing and a blight.

If you say nothing else in this section, please make sure that the sentence "VOICE MAIL IS NOT SECURE!" appears in type no smaller than it does here. For some strange reason, people who cannot reach their party feel absolutely safe in leaving information they would be whispering, even in the office.

If someone needs to talk to someone about something sensitive, the voice mail should only indicate that something important needs to be discussed. Do not elaborate in this medium. Make sure to put those last couple of sentences in your standards.

Telephones, like e-mail can be easily abused. Without sounding like a scolding grandma, state clearly that company phones are for company business. There is little reason to say much more.

Violations

We have talked about a lot of potential misuses throughout this chapter and, of course, there will be results from the detection measures we have described. To make use of those results, some means are needed to notify violators of their transgressions and take the necessary steps to prevent its recurrence. Now, the provisions of this section are really for only a select few to execute: the analyst who discovers the transgression, the information security person who must contact the individual or his supervisor, and the supervisory staff themselves. Still, knowledge of these steps can in themselves be deterrents, hence making its inclusion here educational as well as directive.

In the standards, list the types of activities for which violations may be tracked and responded to. Be a bit vague, as we are not trying to write an instruction manual for people trying to misuse systems and avoid detection.

Note: This is a place where I always like to make reference to the ability to monitor most systems without going into detail as to what it entails. To be sure, we are going to chase down suspected misdeeds, but we are not going to routinely check the activities of every user. Simply say "E-mail can be traced." rather than going into how it would be done.

Make the definitions of abuse quite clear here, so no offenders can suggest that they were not aware of a transgression.

Your procedures should make it clear how a user's activities can be traced by request from management and what steps may be taken to obtain such a trace. These processes should be similar for e-mail, systems use, Internet abuse, or other activities. Again, outline the potential penalties.

Cryptography

In this section, the use of encryption should be discussed. Previous to the point of writing, there should be some agreements among management and IS as to what should be encrypted, how that should be done, and what is to be done. Some information, for instance, can be in the clear when stored locally on protected media. However, when transmitted, it should be in encrypted form. Having this schema in place is the basis for your standards. Iterate all of what must be encrypted and under what circumstances. It is suggested that levels of encryption (NNbit, etc.) and the technology and types of keys be kept under closer guard.

The procedure should indicate how to recognize what must be encrypted and how to go about getting the matter accomplished. Most of the concerns should be in the hands of IS, but the user has to know how to go about obtaining that service.

Personal Responsibility

This is the final section of what I refer to as core concerns for a standards and procedures manual. It details the expectations of management with regard to the performance of each staff member. The standard must make a statement that each individual who handles sensitive data is responsible for its safety and security. It should go on to state that knowledge of mishandling, misuse, or misfeasance should be reported to proper authority.

Additional sections will deal with the physical security of the physical site. For instance, if you have a badge system that requires visible wearing by all employees, someone seeing an unrecognized person without such identification should either challenge the individual or contact security to do so.

Your central theme? Security is everybody's business.

The provisions of this section should be reflected elsewhere in your overall program. Each part of it will stress that no matter the rules, it is up to the individual to provide the strongest link in security. As we progress through this book, you will see more and more how we hope to accomplish that sense of responsibility among staff.

So, we have listed a total of 18 areas for which standards and procedures must be prepared. As stated before, although these areas are pretty standard among installations, there is a chance that not all will fit into your environment. That's fine, as is the inclusion of extra sections, as you see fit. The format is clear and we have tried to give good examples that not only demonstrate how each area should be addressed, but further define the differences between standards and procedures.

Summary

We have, in this chapter, defined the differences between policies, standards, and procedures. These, for our purposes, are the most important aspects of setting up a baseline for your program. A few things to remember:

- The policy statement is the foundation of these publications. It states the company's position with regard to information security and clearly defines the philosophy under which the information assets of the company are to be managed.
- The standards document defines the company's expectation in terms of performance. It states how the provisions of the policy are to be carried out and what considerations must be made.
- The procedures may be intermixed with the standards or may be kept unto themselves. As a two-part document, they present the opportunity to explain to the reader how to go about complying with and implementing the provisions of the standards.

The examples we have provided in this chapter are good, workable documents, but are as generic as possible. What we have attempted to provide is a jumping-off point for the creation of similar documents for your organization. While the "ABC Company" is pretty generic, your employer is not. Fit your needs into the frameworks provided and the outcome will work. You can become more original later, when time and your enhanced knowledge allow.

Once these three documents are complete — in workable form, they will never be complete — you have the baseline for the launch of your program. From here on out, we will explore the means to get the word out and to verify the quality of the program once in place.

Chapter 8

Forms, Roadmaps, and Higher Education

Now, at last, we are coming to the point of talking right to our audience. We are hand-feeding them information that will provide them with an entry into understanding information security and what they need to do to comply with the company's wishes.

I freely admit that the title of this chapter is a bit of whimsy that I am treating myself to at this time. To be sure, we will be discussing the forms that need to be put in place to allow for the employee's acknowledgement of receipt of copies (or links) of the documentation that we have slaved over in the last two chapters, an understanding of their responsibilities in terms of that documentation, and of course, the ever-present access request forms.

The "roadmaps" mentioned deal strictly with the issuance of those forms and the relating of them to the standards and procedures directions given to request access. We can count on supervisors to present the majority of them at orientation time, at least for the basic accesses that all employees will have.

Once we get into the more specialized authorizations that might pertain to specific job duties, the fledgling staff members will seek out and secure the necessary forms and run down the signatures needed to get the authorization they need. And, as they follow the instructions they have read in the manual, they will move effortlessly (we can only hope) towards the access they require.

"Higher education" is my own little play on the ideas surrounding what the new employees will learn from the exercises listed above. At each step, they will learn that the provisions of the standards and procedures will lead them unerringly towards the right places to gain signatures and to submit the forms.

Note: The terms *forms* and *signatures* may well mean online approval and routing in today's company. However, the service provided is little different from what we did a few years ago with paper and what, surprisingly, many companies still do. Whenever you see those terms, consider them to equate to the electronic versions as well.

Let us talk a bit as to the forms we are dealing with here. They will start with the issuance of an agreement that will be presented during orientation, after the policy and a bit more of the company's position on information security has been covered. This form — paper or electronic — will be kept in the employees' files throughout their tenure with the company. Should any issues arise due to the employee's failure to live up to the provisions of the listed documents, that form is proof positive that the employer was notified of their existence and knew of the responsibility. The employee's signature, whether physical or electronic, signifies that at least at the time of hiring, the employer admitted to knowledge of these responsibilities. Believe it or not, this simple action has been the pivotal point in many wrongful termination suits.

We have included a sample of that document in this chapter (Exhibit 1).

As we approach the subject of forms, we will consistently reference the means to perform the same functions online as they are done by many companies today. It is my considered feeling that more, rather than less, organizations will go this way.

In most instances, whether Internet based and using HTML or something less known or more exotic, the scripts will be written in a manner to check an agreed-upon list for the proper approvals for the form and will route them accordingly. For instance: An access request might be initiated by an individual and, upon entering it, a check is made of some aspect of personnel records or others to locate the reporting structure within which the applicant is working. The form is then routed to the individual's supervisor for approval and continues thereafter to the next required signatory (in this instance, electronically) and, finally, to the person chartered with making the system change. As with so many things, once it is left to the machine, there is little chance to forget or have the access request slip under a pile of papers on one's desk. It will be awaiting them in a queue as soon as they log on.

Just as an aside, I have found that these things will remain in queue in some peoples' in box for days before forwarding. Then, approximately ten minutes after having approved it (after ten days in their queue), they call me and want to know when I am going to approve it. After all, I am the only obstacle to getting this access updated!

Personally, I am a large fan of the multipurpose access request form (Exhibit 2) that minimizes the number of separate forms and the accompanying instructions that have to be created, made available to the general population, and filed. Particularly in a computer-based system, the forms can be routed according to the approvals needed from the owners of the resource to which access is being requested. An archive of such requests, best kept in an individual's user profile, makes an effective audit trail as to accesses requested, accesses held, and the electronic signatures of the approvers. This record allows auditors to review accesses, check for proper approvals, and see a user's exact authorizations at the time of termination. Literally, the ability to remove all accesses, via checklist, is now available. Put this information into a database, build or buy the proper tools, and these profiles become a complete

Exhibit 1   Information Security Agreement

Information Security Agreement

In accordance with the information security policies, standards, and procedures of the ABC Company, I, the undersigned do fully agree with each of the below noted points:

1. I have been given a copy of the ABC Company information security policy.
2. I understand that there are specific standards and procedures for the handling of ABC Company information assets and have been informed as to how to review them. I will do so before any attempt to utilize those information assets.
3. I know that I will be issued specific access capability to ABC Company systems and will not attempt to expand upon that access. I will use all information assets as intended by the company.
4. I will keep any user IDs and passwords issued to me in full confidentiality and will not share them.
5. I will either lock or log off any terminal that I am using when I leave that position.
6. I will not discuss ABC Company proprietary information with anyone outside of the company nor any other employees whose job functions do not require access to it.
7. I will make certain that waste materials that contain ABC Company confidential information are destroyed and not included with common trash.
8. I will conduct myself in a manner so as not to place any ABC information assets or the systems upon which they reside in peril of destruction, contamination, compromise, or loss.
9. If I detect the misuse of ABC Company information assets by other parties, I will inform my supervisor immediately.
10. I understand that failure to comply with any of these points could lead to disciplinary action up to and including termination and prosecution.

I have read, understand, and agree with all of the statements made above.

(Signed) _____

Employee printed name _____

Date _____

Witness _____

record of what an individual may do and, searched by application or platform, who all have access to that resource.

As we continue along these lines and when we get to the review and evaluation section of this book, we can better demonstrate the advantages of security databases. For now, suffice it to say that if you are not a competent database analyst, this would be a great time to begin making friends in that area.

Let us move our discussion to the first form that we suggested. That is, the acknowledgement form that is issued for signature at the conclusion of the information security segment of the orientation process. We will talk extensively as to how to prepare that segment, by the way, later in this book. It will be one of the most important parts of your program.

The form in question is directed at getting the employee to acknowledge the content of the class or presentation. It will cover aspects of what was learned, what is expected of employees, and an understanding as to what can happen as a result of not complying with the company's information security policy and standards.

Easily, the best way to put one of these together is to follow the example of the sample. In the sample, we reduce everything to a series of numbered statements, each a complete thought and each using "I" as the central theme. The statements are all in first person.

At the bottom of the form there is a place for a signature and, depending on the culture within which you operate, the signature of a witness. You will also note that there is a place for the printed name of the employee, lest the signature is illegible.

Note from the sample that the objectives of the document are quite simple and direct. The employee, by signing the page, agrees to certain standards of performance that can be measured and is fully aware that failure to comply could result in termination or even, in rare cases, prosecution. While this may seem a bit strong, it does provide the vehicle by which such actions may be taken without violating any of the rights of the individual. I can assure you that the spirit of the document will remain with the signor long after the ink is dry.

As mentioned above, there is no reason why this entire document cannot be put online, with the punching of an "Agree" button effectively replacing the signature. This is best done while assigning user IDs and passwords. That way, when new employees change their passwords from the default, they can, under guidance of a trainer, go to the page and post their agreement. If the personnel record profile that I mentioned earlier is in place, the information goes to it immediately. As far as the database is concerned, this is strictly a check-off item. The form can be compressed and archived in case it might be needed later. As additional accesses, facility entries and egresses, and company property are entrusted to the employee, the profile record can be updated.

Remember what I said about cultivating the friendship of the database administrators?

Let's dissect the information security agreement document in Exhibit 1 and see just what it is that we have accomplished.

First, it is imperative that the single page policy statement be included in the documentation that the new employee gets at orientation. Here again is a good reason to keep it brief and to the point. Note that this concept is first, as is the policy among the documents you have thus far prepared.

The second issue is in regards to the standards and procedures we have recently completed (haven't we?). Make the informing of all new employees as to how to find the manuals and to use them a part of any orientation package. If your company still operates a full-scale paper mill, go ahead and give them a copy right then.

You have, once you have shared the information, made the finding of and familiarizing with the standards and procedures their own responsibility. It is not a bad idea to check on that at some later date with a generated e-mail. Check with personnel on how to produce a follow-up of this nature.

The third and fourth points are designed to make them aware of their responsibility with respect to the log-on information they get. This, too, serves as a reminder as to the value and confidentiality of company information.

One of the issues that is famous for giving information security professionals gray hair is the tendency of people taking a break to jump up from their position and leave their terminal logged on. Whatever access they have now defaults to anyone who sits down at their terminal. The next point will inform them as to how important we think locking a terminal or logging off can be.

For some reason, a person will protect what they have on the screen in front of them in any way possible, right down to blocking another party from seeing it with their body. Yet, they will print it and leave it lying on a desk, throwing it in a wastebasket with common trash or taking it home to use for scratch paper. This is a reminder that no matter the location or form, information is information and must be protected from accidental or intentional exposure. By agreeing to it, new employees recognize their responsibility and understand they will be held to it.

The same condition applies to the next point on the form, the only difference being that the materials in question are to be destroyed. What we will do here is make sure that even in this condition, proprietary information is recognized for its value to the company.

The last two points are express an understanding that work conversation stays at work and that, as an employee, each of us has the responsibility to minimize potential exposure either by accident or on purpose and by ourselves or others. Care must be taken in the original presentation of this concept to make certain that the employee understands that the company is not trying to breed a strain of rats but with the understanding that any loss to the company is a personal loss, as our paychecks depend on the continued success of the organization. In that light, seeing someone else compromise information that could cause a loss to the company is more a reflection as to how it can affect us personally than it is a remote bottom line item.

The last point is almost pure boilerplate. It states, rather effectively, that we are held accountable for our behavior and that failing to act in a responsible manner has its costs. While I doubt that many prosecutions occur, it does give a bit of pause to one bent on damaging or revealing proprietary information.

What we have created with this form is a contract between the employee and the company. Responsibilities have been spelled out and the employee is given a chance to revisit anything that is unclear. Once the employee's signature is on the paper (or electronic profile), the contract is in force. Both parties are protected and both parties have a clear view of what their specific responsibilities are. Yes, the company has responsibilities in this agreement as well. The standards and procedures you are demanding compliance with had better be readable and complete and must not leave any blanks. For employees to comply, they must know how to go about doing so. With any ambiguity in the rules they have agreed to follow, not only is the company at risk, but their chances of redress are slim.

Another major "form" that needs to be addressed is not really a form at all. It is the template profile of access authority given to any computer-using employee. It usually encompasses the office tools needed to function and may grant access to other areas of the information base, such as company Web pages and informational files. I refer to this as a form for a single reason. In most instances, this suite of accesses will be changing often, as new tools are adopted, production processing changes, and new systems come in. While it may be the headache of information security to bring older profiles up to date, the template should be maintained by committee, whether it is management or the team leaders of the projects that alter the needed access authority. Whomever is charged with making the changes, this template must stay up to date.

Finally, we come to the forms needed to alter that template profile according to the needs of different areas of responsibility. There might be additional access needed to programming tools by those charged with programming or specific financial access for those in the accounting department.

However, with such needs being relatively similar among people with the same job responsibilities, why not have departmental, or functional, profile templates as well? As you will see from the sample contained in this chapter, an individual can request a modifying suite of privileges to be appended to the initial template that will produce a final profile equal to that of most others in a given functional area.

Now, let us take this a step farther, as well. What if a series of accesses or transactions can be assigned to staff in a number of areas, as their responsibilities require such access? Perhaps it is a set of six financially related transactions that can be used by finance, budget, purchasing, and any other department involved in the accounting process. If this block of transactions is known, it could be used as a building block in constructing more detailed profile for the individuals in each area. In other words, we could have that block, which we will call Group A for the sake of identification, added as a norm for a financial-based person, but add additional groups to build out a functional profile. As an example:

The following functional profiles are for the respective job responsibilities noted:

> Accountant I   Basic profile + Group A and Group B
> Accountant II   Basic profile + Groups A, B and C.
> Purchasing Agent   Basic profile + Group A and Group R
>   (with purchasing transactions)

A relatively simplistic example, but it demonstrates how functional profiles can be constructed by adding in previously grouped transactions rather than adding them one by one.

Exhibit 2   Systems Access Request

Systems Access Request

Please use this form to request access to ABC Company information systems. To do so, fill out the necessary fields and check off the systems to which access is required. Then:

1. Make sure all fields are filled out.
2. Sign the form
3. Forward to your supervisor.
4. Your supervisor will sign it and forward to the _____, who will approve or deny the access.
5. If approved, information security will implement the access.

Name: _____

Department:_____

Date: _____

Reason access needed: _____

Check systems to which access is needed:
- ☐ NT network   ☐ Accounting
- ☐ UNIX   ☐ HR
- ☐ IBM   ☐ Purchasing

Note: Systems listed are both OS level and application. This form can be used for both with application owners being approvers of the form. These are strictly samples with the actual number being as large or small as you need.

Supervisor: _____   Date: _____

System owner:_____   Date: _____

Information security: _____   Date: _____

Note: Add or delete signatories as needed

Think about this when designing your access profiles. Wouldn't it be easy to construct a profile by only having a job title on the form presented to you? Remember, every piece of paper, every manual, every e-mail, Web page, poster, or other contact you make with the staff of your company is a selling chance for your awareness program. Make sure that you take advantage.

Obviously, the form in Exhibit 2 is pretty basic. In fact, I made it up strictly as a demonstration of a layout that can be used. In the instance of the approvals, names or functions can be easily interchanged. In most shops today, systems administrators take care of adding and deleting users. That being the case, their signature or approval would replace that of information security. I think you can see the potential here.

Make certain to abbreviate the form sufficiently so that the instructions for its use can be contained right on the form. If you have a series of questions or instructions to offer, you can make them a separate lead-in section or intersperse them within the body of the form. Either way, make certain that there is no doubt as to what information is required.

The "shopping list" layout of the form is excellent to make certain that we minimize the number of different forms used. While I just listed a few platforms and applications, we could as well use it for others such as granting dial-up or Internet access or receipting equipment needed to perform company business (laptops, modems, tokens, etc.). Your imagination is the only limitation.

If the form is online, so much the better. It takes little to route the form to any person or department that needs to authorize it and make certain that it ultimately gets to the individual needed to perform the access change. Try to use this medium in any way possible. Have you started buying lunch for the Sybase, Oracle, and SQL programmers, yet?

The important thing to remember in the creation of any form, paper or electronic, is to make certain that it is usable, simple, and complete in the needed factual input. No one wants to rupture their brain in trying to figure out what is needed on any form, nor do they want to go to several places to find forms for similar applications. Any form loses its effectiveness when using it requires a separate procedure, and that being true, your effectiveness suffers as well.

We in information security are often viewed as an obstacle to getting things done. A large part of what we will be discussing in ensuing chapters is the means to make ourselves apparent as vital parts of the overall scheme of operating an information-based organization. This means making certain that what we do is in support of the organization and that our customers, the users, management, and the IS community see us as allies, rather than roadblocks. Moving forward from here, salesmanship will become one of our most important skills and, therefore, tools.

A great form to use in an awareness program may fall under the heading of masthead, or letterhead. This may be a trademark that appears on any publication from the Information Security Department or a specialized stationery that can be used for issuing bulletins or new information for widespread distribution. Once you have built a recognizable trademark or icon, the sight of it will ring out "information security" loud and long. Use as a means to set your publications off from the others that emanate from most companies like bats from a cave on a warm summer evening.

This item will be a central theme as we get into the "Communications" section.

Summary

There are a number of reasons to produce standardized forms for information security processes. Whether they are contracts with employees, as in the case of the security agreement we spoke of early on in this chapter, or request forms used to gain access to specific systems, applications, or other resources, they must be formal and, at the same time, simple enough for anyone to utilize.

We have looked at forms designed specifically to create a bond between the company and its employees in which the employees responsibilities are outlined and their agreement to live within the bounds of the responsibilities is recorded. A sidelight to that exercise is the ability to teach how and where things are expected to be done within the organization and to give employees their first insight into the company's expectation. Further, you have created the image of the information security function and have likewise made the new employee aware of its existence and function.

By referencing the other documentation in this form, you have introduced them in concept and function. The employee now knows where to find them and what they are there to accomplish.

Should the security agreement meet with resistance, it will no doubt be because the employee does not fully understanding its meaning. That in itself is a check of how effective your presentation is. Always be ready to explain further and, should a question be recurrent, alter the presentation of the agreement to remove any doubt on the issues noted.

Access request forms are the next items of importance. They should be made multifaceted — usable for a number of different functions — and be self-guiding, with the instructions embedded in the form itself. There is flexibility in this type of form, study what you need to include before making it up and add items in as check-offs in the overall scheme.

Under no circumstances limit yourself to doing this on paper. The inference of approvals means moving the form among people and places. This could entail loss, damage, or worst of all, pigeon holing. The latter pushes the request into a black hole from which it might never reappear and the entire exercise will have to be repeated.

An automated system, on the other hand, can be built with automatic routing right in it.

To be effective, the form should be a product of a database application in which the initiating of the form causes a check of files that may have a list of required signatories for applications or systems, the requestor's management chain of command, and even a tracking system that can see where a request is at a given moment. When a request gets sidetracked, the system can verify whose approval is holding it up. It can look at the personnel records and can route automatically as the script defines the necessary signatories.

Have you taken your database programmers to supper yet?

Forms are the vehicles by which agreements are reached and all parties with access to a given resource are asked if they agree with giving a specific individual authority to use that resource. They are also the place where a company and the people that work for it indicate their agreement on what each is to provide to their relationship as it applies to information assets.

Finally, it is a means of introducing employees to the information security department and its functions. It is here that they will first become familiar with the images by which the department can be identified.

Use forms wherever needed, economize on the number of different ones used, and brand each carefully, so that all involved know that information security is the place to take questions and comments.

Chapter 9

Finishing Touches

By this time, you have begun to find ways to link pieces of what we have accomplished into a semblance of order. This chapter is devoted to making use of the connections you have made and the credibility you have built. Now, after you have applied the research we embarked on in the first chapters, you have synthesized a full set of documentation with regard to information security. As a matter of form, do not lose track of the other contributors: the ones whose work you included, paraphrased, or built from. Also, remember the help you got in review and direction: the builders of what formal documentation currently existed and the actual documentation team, who helped you make certain that what you were toiling over met company standards and form.

As with any set of rules that will impact the company as a whole, there are a number of steps yet to take before you can publish and distribute. Let us, for a moment, reflect back on those.

One of the first things we did, as you might recall, was get a good feel for how things are run at this particular company. We did it by using anything from organizational charts to talking with other employees at a number of levels. Not only do we now know the reporting structure that the stockholders know, but we also know where the real power lies. We know the "Big Gorilla," and we also know who makes sure that he is happy.

Another thing we did early on in the game was to interview management to find out what their greatest concerns were with respect to information security. Our interviews gave us our first marching orders as to what to address first.

Combining what we learned from those exercises, we constructed a document set that reflected good information security practices and paid particular attention to those things they held dear. In reality, we custom built our manual (or manuals) to their particular specifications.

Now, we have a product to show them that is not only responsive to corporate needs and addresses good security practices for the industry in which the company operates, but also responds to their concerns exactly. We are going to have to get buy-in and approval, but are doing it with a product built to their specifications.

The creation of these documents was the product of all of what we have done throughout this and the previous sections. Still, I do not want to make it sound like we put that work into a mill together and, after a sufficient time for brewing, we got this single product back out. In reality, we produced these documents in the order they were discussed in earlier chapters and were completed in a similar order.

Remember, once we had completed each segment, we passed it along to the documentation people (assuming their existence) to put it into corporate-speak for the organization. Now, in the same order of completion, we have something to give to management for approval and, we hope, subsequent acceptance and implementation.

To begin, your immediate superior should have a very good idea of what you did and how you constructed it. Although we have not looked at this particular item in earlier parts of the process, we assume that you are accountable to someone for your time and a lot of it would have been spent composing these documents. Now that the first complete one is ready, it is time for a quick read for the characteristics needed by the company. Begin at the beginning and have your supervisor and, if possible, his supervisor give it the once over.

Note: If we try to stair step this one to the top, we will be at it for a significant segment of human life expectancy. Where possible, try to cover at least two levels of line management with each submission.

Put a target date in your cover memo (e-mail) and try to make it aggressive but realistic. In the instance of your immediate superior, it is a good thing to walk through it with him. As the approvals get farther down the road, use a similar *relatively* aggressive time frame with the disclaimer that "If there is no communication by that date, acceptance of the document as presented will be assumed." Word it in a manner so as not to get anyone riled up, but make it clear that although you are aware of their busy schedules, this is a hot item and really needs their attention. Know what? If they feel it is an issue that they cannot complete in the time allowed, they will contact you, thereby accomplishing the original aim, to convince them of its importance.

As mentioned, you might have to go through a few steps in the organization before the product is ready to introduce to the blessing agency, whether that be the CEO, an executive committee, or a standards committee. Pray that it is the last, as they are more likely to recognize the need and give it full consideration.

When you have to go through the top dog (Big Gorilla?) in the organization, you are at the mercy of his or her schedule and such whim as may come along. In this case, it is one person who has virtually complete control over his or her time. Personality also can play a big role in this. All of us have had experience with the executive who uses delays to impress upon one and all his or her importance. Sounds juvenile, but you may have to live with it.

An important aside: if the company is not overly huge, you can often get an interview with the CEO early on in the game, usually while you are doing the other ones. This is a big plus in that you have already intimated the arrival of such document during that interview. He or she will be expecting it and will no doubt review it more carefully, as a measure of how much of his or her statement was addressed. Am I reaching you with the importance of that first interview and the collecting of management concerns?

More likely, however, is that it will go to a management team in the form of a standards committee or executive committee. Again, a lot of them will have been interviewed at the outset and should likewise be looking for your offering. Even if they were not among the interviewees, the documentation people with whom you have conferred throughout the process will have warned you and even structured the document into what they expect to see and are likely to approve.

We have probably gotten a bit ahead of ourselves in the discussion of the approval process as we have been talking about getting it to the top without giving real attention to the interim steps.

Almost without fail, there are going to be questions and suggestions made along the way to having a "perfect" example to send forward to senior management, in whatever form it takes. Initially, there will be discussions with the documentation people. This is the place where you want to take whatever time is needed.

There is really little chance that whoever massages your document is knowledgeable with regard to information security. That person's job is to "make it English" in whatever form the company likes to see it. Your document, once within this language mill will be massaged to appear as do all others that control the way the company runs. Areas will be broken out to delineate the order required (statement of purpose, goals, etc., at the beginning) and sections will be broken out from the whole cloth of what you have produced. We have stressed the need to put in all of the detail necessary to make the document responsive and now we have to trust the wordsmiths to slice, dice, and reconstruct it in the manner required.

Assuming that you have done as suggested and kept in good contact with those folks, this can be relatively painless. You will be writing with their standards in mind and they will feel comfortable enough to be in constant contact with you. If they do contact you with a question, give it full time and thought. Generally, it will have to do with concerns about diluting meaning when revamping to fit the accepted format. If you read carefully and verify that your message has not changed, the output will be acceptable on the first pass.

Even if that seems to have gone well, once you get the draft back, you will have to read it critically, with an eye to your original message. There will be, no doubt, a couple of return trips to iron out some inaccuracies or to agree on more effective wording. Again, give it due diligence, to make certain that nothing is lost in translation.

Actually, it is not a bad idea to keep your supervisor in this loop, as well. Never forget that the outcome product of this exercise reflects directly on the supervisor, and you want the comfort level to be as high as possible.

When it becomes time to present it as mentioned earlier, you had best prepare yourself to do so with an eye toward potential questions. Before your standards go for approval, the policy statement will have been seen and approved. Likewise, the standards, if presented as a separate document, will follow that and the procedures will come thereafter. If the latter two are incorporated, as suggested, it will be a single shot.

For the most part, the act will involve submitting the document(s) for consideration and waiting for fallout or questions. In all likelihood, you will not send it forward personally, that usually being done by someone on a similar level with the members of the committee. This may be your boss or someone above your boss.

Note: We have continually assumed that there are no more than two positions between you and where it all happens — the top. If this is not true, you are probably facing a far graver situation than simply trying to get a process approved. You are at a level where your credibility will be constantly challenged as being too far down in the organization. That, in fact, is true. If the information security officer (ISO) is graded like an analyst, there is little chance that person will be able to perform effectively.

There is, however, one potential exception to this sad rule. If your immediate management, up at least two levels, is aware of the importance of what you do and have brought you into the company where they could, just for the sake of getting you in the door, there is still a chance. Generally, this will be a part of the agreement that brings you in. We will assume that their vision is at least that far-reaching and that a large part of their "carrying the mail" from this point forward is to give you exposure and push for the elevation of the position in the company. If anything else is true, you have a major problem.

The issues around positioning of the ISO could easily be the subjects for another book.

Let us assume that through your efforts and that of line management, we have gotten as far as the final authority, be it any one of the three entities already mentioned. Now, we need to find out what the package must look like to get through their deliberations.

In most cases, a short, management summary should be prepared, no matter to which person or group you are addressing it. The content should simply state the reason for the document, give a brief overview of the content, and present a full table of contents. From these few items, the readers know what they have received and what it is intended to accomplish. Some will read further, some will read excerpts, most will fan through the pages as though expecting something to pop out at them. Few, if any, will read it through. If the form and expected content are satisfactory, the item will be approved.

Always check with your documentation people, again, about what that summary should look like. They do this on a regular basis and can give you a good template for preparing it. Of course, they will be available to put it into acceptable form before presentation.

There will be an occasional event where you are asked to present the document orally. Rather than be concerned with the prospect, I recommend that you use it to its full potential toward getting support for your overall program.

Your presentation, even if no longer than 5 to 10 minutes should contain the management summary I suggested for the written proposal, a copy of the table of contents, and a few sample pages. Of course, the entire document should be readily available, either printed or online. If at all possible, present it with overheads or an online demonstration product. The components I mentioned bear much more impact when placed in a logical order and presented in a theater setting.

In such presentations, always make a point of introducing the document or documents in question as they apply to the overall information security awareness program. Often, particularly in these surroundings, it is possible to put in plugs for other aspects of the program as well as these items. Point out exactly what we have pointed out thus far: that the policy, standards, and procedures are the foundation for the overall program. Always place it in perspective as to what it does for the company, why things will be better with this program in place.

Never, ever, miss a chance to sell your program above your station in the company.

If your presentation draws people's attention to the extent that they make suggestions, you have succeeded any expectation you might have had. Get them to explain their ideas and decide how you can use their input to improve what you are presenting. In most cases, you will find that you have covered the subject in your narrative — after all, it was based on their initial input — so you merely have to point it out. In many cases, the comments might well indicate that they have indeed seen it, but had some difficulty with the concepts. This is an excellent clue to where your document might have weaknesses.

If this initial presentation was for the policy statement, you will be setting the stage for the other documents that you will be presenting at a later date. What you do here, then, will build an image of your credibility for the next and the next submissions. If you carry this off right, the later ones will be more rubber stamp exercises. You have established credibility on the basis of your initial effort. And by all means reflect back on that policy statement as you move forward. Demonstrate how each document supports those preceding it and those following.

These audiences can be difficult to come by, so it pays to leverage them for all they are worth.

Let us assume that all has gone well and you only have to go back to the drawing board on a few items. Be able to tell them at the meeting just when you will return the amended copy and what changes you propose to make to meet their requirements. Then, go back and get to them immediately. Make certain that, when you put in the changes, you use a different color or typeface so that the changes stand out.

When you return or forward the changes for approval, make certain that your cover sheet or e-mail spells out specifically how you expect to be notified of their approval of the changes and that they now accept the document in its entirety. The latter is extremely important as failure to do this could result in the whole thing getting on a never-ending merry-go-round. This is your chance to request specific approval of the amended document; do not let it slip past you.

Assuming that the approvals received were only for the first document (policy), it is now time to get back to the others. Prepare them for presentation in the same way, making certain to amend your approach by whatever you learned from the original presentation. If the changes that were requested reference anything in subsequent documents, make sure to address them before doing the presentation. Let us make sure that we do not have to go back and fix a more detailed reference to something already fixed.

Use the same approach that was successful in the first effort and get about each following document.

Summary

The reward for getting all of the documents we need completed is the opportunity to present them to the powers that be that need to approve them to put them into place. Your job, now that you have them ready for review, is to prepare them for that presentation.

Working with your management and the documentation people within the organization, make sure that your product is in keeping with the style most acceptable to the company and contains all that it needs. Then, you can put together your presentation.

If you have to present it remotely (that is, by e-mail or submitted paper), prepare a management summary that gives an overview of the content of the document in no more than a page and a half. Include a copy of the table of contents. The document itself should follow. In the case of the policy statement, the summary is overkill; just describe the function of the statement and attach it.

If you do get the opportunity to present the item in person, make sure that the same elements are available, but try to put them into a slide presentation in some manner. Cover the same materials as with the written version.

In all cases, set a time limit for their review and acceptance. Obviously, you cannot dictate to senior management, but you can word it to place a reasonable date before you contact them for additional input. In the case of a written — rather than interactive — presentation, it is valid to set a date by which you expect to get their input. Even if the date is unacceptable, they will get back to you with an alternative. Now, you have a date they set themselves.

Make your presentation accurate and informative. Look and be prepared. If they have additional input, based on their review, discuss it, in case it is addressed elsewhere, or accept the input and make the changes. Agree to a date by which you will have it ready and make certain that you hit the date.

Run the changes through the documentation process and highlight all changes by using a different color or typeface. Resubmit only those items that changed.

Once the document has been accepted for publication. Set about finding a way to publish it that uses all of the vehicles the company currently possesses and attempt to create some of your own.

We will treat the last subject in depth in the next chapter.

Chapter 10

Taking It to the Streets

At last, you have the building blocks set into the foundation that your entire program is going to be built upon. Your issue now is to get it in front of as many people as possible, in as short a time as possible, and with the least amount of effort on their parts. Make it fall into their collective lap, so to speak.

In this chapter, we are going to talk about the places to put this documentation and the means to make certain that it is read. We will, of course, use most of the time-honored means to distribute the documents, but we will discuss a few novel means as well.

The usual means for getting a procedures manual out is to print it, bind it, and send it out to all current employees — sometimes just the supervisory staff and above — and make sure that it is a part of the package, the heavy part, that all new employees get. It will then be placed carefully on a shelf, where it will reside, untouched, until the next Ice Age. Not generally considered the best way to do business, but in terms of management expectations, it works just fine. Everyone has access to it, even if they never have any reason (as they see it) to ever open the book.

With this chapter, we are going to begin putting together the parts of a program that will be so interlocked that no one will be able to view one part of it without getting an inside glimpse at all of it. We will use our baseline documentation to create an environment where all employees or others who handle company information assets will be exposed to all of it and will have legitimate reason to look at it. They will, in fact, not only be urged to make themselves familiar with it, but will have solid reason to maintain familiarity.

Much of what will set up the situation described above will be covered in greater detail in the next section. What we are doing here is placing the background documentation for the entire information security program — not just the awareness aspect of it — in front of them and creating circumstances that will draw them to familiarize themselves with the documents. Stay tuned, as we move in that direction.

Now that we have a complete set of baseline documentation, we need to make certain that it gets out to the troops quickly and in a manner that fully states its importance. Let us explore means to do so.

The policy statement should be the first thing written, the first approved, and the first to be presented to the staff. Let us discuss a number of ways to handle that chore. We must remember a number of things about the nature of the policy in our efforts to make its contents common knowledge.

First, it is a full statement of the company's stand on the issues surrounding the value of its information assets. It defines information as an asset, it states that the company recognizes the value of information, and it further states that the organization is committed to protecting the information. The principle of least privilege that you included even defines just how much access (in general terms) an employee is to have to those assets.

Best of all, the document is — assuming that you followed my advice — only one printed page. That rather minimal size serves a number of purposes:

■ It is so general so as not to get caught up in exceptions or detailed descriptions.

■ It is short enough so that even the employees with the shortest attention span can go over it in a minute or two, well within their range of focus.

■ Because of its short length, it can be independently plugged into other documents without damaging their integrity nor increasing their size significantly.

■ The generality listed above also makes its basic intent easily under-standable to those with little or no background with the company. New employees can understand it as easily as more veteran staff. This is their first written statement of the value the company places on their information assets.

■ The content begs further interpretation. This is the basis for the other documents to come.

There are a number of ways to distribute the policy, but the first place to go is to human resources or, in a few instances, to whoever else conducts new employee orientation. What you are searching for is the package of information given to each new employee. Somewhere in that confusing mass of paper is an employee handbook of some type. Some are nothing but folded cards, others are loose-leaf notebooks, while still others are slick, bound publications.

Assuming that the employee handbook exists, in whichever of the above mentioned forms, one of your first issues is to get that single page document into the book. You will, of course, want to put a bit of introductory material with it, usually only a few paragraphs about the information security program and the policies and procedures that lie behind the policy statement. Make certain that the reader knows that they exist and realizes that they will be encountering them soon. How soon depends on a number of issues that we will discuss later.

If for some reason such a handbook does not exist, that fact can be used to add even more credence to your program. Immediately prepare a brochure, outlining the bases of the information security program, notifying new employees that they will be receiving their user IDs and passwords in the near future, and presenting what the company expects of them in terms of maintaining secrecy of their passwords and how they are to treat company information assets. Use the policy statement as the centerpiece of all discussion.

Make sure to isolate the policy in the body of the brochure as well. It should be in a different typeface and, if the size of your vehicle allows it, on a page of its own, separated from the other text. If possible, border the page. Whatever it takes, make sure that the policy is treated like the gospel according to you.

Assuming that you get this brochure (even if a handbook does exist), there are a number of other things that can be accomplished with it. We will discuss that later when we talk about your overall new employee orientation program.

If your company has an internal Web presence, make certain that the policy gets onto it as quickly as possible. Assuming that the webmaster has a relatively sophisticated page, you can introduce the statement in that manner. A spotlight that links to the location where the policy is stored calls everyone's attention to it and, at the same time, makes it readily available to read. This is far superior to trying to distribute it as an attachment to a memo, particularly if your organization has more than one site. Of course, in a pinch, that will do fine.

The reference we just made to "the location where the policy is stored" can have a number of other advantages as well. Rather than simply have the link retrieve a document from whatever management system you might be using, why not have it link to the URL of your own, information security Web page? More about that in pages to come.

We have now discussed means that will get your newest contribution to internal literature in front of the entire staff of your company. Thanks to modern means and the communications technology now available to us, we can literally spread the word worldwide in a matter of moments. By the way, if your company is worldwide, and English is not the language of choice at any of your sites, you might go to the measure of having the document translated into whatever languages you want it presented in before the initial release.

Under normal circumstances, there are good translation facilities available within the company that allow communications among shops. Find out who performs that function and get the policy to them for translation.

There are a number of ways to use second, third, and even further language versions in distribution. First, if you are using the Web facility for distribution, find out how the webmaster normally handles such language challenges. Usually, he or she will have the main page available in all languages that are being used. It is not a difficult job to have different versions being used at different ranges of IP addresses. Or the webmaster may use a single page sign-on form with the ability to select the language of your choice from that point. Under either set of circumstances, make sure that the policy is available in each language version and that the reader is pointed to it at the home page.

One final thought on the policy, before we move on:

Most people in the company will not know you, who you are, or what your function is under normal circumstances. This will be one of your first public acts, so they have not had time to become familiar with you. However, each of them is aware of who the CEO or president is and knows exactly what that job is. Why not, then, have the CEO introduce the policy?

This might sound like a function that CEOs or presidents would consider beneath their normal role. Still, if you did a good job in your presentation, your leader will be aware of the document and what you are trying to accomplish with it. If you prepare the copy the CEO or president is to use to present it, getting a sign-off on it will be, in 99 out of 100 cases, a slam dunk.

By using this presentation, you have gotten the word out, brought peoples' attention to it and placed it where they cannot miss it, and by dint of who presented it, tacitly reminded the readers that management, as high as you can go in the company, supports this program.

I have spent a lot of time on the distribution of the policy and have done so with good reason. Along with talking about getting the word out, we have explored a number of different approaches one could take. We have introduced the concept of putting information security facts into the media distributed at new employee orientation — right down to producing an information security brochure — and have explored the ways to get it out to the current populace. Now, these outlets were mentioned in terms of the policy, but can be applied elsewhere. In future chapters, we will discuss the use of internal publications and your company's Web presence as tools of communications. For now, let us just leverage them for our own use.

The standards and procedures manual creates an entirely new issue that must be addressed if it is to be known and referenced by the total employee populace. Let us take a look at a few ways to do that.

This, or these, document(s) will be quite large by comparison to the policy statement. In most cases, they will certainly exceed 50 pages and may be double that. This little circumstance unto itself creates new issues that must be addressed before distribution. How, then, do we get people to read a lifeless tome of do's and don'ts to make sure they understand their own responsibilities? Let us take a look at a few facts that might shed some light on potential methodologies:

First, we have gone to a lot of trouble to make this thing readable: the sections, the rewrites by the documentation folks, the references to points in the policy. Now, we have to make the medicine go down.

Let us take a look at the standards and procedures document (for purposes of this section, assume it to be one large document) and try to define its function. The policy talks about what and how; this form is only detail as to *exactly* what and *exactly* how. From the policy and, by the time they get their hands on a company computer, security agreement, they understand the basics of what is expected of them. The only thing they might be curious about, and that only when the need arises, is detail.

That last word, *detail*, pretty much describes the function of the manual. It is a *reference*, not the lifeblood of day-to-day operations. Its major function is to describe exactly what correct conduct looks like for each of many specific circumstances.

What if we structured the document so that it could be more easily read and could direct the reader to exactly the spot they needed to answer their question, rather than make them start on page 1 and not stop until they find it? What if they had an abbreviated version of the manual that had all of the same sections and subject matter as does the manual, but was stated completely in a few pages? Would that not be easier for a user to relate to?

The advent of Web and database applications has created a huge flexibility in the way we do things. We can look at something superficially or drill down for more detail. Ultimately, we can learn as much or little about something as we wish. As long as we are discussing readability, why not explore using that technology to give persons a quick overview of the subject while proving links to get more information on a subject-by-subject basis? We could give them a short breakdown of the theme of a given standard, for instance, and offer a link to an area where far greater detail is available. Some needs will be satisfied by that overview, others will have to be researched through the deepest means possible.

Let us build a small example of what I mean when I speak of a short breakdown:

Using an example from the list of subjects that was mentioned in Chapter 6 we can demonstrate what is meant by a short and long form (no, not a 1040!). Let's take the subject of passwords as a means to illustrate our point.

In the short version, we will say:

- "Every account will have a password."
- "Passwords will each be of a predetermined length and makeup."
- "Passwords will be changed on a regular basis."

Those three statements are the basis of the password standards to be used. Although they are simple, they do give the necessary framework for what a password should be. Although they are accurate, they do beg a number of questions: How long must a password be? What characters are acceptable: alpha, numeric, special characters? What is the maximum number of characters? Are there limitations to what can be used (family names, proper nouns, nonsense strings of numbers)? How often must a password be changed?

All of these questions should be explained in the detail section.

One of the beauties of the modern approach to this is the use of HTML to link several pieces of information together. By having a link from the main page to the short version of the standards and procedures, you are able to get a quick overview of the entire document in just a few pages. To be sure, there will be little detail — witness the password example given — but there may be enough to satisfy the need. However, if an additional link associated to the detail — by subject — is available adjacent to the short version, readers can use it to go to the detailed version to get as much information as they want. The detail may run something more like the example shown in Exhibit 1.

We can continue along these lines for a number of additional requirements for password life span and structure, but by now, you have a good idea of how this can work. The brief version states the general, the detailed version contains the more finely distinguished characteristics.

Exhibit 1   Detailed Version

I. Passwords
  A. Passwords must be used as ad adjunct to a userid when gaining access to any production system.
  B. A password must be a minimum of 6 characters and a maximum of 32 characters.
  C. The password must be made up of a combination of alpha, numeric, and special characters according to the following pattern:
      1. There must be at least 1 numeric character in any password, but not to the exclusion of at least 1 alpha character.
      2. Passwords may not repeat the same character more than twice consecutively in a given password.
      3. No iterations are allowed in creating passwords, i.e., password1, password2, password*n*, etc. The system is set up to detect and block such re-usage.
      4. No password may duplicate any password found in a hacker's dictionary that will be checked against your password. These will be treated as system reserved words in practice.
      5. Special characters are allowed in a any password.
  D. Passwords will have a defined life span of a maximum of 30 days.
  E. There will be no minimum period between password changes.

This process can be repeated for the 18 items that we listed earlier as well as however many other points you wish to add. We paid good attention to the structure of the standards and procedures earlier and need not readdress it here.

As mentioned earlier, this structure lends itself well to the use of HTML presentation on a Web page, but can actually be used in the more primitive system of paper manuals. In the case of the latter, page and section numbers in the overview can steer the reader to the detail as easily, even if it takes a bit more work.

Although we have talked about the ways the end product can be presented, we can use other means to let people know of the existence of the documents.

We spoke earlier of publishing the policy statement in the new employee's handbook, the place to give input on the company's position on information security. In addition, we can place the short version of the standards and procedures document there as well. If the detail exists in an online dataset or on a Web page, the links to that document can be presented along with the policy statement.

Most companies today have some form of document management in place for use by all employees. It simply makes no sense to not have important documents available to end users, be it with regard to personnel issues, insurance programs, or the policies and procedures we have prepared here.

Once again, the way to get your work into that repository is to go back to the documentation department to locate it and to have your work included. Generally, they will control that repository and, due to your excellent work up to this point in keeping them involved, will make it possible to include your work in their archives of important documents.

So, after exploration, we have found that there are actually three different means we can use in publishing the standards and procedures documents. We have already included the policy statement in new employee orientation, any class work that might be presented at orientation time, any company overview documents, and such Web or news media that might exist for the purpose of presenting information to the rank and file.

The standards and procedures, on the other hand, are far more weighty in form and substance and getting them in front of staff is another story altogether. They must be trumpeted upon creation and installation in whatever form they are available and must hearken back to the policy statement.

The document can appear in at least three different forms: paper, as an entry into a document management system, and a Web-based dataset. The latter two are certainly more state of the art, but do not lose sight of the deforestation method of information transfer. Someone, somewhere will get a paper copy of it, even if you use one of the online options. Guaranteed, someone — probably a lot of someones — will print it.

Summary

After having gone to the extent of producing a document, having it reworked by the documentation department, submitted to the standards committee or executive committee, you are now ready to put your hard work in front of your selected audience — the rank and file employees of your company.

The first item you will concern yourself with is the policy statement. Once approved, this statement should be plugged into any other document that describes the company, discusses employee duties and responsibilities, or is used for any type of news presentation.

As a short and important piece of work, it can be added to almost anything else that is distributed without disturbing the integrity of that document. When it is first presented, for instance, it can be included in a company newspaper, an employee manual, or on a Web page, the latter either by printing outright or linking from a symbol or statement. To get the best possible exposure for the Web presentation, make a point of working directly with the webmaster to get a spotlight location.

If possible, create an entire brochure on information security policies, standards, and procedures. This booklet, placed in the hands of new employees gives them a complete source of the detail for the way the company wishes its information assets to be protected.

Yeah, I know that this would be a paper document, trees would perish, and more paper would be spread around the company. However, if this is the only way to get this documentation in front of the employee base, so be it. We plant more trees every day.

Assuming the availability of some means for putting the longer standards and procedures document online either via Web presence or document management product, make sure that the detailed form — of the detail and overview versions described in the body of this chapter — is available there.

Then, your printed or Web-based document can be limited to just the policy and overview. Make certain that the latter has references to the location of the detail accompanying each entry.

Of course, in the best possible scenario, the policy statement is spread far and wide and is one of the first things the new employee will see. Then, with a Web page available, the overview can be linked, item by item to the detail. That way, anyone needing simply a rough idea can scan the overview and only drill deeper if greater detail is needed. This makes a more flexible and, therefore, more complete document.

Whatever manner of distribution you choose or are forced into, it is absolutely imperative that this information gets to the people for whom it is intended. On cannot expect compliance with the rules if they are not available for the reading or in a form easily used by staff members.

Take advantage of all of the resources available to you in preparing the document and making sure that the form and content are in keeping with company standards. The documentation department is the best possible source for that input. Not only can they help get your documents in shape for presentation, they can usually offer ideas to smooth your way in presenting them to the approval system.

Once approved, use the new employee orientation to make the first presentation of the policy statement and an introduction to the underlying standards and procedures. If you have a forum in the orientation, create a brochure that contains minimally, the policy and the standards and procedures overview. Worst case, make sure that the policy gets into the employee handbook.

As we progress through this book, we will attempt to leverage one of the best tools available in the contemporary office to communicate across a large population of users. That is, the Web and the internal network. By building a Web page for information security, in coordination with the company webmaster, you can not only place these documents in front of your chosen audience, but can use it for any communications ideas you might have. This tool will get a lot of attention as we move forward, but suffice it to say that this is the best medium of distribution you have available. Try to avail yourself of its advantages.

For now, you have completed the baseline materials and placed them into place for the springboard for the entire program. From here on, we will talk about the other things that can be done to build a well-rounded program.

Section 3

Communications: You Know, Now Let Them Know

If the road to hell is indeed paved with good intentions, then the sidewalks are built of grand ideas that either never saw the light of day or languished as the best kept secret within the corporate walls.

There is no such thing as a perfect resolution to any problem if it is never applied nor is there an unspoken answer to a burning question. *Unspoken* is the perfect synonym for *unknown*.

We have spent lo, these many preceding chapters, digging through company documentation, directives, and detritus, seeking out whatever wisdom remained from those who preceded us. Many hours were spent, locating the chinks in the armor of protection fashioned about the corporate information assets and filling those gaps with freshly minted policies, standards, and procedures, designed just for the purpose.

Now, does the preceding sound high-minded, or what? While the attempt at humor is apparent (I can only hope), the issue is very real. Far too much good work goes unnoticed and unapplied simply because no one got the word out. Writing the dust-covered manuals we referenced earlier was no doubt a time-consuming labor for someone and, I am certain, that their aim was not to take up shelf space eternally without being read.

The next several chapters will explore the means to make certain that every person within the organization sees the documents that you have produced and is provided with the impetus to *want* to read and understand them. There will be no threats or cajoling used; only logic will be needed.

In today's world, communication is the all-consuming buzzword. It has been a boon and a curse to people in our line of business for years and will multiply our concerns in the not-too-distant future (how about tomorrow?). Still, rather than fight the whirlwind, why not climb on and enjoy the ride?

As you look around your company, you will see that they use at least a subset of almost every medium of communications known to mankind: Paper manuals, electronic mail, Internet and Web broadcasting, using the same media for the search for and retrieval of information, audio, video and any number of hybrids of two or more of the media listed.

We have, in barely ten years, watched a 360 kilobyte, 5 _ floppy diskette turn into a 720K, a 1.2 Megabyte disk and seen the advent of compact disks that house information, music, and movies. The old desktop PC that in 1983 held all of its information on one of those smaller diskettes now cannot function with less than 30 gigabytes of internal storage. We have the ability to pack information into a simple desktop computer, pass it through, and distribute it to the world. And, no desktop seems to be without one anymore.

Electronic communications ship huge files about like leaflets dropping from a plane, blanketing target areas and often overlapping into less interested regions. We can upload or download movies, music, or the information that our company runs on. Damn the Postal Service, long live FTP!

Still, despite all of the modern day marvels we have mentioned, getting our message out, received, and given the proper attention will require the human touch. It will not be strewn about the plant, but will be targeted to where it will do the most good. We will know our audience, have our ammunition, and fire only when we see the whites of their electronic eyes. We will have a plan.

As we have stated innumerable times before, our biggest barrier will be the dearth of resources under our own control. We have the ability to print manuals and probably will be able to e-mail folks that we need to reach, but the tools that we really need, the weapons of mass instruction, are usually safely in the hands of someone else.

In the next few chapters, we will explore the means to exploit the sophisticated media of transfer of knowledge by the human resources department, the training department, the public relations department, and any other group within the company that has control over any means to bring news to the masses. Where need be, we will use a trailer hitch or a saddle, but we will go along for the ride.

Away back near the beginning of this volume, I related a story about having gotten out an independent bit of information and was roundly chastised for daring to be creative. My first response was anger and frustration, that anyone could actually try to stop the distribution of needed information. Later — fortunately, not too much later — I came to realize that had I checked first about how such things were done, I would not have come down on anyone's toes with quite the force I did. Lesson learned.

We will, then, talk about finding the resources and the best ways to leverage them for our purposes. This will be a mix of equal parts of creativity, writing skills, timing, and diplomacy. The last will be more liberally applied than the others will, as it has to be refined for consumption by our cooperating partners, management, and the perceived audience. Now, you can add political savvy to your portfolio of accomplishments.

As we go through the measures covered in the next several chapters, let our imaginations expand on the issues we discuss. As certainly as this is being put down on paper right now, someone, somewhere is creating a new and exciting means to convey information. By the time you read this, you may well be aware of it and be able to see how the new technology can support the ideas contained herein.

And now, on to the meat and potatoes.

Chapter 11

Ride the Tame Horses

The title of this chapter has, I am quite certain, caused a certain amount of consternation for the reader. Why, you may ask, would I be talking about riding horses in a book about security awareness? Actually, the answer is as simple as the play on words that became the title of this chapter. What does it mean? That one is simple: it simply means to never get stuck trying to invent something new when an old invention works at least as well.

Let me explain, using the same metaphor:

When you embark on your campaign of informing the select audience, your should first find out what vehicles currently exist for information distribution. If something is there, figure out how to use it, rather than going off on your own to come up with another means to get the word out. Paraphrased to what was noted above, there is a good saddle horse in the corral; do not go out to catch and break a mustang to ride. (Gosh, doesn't my Western upbringing show up every once in awhile!)

Getting out of the corral and into the world we have to live in, let us take a hard look at what we are trying to do with this concept.

Every company has some form of newsletter that is published on some general schedule. In the best cases, it will be monthly; in others, less often or, worst of all, occasionally. This type of publication, particularly if it appears in a predictable manner, is among the finest tools we can use to get the word out. People are aware of these papers and, to one extent or another, look forward to receiving them.

Unfortunately, in the majority of cases, these papers are pretty badly done, despite their often being staffed by experienced and thoughtful journalists. You see, the public relations function will usually be ahead of you in claiming space in the publication. Unfortunately, their idea of "news" and "of interest" usually involves articles about the activities of senior management and pictures of the same. Often, the only pictures that will appear are of said management. You read it and find the same copy that appeared in the local paper two weeks ago. However, this version will have even more detail. and more pictures. If there are pictures of the rank and file, they will appear well toward the back page, along with the service awards, retirements, and other things that would interest the average employee.

Now much has been written about this particular oversight over the years. Yet, despite the protests of those charged with preparing this paper, the tide never seems to turn. Commentary on the "culture" we discussed earlier? Perhaps, with the message being that we are all one big, happy family, but certain members of the family are just more important. Go figure.

Assuming that the folks that run the paper are as conscientious as I think they are — my experience has been almost unanimous in this area — they will have included enough material to get the staff to pique the interest of the average employee and that guarantees readership.

Another important point to make is that the people that run the paper are usually journalism professionals, many with extensive experience. They are forced to do some of the things they do and they generally write all of the lead articles. No matter how good they are, there are usually very few — often only one — of them to do the work. By providing good copy on a predictable basis, you will be viewed as an ally. Guard that status jealously. As we will see later, that level of credibility is golden and can be exchanged for favors at a later date. Also, pay strict attention to deadlines and make sure that your contribution is not just on time, but early. Make certain that no one ever has to ask you about the article that is due for the next edition. Promptness, like exemplary writing, is a good characteristic to be remembered for.

So, here we have a ready-made vehicle with which to carry our message abroad. Despite its shortcomings, it is probably the one way to get your message in front of as many people as possible quickly and with a certain amount of authority.

Introduce yourself to the editor of the paper at your earliest convenience. Try to find out the nature of the staff and as many of the standards for publication as possible. Be inquisitive about getting a bit of space in the next issue at your earliest convenience. Get a good look at what is expected of a contributor and make sure to get clearance to prepare an article. Get the article done as far ahead of the deadline as possible and stay as close to the requirements that you have learned in every aspect of the piece.

Now, many of the people that will ultimately wind up in an ISO position have extensive technical backgrounds, historically coming from programming and operations management areas within information systems. Documentation has been, in general, an important aspect of writing code and making a data center function. Most of us have had the chance (in most cases, forced into that chance) to take a technical writing course. Here is class work dedicated to teaching you to write formulaically and to make sure that all aspects of your writing are clear, concise, to the point, and boring as hell!

Folks, I am going to tell you right here to lose that tech writer mentality as quickly as possible. I do not, in any way, shape, or form, mean to denigrate the functions of the technical writer. What they do is indispensable in the information processing field. However, you are not writing for a technical journal (although most of them could stand to be "un-desiccated" a bit, too!). You are writing for an audience who, for the most part, could not decode effective technical writing, must less thoughtfully parse their way through your overall message.

The information you are wishing to present is issue based, not technical. Your audience needs, indeed wants, to know about what a virus can do to their hard drives, not how it goes about its dastardly work. They are not, for the most part, technicians.

What you are trying to create is a comfortable relating of your message to your audience. If you want to be successful at that, you need to talk *to* them, not *at* them. Make your tone comfortable and easy to understand, and stress the importance of the subject matter. Give examples of what the situation is and can do, whether you are talking about a virus or logging off your network attached PC when you leave. Talk about how easy it is to forget to log off — in the latter case — and about the potential upshot of such an oversight. Talk about how if someone were to sit down at your terminal in your absence and perform transactions against applications to which you have access, the logs would show that you did it. Simple message, but it involves the time-honored "what's in it for me?" question. They now know that this security issue can fall right into their individual laps.

And, for heaven's sake, do not forget to apply a bit of humor to your writing. There is so much stiff and stilted copy in that particular publication that a bit of humor will work wonders in getting your message across.

Now, I am not talking about printing out a stand-up routine; I am just saying lighten up. I have often used one of Mark Twain's favorite ploys — huge overstatement — to make a point. When you refer to hoax viruses, for instance, and are cautioning your readers against forwarding the "message" as was intended, you can refer to the usual message in the hoax as warning against "a new and virulent virus (usually dutifully reported by IBM or Microsoft) that will wipe out your hard drive, sour the milk in your refrigerator, and impregnate your dog." This statement is clearly in jest, but replicates the tenor of the notifications that most hoax viruses portend. However, your reader will get a chuckle while getting the message. *However, it is the humor that will get him to look for and read your messages in ensuing issues.*

And that, my friends, is your goal.

As in most technically oriented organizations, you will probably be given the opportunity to attend technical writing classes. If you feel that you can use the skills, by all means enroll at once. There are many skills that will be of great value to one involved in information systems, but this is not one of the places where it can be applied. If a course in creative writing is offered, take immediate advantage. Writing is like photography. You want your work to shine forward with radiant colors. Technical writing is in black and white (faded, at that).

Despite the apparent joking manner of my last several paragraphs, I am serious as brain surgery about the aspect of entertainment in your contributions to this paper or any other publication. You must get your message across, but like sugar coating a pill, you must make it as palatable as possible.

As mentioned earlier, your efforts, particularly the first ones, should be to the letter as specified by the editorial staff of the paper. Their job is difficult enough without having to go back over contributions to bring them into compliance. The less work they have to do with yours means the higher their regard for you. After awhile, you will be able to take a few liberties or request additional space for special messages.

Remember, these people write the majority of the publication for each issue. They are usually busily trying to get it together and finding enough copy to fill it out. Remember the comments I made earlier about timeliness, clarity, and sticking rigidly to the standards they set up? This is your chance to make an impression about how perfectly suited your copy is for production and how they can always count on your work for quality and timeliness. Can you now see how they will view you if you continue to supply them with good copy in full keeping with what they need?

I can hear the comments now about how "I'm not a very good writer," or "I just hate to write!" Well, folks, no one is born an accomplished writer. You took a lot of time to learn the IS skills that you have exercised for a living up until this point, something a lot more foreign than putting the words of the language you communicate in daily down on paper. Despite the assurances of many literary critics and authors of varying levels of talent, writing is craft, not an art. One can learn to do it as readily as one can learn to paint furniture. To paint the Mona Lisa took genius; to paint a chair takes an earnest effort to learn how to choose paint and a brush and to apply it correctly. All you have to do is get the color right and put it on smoothly and evenly.

Perhaps that sounds pretty simplified, and it just might be. However, you can learn to use correct grammar and to construct a sentence effectively. If you can tell them what you want to say orally, you can put it on paper. You are delivering a message, not the Great American Novel. Creativity takes a back seat to clarity, in this case.

Besides, Spell Checker and Grammar Checker are still there for the using.

So far, I have directed this chapter toward the newsletter type publication, the monthly or bimonthly sheet that almost every company has. Often, particularly when there are other areas of the company that are remote from your location, there are supplemental sheets specifically at those installations or versions of the home "paper" modified to fit into the other environment. When the company has foreign locations where language might be different, another set of challenges must be met.

Translate, you say, and the message can be transposed for the staff at any installation. Not true! You may be working with different function areas of the company or be in a location with vastly different problems or even legal situations. If, for instance, a subsidiary makes a product — building materials, let us say — entirely different from your headquarters/research and development/engineering installation, the things that interest them and should interest you may be entirely different. Worrying about software utilization standards might not be of great interest to the framer that is putting prefabricated roof joists, as a simple example.

The same thing is involved with legal issues in foreign countries. While we view some areas like personal privacy one way in the United States, other countries have far different viewpoints. I would not, for instance, be talking about how the company can monitor Web surfing in a country that has extensive laws protecting personal privacy.

As far as the quarterly or annual distribution is concerned, check into what the content is normally and try to find a "hook" where your message will fit. If, for instance, the Christmas issue of the paper is devoted to looking back on what has occurred with the company in the preceding year, try to recap specific challenges that have been faced with regard information security. However, mention only the positives, as they are the ones that are not likely to be embarrassing. For instance, I would make a big issue as to how, through the cooperation of all system users, a virus attack was thwarted. On the other hand, I believe I might not mention the $2.5 million loss from the assistant bookkeeper's embezzling by elevating creative bookkeeping to an art form. Not a good subject!

Continual, I have stated that one has to perfect the craft of writing if these wonderful vehicles are to be used to their greatest advantage. Make sure that your copy gets in and that the rank and file read and enjoy.

This is probably a good point at which to start going over the things that make an effective entry. To that end, let us go over a few rules for making certain that you article hits the mark:

1. Limit Yourself to a Single Subject.

For whatever reason, some people have a real problem limiting the scope of anything that they put on paper. Yeah, I know, right now you are just worried that your vocabulary and imagination are not equal to the task of constructing a meaningful 500-word article. Trust me on this one: sooner or later, you will find that size constraint far to limiting for your flowing prose.

No matter how often a thread appears to logically lead to a second thread (e.g., a discussion of e-mail attached viruses can lead you down the primrose path of e-mail security issues in general), resist the temptation and get back on track. On the other hand, you can use a single sentence — using the example from the previous paragraph — and announce that a future column will explore the e-mail issue in greater depth. Use something like "While this column will not go into the intricacies of e-mail security, it is far too important a subject not to get some attention. Watch for an upcoming column on it." Wasted a few of your precious 500, but well worth it.

Note: I have continually used the 500-word limit as an example. Actually, that is more often than not the limitation placed on an internal periodical article. Practice keeping everything within that limit; you will not miss very often.

If, for some reason there is a second item you wish to cover, identify it clearly and make a decision as to which of your two ideas is the fodder for the main column. Remember how I have been stressing becoming a trusted contributor and a real aid to the editorial staff? This is the place to take advantage of that status. To be sure, you will have to be content with just putting forth your basic article for the first months until you have paid your dues, demonstrating that you will consistently provide insightful articles on time and in complete accord with company standards. Then, and only then, can you embark on the undertaking covered in item 2 of this list.

2. Open the Window!

This is a simple way of demonstrating how to approach the second subject in a given issue of the newsletter. Make a formal request to the editor of the paper to have an "emergency" announcement as a part of your article for the period (month, etc.). Make it in the form of a "news flash" or some other means to separate it from the main body of your article.

Say, for instance, that your main article is about backing up important files, but you just can't wait to crow about how your team knocked down a virus that had caused havoc around the world before it could do any damage to your company. To do that, make the statement short and introduce it with a short fanfare type introductory headline, like:

ABC Company Virus Response Team Stops Melissa Dead in Her Tracks!

Overkill? Of course, but it will get attention. Give a few details as to how they did it and limit it to ten sentences or less. Enclose it in a box — a window — and make sure that it is printed within the body of your main article. Your blurb should serve the purpose of complementing the virus response team and illustrating to the readers how important you think virus protection is — Two-edged sword.

Note: Do not do this without first clearing it with the editors. Presenting extra or out of pattern copy can cause a certain amount of stomach upset with most folks in this business. Ask permission first.

3. Try to Introduce or Explain Your Article with Anecdotal Material.

Tell a story that illustrates the problem you face, or the solution you recommend. For instance, once, in a column about passwords and their generation and maintaining privacy, I used the story about my son — at the time of the story, all of 11 years of age — and his selection of a password as described earlier.

Now, the readers thought that was pretty funny, but it pointed out a trick that they could employ in building their own password. Plus, it humanized the writer (some would contest that), speaking of his own child.

4. Relate the Anecdote to the Subject of the Column.

As in the case above, make sure that you have gone into the need for passwords, the shortcomings normally found in weak passwords, and ways you can go about keeping passwords unique and not easily guessed. Having a story like the one that I related brings it back to the human level.

5. Make Sure to Relate the Entire Column to a Business Need.

In the cited case, a good password keeps someone from guessing it, thereby protecting access to your account, protecting company information assets from being compromised by someone else using your access authority. Simply relate what it does for you, what it does for your account, what it does for the company.

6. Enlist Feedback.

For years, I have made sure that my phone number and/or e-mail address were always a part of the column. Whether in the byline or as a special access for anyone might have a need to know more about the subject, a means to contact you must be available without search. Anyone needs something about information security needs it right now. Failure to come up with that means of access will quickly dull the interest in reaching you.

Note: Although it will be discussed more thoroughly later, this is a good time to note the value of having a common e-mail group (InfoSec, for instance) or central phone number to make yourself more available and, therefore, more credible to the company staff. Try to work something out to stand out in a crowd, particularly a crowd that might want to talk to you.

7. Close Out the Article with a Summary of the Message You Are Trying to Get Across.

There must be a final statement that has a strong implication that if the reader fails to act on what you are saying, the information assets of the company could be at risk. And, what costs the company costs each and every employee.

The last item is a lot easier to sell if your organization has profit sharing. That being the case, go right ahead and state outright that the more profitable the company is, the bigger the profit-sharing checks. That has a real emotion hook. There are strong circuits between the heart and the billfold.

There are a number of other things that we could discuss in terms of using the English language (or others, if need be) and putting together a compelling article. However, that type of undertaking is more a subject for a complete book or a class. That is really not my aim here, but if such a tool does become available, by all means take advantage of it. Remember to lean more toward journalism than technical writing.

A final thought before we summarize this chapter:

Today, more and more companies are going to company internal Web pages for many purposes. Usually, there is a home page with links — in one or more forms — that everyone's log-on script defaults to or is one of several icons on the initial screen. Here is a means for publication that is not limited to the written word or a publishing schedule. If such a vehicle exists, you can not only put up a Web page devoted to information security, but can leverage the home page for special items.

Most home pages are extremely flexible and have regular appearance changes to highlight current events or concerns. If something special happens in the information security field — such as the virus infection episode that I used in my "window" example — you could create a spotlight, or headline item on the homepage that is linked to a bit of text much the same as what was printed. In addition, that item could be easily linked to further information about viruses or whatever else is covered in the spotlight entry. Do you recall how we discussed having the policy, standards, and procedures on a Web page back a few chapters? Here is a chance to link a live event to the areas of company regulations that relate to it.

Often there will be Web-based newsletter as well as the homepage itself. The usual means for circulation of such an online document is the distribution of an e-mail with a link to the newsletter. Your job is to find out about that letter and make contact with the editors of that, as well.

Often, this type of news release is associated with a given department, rather than being companywide. It is available to the rest of the company, but advertised only within certain areas. In such cases, your contribution will have to be written in a manner that can be acceptable to the selected audience. Check carefully, usually by reading a few back issues, as to what means will best reach the intended audience.

If the intended audience is an IS department, maybe you should have taken that technical writing class!

Finally, I want to visit on the idea of bulletin boards. There are generally a number of such boards around most companies of any size. Depending on company regulations, the posting of information on these boards may be as simple as finding a tack or as complex as having copy approved by your management and someone above them. Make certain that you trod on no toes, assuming you see possibilities here.

Take a good look at the boards and try to get an image of what is on them. Often, they will be employee advertising media altogether, with items such as ads for cars, apartments, homes for sale, and Tupperware and will be completely unregulated. Others, a bit more regulated, will require that entries be approved and date stamped before posting; others will have a majority of the space reserved for company postings. Often, you will find all of these levels within one company, but in varying locations.

Your aim is to get on the company info board, assuming that it is a good vehicle for getting information out. In too many cases, messages are posted and left there for the entire life of the sheet of paper used. Barring dry rot, they'll be up there for eternity. These are the boards that become wallpaper — everyone acknowledges their presence, but could not describe any detail if their lives depended on it. This type of board is generally a waste of time to use. Still, if you have access to someone with time and a bent toward creativity, new and fresh ideas can be posted there. Try to stay with the pattern of company postings, but be different enough to catch the eye of the passerby. For instance, try bright colors or a different typeface than the norm for effect.

Several items should be remembered before even attempting to use this medium:

- Is the bulletin board used for updates that are important to the company?
- Is it located in a place where a majority of the staff will pass by on a regular basis?
- Are there regulations for posting? Definitely familiarize yourself with those.
- Does the company culture seem responsive to writing on the wall? Often, things posted in this manner are assumed to be of little value, and rather than getting your message out, you may be downplaying it.
- Can you produce copy that will grab attention? That creative soul, a graphics department?
- Can you produce and maintain enough copy to get to all boards involved in this type of news out? In a multibuilding campus, this could be a daunting job.

In short, bulletin boards are a mixed bag, particularly if vehicles such as those described are available as an alternative. As a rule of thumb, I would say that if you have more than ten boards to get your message up on, there are probably more sophisticated methods available. Use your energy in exploiting them.

Summary

With any kind of luck, your organization will have not just one but a number of employee informational vehicles available for you to exploit. Your main function is to locate them, find out what their standards for publication are and make certain to produce solid copy to be entered.

We have talked a great deal about you and your ability to wax poetic for purposes of entertaining and educating the employees of your company. This is great for a one-person shop, but there is a good chance that you will have some help. That being the case, I would make a point of recruiting for writing as well as technical skills.

So the vehicles we may use are:

- The regular periodical, printed on a monthly (usually) basis and with a fairly standardized format. This is where you want to get a presence as quickly as possible and make sure that your interests are represented every month. Learn their standards and make certain that everything you write is scrupulously adherent to them. Know the deadlines and beat them comfortably every month.

■ The more spread out quarterly or biennial company updates. This one is often in addition to the regularly scheduled periodical. It often gives the opportunity to give a bit more detail — more column inches — and put more teaching into the article.

■ The peripheral newsletters: these may be foreign language versions of the regular newsletter or they may be published at remote installations and only for their consumption. If the issues that you are writing about include concerns there, by all means find a way to get your articles published there. If time allows and the issue is pressing enough, prepare special articles for those papers.

■ The Web-based newsletter — the wave of the present and with very little continued growth, the future. You can get articles into the periodic publications and work with the webmaster to get more pressing issues on the main page. These can be in the form of "spotlights," or headlines and/or links to greater detail and even to your policies, standards, and procedures. This is a powerful tool and the use of links lets you corroborate what you write with documentation from a number of sources. Do not forget that you can use outside URLs to make your readership aware of issues in the field and the experiences of others. Make a point of applying any such medium that is available and if possible, take an HTML class to empower yourself to do some creating.

■ The department-specific newsletters. Not usually reliable as to time of publication, but generally looked forward to by its normal reader community. Review back issues to get a feel for writing style, grade level, and type of information presented. Preparing an article for this type of publication will take a sharp focus toward the end reader, perhaps more so than with the earlier mentioned vehicles. The interests will be much narrower here.

■ The good, old bulletin board. Put up an ad to get rid of Old Shep's illegitimate offspring ("mother purebred German Shepherd, father from a good neighborhood."), a car, a house and, oh yes, a warning about not opening e-mail attachments from people you do not know. The previous sentence gives you a pretty good idea of what you are usually up against. In those areas where formal postings are available, your message will get far more notice and might just be effective. Try to make your contribution a bit outside the run of the mill and make sure it appears on all boards that have sufficient traffic to ensure that the majority of employees are exposed to them. If there are multiple boards, try not to miss any. If the number is greater than ten of those, you might well spend your time using the previously mentioned means. A company big enough to have that many formal bulletin boards usually has more sophisticated tools that will better serve you and make more efficient use of your time.

In any company, large or small, there are usually a number of ways to get information to a majority of the staff by using a known and predictable means. We have covered a number of them in this chapter. It is, however, up to you to evaluate each and put your effort into those that will best serve your purpose. What I have said works in generalities, but might not be best in your particular environment. Look carefully and invest your time wisely.

If all else fails, you can go out and catch a mustang and, with a bit of time and effort, break him to ride. However, if there are broken saddle horses available, climb on the best one and get the ride you want.

Chapter 12

The Best Toys in Town

We have continually pounded upon the necessity to get our message to everyone and repeat it until it becomes as familiar as their own birthdays. That's really fine, if you have the proverbial staff of thousands to preach the gospel on every street corner. Unfortunately, it is probably just you, or perhaps you and a few staff members of your own. Your audience outnumbers you by at least hundreds and maybe thousands to one.

Now, what we discussed in the last chapter is a good way to get information on a given topic out to the masses, but it does not have a continuing presence, something that is needed to make certain that the concepts of information security are readily available — with or without a voluntary effort by each member of your selected audience — and presented regularly.

Let us explore a few ways of doing just that:

Note: We will make some assumptions in this chapter, based on probability. First, the fact that you are in your position is a good indication that the company is serious about protecting its information assets. They obviously have a certain commitment to that. Second, we will assume some level of sophistication in your training department. Under normal circumstances, the training department manages to come up with more new technology and ways to deliver training than does any other area. These things being only partly true, we have a great partner to get started with.

There are tools available for training today that were not even available just a few years ago. Once we watched 16 millimeter movies that were made using actors more closely related to crash test dummies than Shakespearean thespians. You got a bunch of people into a room, pulled down several blackout curtains (remember them?), threaded the projector, pulled down or set up the screen, and set forth with your movie. The grinding of the projector always gave the presentation that thrown-together, amateurish character that I can recall today. Training films, they called them, even in the military, where they reached their apex or nadir, your choice.

We still have movies today, but more often than not, they are shown in videotape format. You pop it in, turn on the TV, and away you go. The films are very professional as the equipment is better and easier to operate, the video cameras have autofocus, gyros for balance, and almost everything else needed to make the operator superfluous. The film — or in this case, videotape — is less grainy, more light sensitive, and more tolerant of changing conditions. If you shoot it yourself, there is a chance that you can prepare something even better than the old training films.

However, along with the recognition that a film image could be leveraged to present a concept to far more people in far less time than a road show, companies have sprung up that specialize in delivering your message to your audience. They have studios, but they really are not shackled to them. They can come to your site and, with a bit of preparation, film an entire class while in session, do the same with a speaker's presentation, or set up a scripted show scenario in a very short time and at quite reasonable cost.

Today, larger companies often have this type of skill available in-house, and depending on size and need, some of them match specialized business facilities. Often the staff of the department has the credentials of the best of the private contractors. They can assist you in preparing scripts and setting up "sets" within which to stage your production and produce a final product with titling, graphic effects, and other such special effects that will make your simplest efforts look very professional.

If I might go back a bit to a previous life with a company of modest size, I can recall that the manager of corporate security and I borrowed a video camera from the human resources department and set about making up a film to inform new hires of the safety and security standards throughout the company and what their specific responsibilities were. My colleague sat at a desk, lighted with what lights we had available, and did the talking-head thing about physical security while I filmed. We repeated the same scenario by switching roles — he filmed and I talked — for the information security side. I then prepared a 60-second script and presented the concept and that script to the president and CEO of the company and requested him to sit in front of the camera, in his office, and read that script. This short ingress into his busy day — it took well under 30 minutes, even with retakes — demonstrated to the viewer that management, on the highest level, supported what this tape portrayed. It was a validation, introducing my colleague and myself and talking a bit about how important what we were going to say would be to the viewer.

I think our original cost was something well short of $10 for the tape and some duplicating costs that still never reached the $100 mark to make enough copies to use across three states. That tape became a part of the new employee orientation program for the company and was not only used in that manner, but often shown at branches or other gatherings of staff to make certain that they were well aware of its contents. All for a cost that would not buy a winter coat that was equal to that particular region.

A little aside on the Roy and Mark Video Production Company: As noted, people across three states got to see the tape at various times, including at small branch banks. It is a bit unnerving to be in the hinterlands of New England, at a subsidiary office, and have someone come up and say "I know you!" Despite the number of times it happened, it usually took a reminder about the tape to get me to quit reviewing my lengthy past and wondering where I had come into contact with this person who was at a location that I had certainly never visited before.

The scenes on the following pages are from Commonwealth Films' Information Training videos (titles follow captions). They address the very real threats of theft of laptop computers and the resultant loss of not only expensive hardware and software copies, but of the potentially priceless information stored on the computer. Even worse, there is a tendency by many to use secure methods in offloading sensitive information to removable storage media, and then storing that media in...you guessed it...the same case the computer is stored in!

Hacking, and the way it is likely done, are also a focus of the videos.. This type of thing is extremely pertinent to today's environment, with the reports of new incursions making the front page on a daily basis. Learning how to protect yourself and making certain that the staff of your organization knows the "face of the enemy" is always strong medicine for prevention.

I used that anecdote to demonstrate that you can often get excellent results with a pretty modest outlay of cash or time. Imagine if the two of us had to wander the three states in question, parroting the same things we said on the tape. The time impact would have been huge. Plus, we would not have had the luxury of having the top "gorilla" in the company blessing it at the same time.

Of course, you can do a lot with what can be prepared by the sophisticated internal or external video specialists that can duplicate our modest efforts but with much finer style. Just like I mentioned about the articles you write, color and pizzazz raise the level of interest. If you got it, use it!

A quick reminder on such videos: We tend to forget these things once they have found their niche in the educational programs of the company. Witness my never seeming to recall it when meeting someone who had seen my smiling face (and survived) on tape. Make certain to review these things at least annually. Even in a 30-minute tape, a lot of things can change rather quickly and the information can become outdated. This is a point that I will develop more as we talk about maintaining and evaluating your program, later in the book.

Along these same lines is another option that takes advantage of the videotaping technology and that is the idea of prepackaged tapes. A few years ago, I would not have recommended any of these on a bet; they were stiff, quickly outdated, and acted by characters reminiscent of the B-movies that are the butts of many jokes. However, and as with other aspects of the technology, they have improved dramatically and cover many areas. Although they are pretty pricey ($350–$500, on average) they do present problems with which we are all familiar and valid resolutions to them.

Exhibit 1   This scene illustrates a laptop computer being stolen using a well-known scam at an airport security checkpoint. (*Targets of Opportunity*)

Exhibit 2   This scene shows a password being stolen by "shoulder surfing." (*The Best Defense*)

Exhibit 3 This scene depicts a laptop computer being stolen at a hotel taxi stand. (*Look Out for Your Laptop!*)

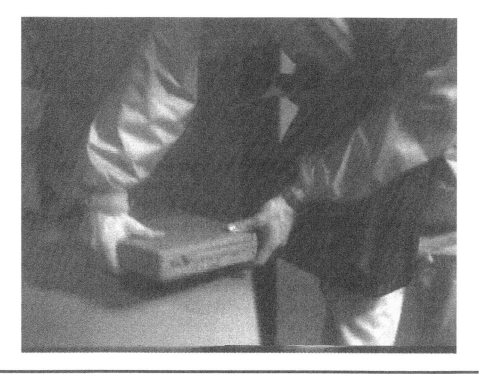

Exhibit 4 This scene illustrates a laptop computer being stolen by a bicycle courier. (*Look Out for Your Laptop!*)

Exhibit 5   This scene shows a laptop computer being stolen by a second shift Maintenance worker. (*Look Out for Your Laptop!*)

Exhibit 6   This scene depicts professional espionage agents searching stolen laptops, PDAs, and cell phones. (*Look Out for Your Laptop!*)

Most of the companies that offer these tapes usually offer a generous tryout period at little or no cost. Should you decide that one or more of these tapes provide a valuable service, I am quite certain that an agreement can be reached on multiple copies if that would better serve your purpose.

I have included at the end of this chapter a list of a few of the companies in the field. While I cannot either approve or disapprove of their products, they have been in the field for awhile and may well have tapes that can be of service.

Depending on the size and the state of technology within your organization, there are a number of online vehicles that may be used at the workstation for purposes of teaching individuals about specific aspects of computer security and their responsibilities. As most of you are aware, Microsoft PowerPoint is an excellent presentation product that can be used in a number of ways: It can be used to build slide shows that can be built into overheads (in the most primitive of environments), punched in for a slide show managed by a facilitator, selected by a viewer in a self-paced study program, or automated with a script to provide a hands-off "show" upon demand.

Now, if such a show were to be hooked into log-on, your message could be presented to a new user at log-on. If you so chose, it could be turned off at its conclusion by a simple "Do you wish to see this demonstration each time you log on?" What with the larger quantity of memory in each new PC today and the multigigabyte disk capacity that has become standard, this small file would be of little consequence in the overall storage scheme but would free up the time of skilled trainers forced to provide training to each new employee (hopefully, in groups) on a weekly basis. The benefit derived from automating this, or any part of the orientation and training scenario, would allow training staff to be assigned elsewhere.

A final thought on automating orientation and training: Today, utilizing the same storage capability noted before, along with the capacity of CD-ROM, an entire video can be prepared to deliver the message about Information Security 101 or other, more detailed lessons. In fact, weaving the technology into a server-based system, you could use any of a number of methods to either push the file to selected terminals or request that they be downloaded. Let us say, for instance, that the assignment of a new log-on ID kicked off a request to upload your basic information security awareness file to whatever terminal initiated a brand new log-on. As the profile was being established, the file could be presented in front of any further system attachment. Of course, in the interest of free choice, the option to not watch it again should be offered at the end of the initial presentation.

Streaming video has become less of an esoteric art in the contemporary world than it might have been in the recent past. Do not overlook the potential of this powerful medium when preparing workstation information presentation. In the next chapter, as we talk more about formal classes, we will take an even deeper look at the application of streaming video.

By the way, there should be a method of making certain that the "101" presentation is available by request with a minimum of effort on the part of the user. That can be done by building a unique screen icon or entry into the Programs directory under the main menu.

We have, to this point, spoken a lot about the means to get information to new and longer-term employees, but very little about what information should be presented to them. Let us go over the makeup of an introductory tape or screen-displayed class. In the next chapter, we will spend more time on facilitator-assisted or trainer-presented classes, but for now, let us look at how to construct a programmed course. For the most part, we will stick to the work that you do or cause to have done, rather than commercially available tapes, CDs, and so on. The latter will be selected to deliver a message, usually in a very narrow vein. In most cases, these will not be exactly what you want but will be a tolerable tradeoff between exactness and the expediency of getting a finished product rather than building from the ground up.

Any orientation-type presentation should begin with a welcome to the company and a statement as to how seriously the company takes the protection of its information assets. If you can get a statement from the CEO, as I described in our little homemade video, so much the better. Nothing corroborates your statements as well as having the top person in the company speaking out in your favor. If you are using PowerPoint or another such nontelevision medium, a slide with a quote, formally reproduced and with a "signature" or citation as to the statement's source at the end, is still pretty powerful stuff.

Let us go over the basic content you need to get across. Now, this will be pretty generic and will not go into specific requirements that might reside in one company and not another, but as we move through it, you will see where limited-interest custom information could be inserted.

We have pounded on the idea of policies, standards, and procedures since the beginning few words of this treatise, so why change now? You have told them what the presentation is about, the top gun has stated his support, so now it is time to go to the basics.

Publish the entire policy statement on the screen. If it does not appear in written form in something they have received up until this point (perish the thought!), invite them to screen print it now. If full publication is precluded by space and time, publish a URL where it can be found. In this case, speak in generalities, outlining the policy and stressing its importance. This is the one single thing that should not be overlooked. Everything else is, to one extent or another, flexible enough to omit or reference abstractly.

The next significant step is to demonstrate what the company finds important for new employees to know and understand. Usually, this will be a description of the type of business that the company is in and the things that they wish protected. For instance, if your company bakes cookies, the exact recipe is probably pretty well protected. Having the world know it would not be good for business. The same follows with any other business from manufacturing to services sector organizations. There are things pertinent to the way things run that would not serve the company well were they known.

Of course, there are certain items that are pretty similar throughout industry. Financials, for instance, may vary in dimension or detail, but have a majority of common details. This falls under the heading of confidential in virtually all organizations.

The next thing to do is to relate the new employee's probable responsibilities for maintaining these company secrets. No matter if you are dealing with a janitor or an engineer, they will all come into contact with all or some of these secrets. Demonstrate a number of ways this could happen. For instance, when discussing housekeeping, the engineer could easily drop something in a wastebasket that could compromise confidential information. By the same token the janitor has access — the responsibility, for that matter — to that same information in that same wastebasket. Does the idea come through?

On the following pages are great examples of the products of the Atterbury Foundation; contact information can be found at the end of this chapter.

Each image is a clear, self-contained message, using carefully crafted statements that remain in one's mind and brightly colored images to support the text. In addition, they are eye-catching and colorful, sure mechanisms to guarantee notice. (While black-and-white images are represented here; visit their Web site for a true view.)

If your budget is limited, and you do not have the staff or resources to create something of this nature, I believe you will find these reasonable and a lot of "bang for the buck."

While I will in no way recommend the products of any vendor or organization, these are splendid examples of what can be done using this simple medium.

Cover the basic rules of using the company communications medium. We will cover this in more detail in the next chapter.

If there are special issues involved, this is a good place to cover them. Virus prevention, for instance, is an almost universal topic at this time. I am certain that you can identify many more within your organization.

Go over the rules for using equipment like the terminal (PC) upon which this presentation is being delivered. Talk about passwords: how to build them and how to keep them secret.

I will not go further into what can be aired in this manner as I am certain that you have come up with ideas of your own by this time. Suffice it to say that once you have located a medium of exchange of data, the materials will appear more quickly than you can address them.

Now, as a closing shot, I will touch on some of the other, more time-honored means of getting the word out.

I do not think anyone has not, at one time or another, come across the trinket system of spreading the word, be it about supporting the company, the upcoming Christmas luncheon or information security. Using this method, all sorts of key chains, coasters, ballpoint pens, and other small, easily lost items are distributed, each bearing a cryptic message. From people having possession of these items, at least until the time that their offspring make off

with them, the message of information security and its importance is carried far and wide.

Likewise is the poster culture, where "SSHH" signs are put up with a picture of someone's finger pressed to their lips, signifying a plea not to talk. These were relatively effective during World War II, so they must still have some effect today. Yes, they probably do, but like a lot of other 60-year-old ideas, some of the gloss has worn off. Most certainly, some messages can be effectively delivered by poster, assuming that you can get them into the right places, but there are shortcomings, as well. A poster, left up too long, turns into wallpaper. Everyone sees it, but no one looks at it. With three or four exposures, the message disappears. Figuring those exposures to take little more than two weeks, you had better be ready with another version in pretty short order.

The same goes for the trinkets. It has always been a trend to pass out little reminders to push the idea of security. Like the poster, they wear out in short order. If you feel that you must use something of this nature, and I caution you that in some companies, it just does not go, try a sticker that can be put on the console or screen of a PC. Use a simple phrase, like "Log it Off!" or "Stamp out Viruses," for greatest effect. If the company issues mouse pads, try to get one of those catch phrases on it, as well.

Another thing you can do is give out mouse pads or T-shirts as prizes for one or another contest. The contests can be staged, as we will discuss in the next chapter, or you can simply set up a table in the cafeteria or lobby with a few of the stickers, poster, or other gimmicks designed to catch people's attention. Have a few things like the T-shirts or mouse pads as prizes in a raffle. If your budget can stand it, have them answer a simple question about security to win one. Only the limits of your time and budget will limit the application of this means of notification.

Perhaps the final means for getting your message out is to produce a printed, e-mail, or Web-based means of notification. By using this system, your message comes across both timely and formally. The latter is of utmost important in that formality often creates the aura of importance.

These things can be done in a number of ways, from a newsletter format, within which you explore a number of topics or a bulletin format in which you hit one subject hard. Unless you have almost unlimited resources, the latter is probably the best way to go.

There is no need to explore writing style again here except to say: keep it interesting. Dry, colorless copy will be ignored, I can assure you. Take your one subject, decide what you have to share about it, and try to keep within those bounds. For instance, if you are having a problem with a lot of virus-bearing e-mail attachments coming in through your mail system, you might want to warn people against opening such attachments. The best way to do that is to offer a set of rules to go by. Number them and list like you were planning on going shopping. As an example:

1. If you do not recognize the sender, delete without opening.
2. If the body of the message says "Here's the stuff you requested" and you didn't request anything, delete it without opening.

3. If you recognize the sender (as with an address-book spawning virus) but did not expect to receive anything from the sender, delete it without opening. In a case like this, you might want to check with the sender — still without opening the attachment. If the e-mail is not genuine, the sender might well want to know that his or her machine is infected.

You can add additional items if warranted. Just remember to use the numbered format as it makes it much easier to read.

Whether on paper or through the network, you want your copy to be easily discernible from any other. That is relatively easy by selecting or building a distinctive masthead. Building one is not exactly brain surgery as there is clip art available in almost any medium you might choose.

For example, a number of years ago, in an earlier life, I built a masthead out of relatively simple clip art images. I took a terminal picture, superimposed a large, old style keyhole onto the screen, created a gothic key just beside the keyhole — as if it were about to be inserted — and arranged the scrollwork of the key head into a gothic "B." The final draft was of this image to the left top (facing) of the page with the key head being the "B" of the word Bulletin. The overall title of the banner was "Information Security Bulletin," Bulletin being the first word of the second line of the title. Not spectacular by any means, but easily recognizable from other form. It is heartwarming to walk by a cubicle and, at a glance, recognize your bulletin as one of the items tacked to the wall.

Online tools give you even more latitude. Remember, the image need only be unique, not necessarily a candidate for any international art awards.

Another thing I found useful with the bulletin system, no matter what medium you finally settle on, was to never schedule it. Have it come out apparently on a random basis. It gives the appearance of a bulletin much more of an emergency aura, something you want to communicate. Although there was never a schedule, there always seemed to be about 12 of them every year. Might not have been exactly once a month, but it certainly was not very far off that. Keep 'em coming on a regular basis, just don't be too consistent with your release dates.

This final means of communication is easily overlooked in our more-technical-by-the-day world, but it is still extremely effective. We communicate in English and that is still the best way to share information.

Summary

Getting your news to the world at large may seem a daunting task at first, until you realize the powerful tools you have at hand. You can use the most high-tech methods to send your message or can reduce the level of cyber technology to paper and ink (toner, I suppose, in today's world). The idea is to leverage what is available to circulate your prepared message.

We have discussed a number of methods and have talked about the positives and negatives of each. Briefly, they were as follows:

- The relatively new medium of video, either commercially prepared or prepared to order. If your company has a multimedia department sufficiently sophisticated to make such videos, take advantage with your training films. Still, we demonstrated that we could produce a pretty low-tech version of such a video with very little expense (and I might add, in the case of our little experiment, no great level of talent, either!) but a marked impact. I would not be surprised if that old tape was still being used, somewhere.

- Commercially prepared videotapes. These will come with a general message but now exist in sufficient variety so that you may well be able to find something "canned" that will deliver your message well. While there is still a wide range of quality among the different vendors, some are quite good. Review them, make a decision and, if you decide to use one or more of them, work out a contractual agreement with the vendor over the application and the number of copies you may need.

   By the way, if you do need something special and can demonstrate that it would be worthwhile for them to add something of that nature to their catalog, you might well get one of these companies to produce something to your standards. They would, of course, have to see where a commercially viable product would come from their efforts before they would undertake it.

- A third medium is the PC screen program. This can take one of three faces in your program. First, you can have a moderated screen "show," with a facilitator presenting the slides and talking around them. Second, you can have a self-paced version delivering the same information. Third, you can use streaming video or scripted slides delivered on an individual's terminal. The latter can be scripted to be presented the first time a new user logs on and he or she can be given the choice whether to watch it again.

- We can also use the technology of e-mail or Web pages to distribute the same information. It can be distributed to a global mailing list, can reference a URL, or can have a presence on the company home page. The only real limitation is the level of sophistication the corporation has available.

- Ultimately, we can go back to the old standby, pen and ink. We can create a newsletter or bulletin logo on a masthead that will identify the document as being from information security and will make it stand out from other publications. Keep the content of the latter form (the bulletin) simple and focus on only one issue. Use a list or bullet type of format to make the points stand out and be easily remembered.

In short, there are a number of means available to get more data out to more people in a minimum amount of time. Now that they are within the organization, you have full access to them. Make sure that the message you send is timely, useful, and easily understood. The rest will take care of itself.

I have really given short shrift to a number of good organizations that create some of the materials we mentioned here. As I am wont to place a valuation on someone else's work at this point, I do not wish to review their product lines. I do, however, want to give you a few names of companies that can provide good materials. Use them, with no input — either positive or negative — from here.

As I noted earlier, I promised to give you a few sources for getting preprepared video presentations. This list is far from complete and other companies have no doubt sprung up since the publication of this book. Check around, look for advertisements in trade magazines, and subscribe to a few. I guarantee those subscriptions will spawn an influx of mail that will inform you of even more. The ones I did want to share are:

Commonwealth Films

223 Commonwealth Ave.
Boston, MA 02116
(617) 262-5634
Fax: (617) 262-6948
E-mail: info@commonwealthfilms.com
Web: http://www.commmonwealthfilms.com

This organization has been around for a long time and has a wide variety of subject materials available. Their offerings include information security and many other business subjects. Your training department is probably familiar with their product line and might even have a catalog. Check there first.

InfoSecurityStuff.com

1627 US Highway 1, Suite #6
Sebastian, FL 32958
(561) 388-8490
Fax: (561) 388-8491
E-mail: kenmcewan@ibm,net
Web: www.infosecuritystuff.com

General films on information security and a number of other business subjects

Here are a couple of companies that make posters and awareness publications:

Locksmith Publishing

850 Busse Highway
Park Ridge, IL 60068
(847) 692-5940
Fax: (847) 692-4604
E-mail: Slasky@worldnet.att.net
Web: http://www.simon-net.com

Monthly newsletter, security technology and design. More for security practitioners.

The Atterbury Foundation
3045 East Laurelhurst Dr. NE
Seattle, WA 98105-5330
(206) 524-3671
Fax: (206) 524-3695
E-mail: chatterbury@seanet.com
Web: http://www.atterbury.org

Posters

Chapter 13

Back to School

Thus far we have taken apart a number of ways to get information across and to stress the importance of what we are communicating to the listener and to the corporation. When push comes to shove, the employee has to understand how seriously the company takes information security and how it is willing to respond to threats to its information assets. That is where your program comes in.

In most larger companies today, where normal turnover dictates that a new employee orientation takes place at least a few times a month, there is a curriculum of short classes that take up at least most of the first day. In some instances, where employment might involve the learning of skills specific to the product line of the company, manufacturing processes and emergency procedures, a second day of classes might be involved.

If you have developed a relationship with management as we have advised in earlier chapters, the kernel of your message has stayed with them. Therefore, it is up to you to request time to send your message to new employees coming on board. The best way to do this? You must set up a basic information security classroom experience for these new people.

Now, writing a class to be given by you or a trainer is an experience not too many people in our line of business have tried. In reality, and based on the writing experiences that we have discussed for several chapters, it is doable and doable well.

Let us then, discuss what we have to put into the class we are creating. First, how much time do we have: one hour, half of that? The material must fit into the time allotted. In most cases, as we begin to work on the content we will need to communicate, we will find that there is a lot more information than we can get into the allotted time. Whether to pare it down or eliminate it can often be the most perplexing part of creating the class outline. The need must dictate what is in and may force a change in the structure of your outside documentation to support the references made in the class work. In short, if you cannot cover a subject that you feel needs to be covered, you may have to give a reference to another source for the information. That being the case, the referenced material must support what the employee goes in search of. Keep a good record of what your class will offer and what must be looked up afterward. Update your standards and procedures appropriately.

To begin with, let us entertain the idea of putting together instructional material that covers the basic points that every new employee should understand. Start by producing an outline of what you want to cover. Do so by considering what issues you would discuss one-on-one with a new hire. What could you tell them that would not only protect the company better, but make them want to participate in that protection. A sample outline might look like the one in Exhibit 1.

Now, that seems simple enough, doesn't it? Just follow the outline and you can create a perfect class, right?

Obviously, there is a lot more to it than simply following an outline. To prepare and deliver a solid class we certainly have to cover all of the ingredients mentioned in the outline, but we have to address them in sensible and effective ways. Let us go over the outline and discuss the ways to address each point.

Your introduction has to be an impact point in the presentation. These folks will no doubt have been exposed to an information avalanche over the past day or two and are near the saturation point. What you must do is create morsels of data that will be memorable and stand out against the background of mostly useless drivel under which they have been inundated.

First and foremost, introduce yourself. Your mere presence is an indication that the company does not take matters of security lightly and that information is considered important enough for you to be standing before them. By the way, even if your organizational culture allows for casual dress, make certain that your appearance is just a step more formal than what they have seen so far. Again, if the subject is important, they need to see that you take it seriously.

Your verbal introduction should include your title and reference to what you do. If you are a trainer, rather than an information security professional, make it clear that you, along with the information security department, developed this class because it was needed. Talk about how your expertise is teaching and building presentational course materials and that your counterpart was the "expert" content manager. This immediately lets them know that you are not operating in a vacuum, far from the world they will live in, but the professional deliverer of professionally originated material.

For the second point, introduce the concept of the company viewing this as important enough to fit it into the tight schedule that, by this time, they have experienced. So important is information security that they gave it its own time slot.

Finally, give a quick overview of what will be covered. Make it clear that all of this is important and you will try to present it in an interesting manner. Urge them to ask questions as they occur to them. Remember, if questions are asked during class time, the class becomes interactive, vesting the student section in the value of the material.

The second section should, by this time, be second nature to you. Talk about the policy statement. Now your material could vary a bit, depending

Exhibit 1 Sample Outline

I. Introduction
   A. Who I am and what I represent
   B. Why we are sitting here
   C. What we will be covering
II. Intro to company policy
   A. Trot out the printed form or a slide. If this has been done right, this should be at least the second time they have seen it
   B. Go over the provisions in the document
III. Talk about information as an asset
   A. Give a solid, memorable statement as to how the company considers information and its processing environment as a corporate asset
   B. Talk about classifications of information
      1. Definitions of the levels of sensitivity in your organization
      2. Examples of each level
      3. Short oral quiz; present information examples; get input as to their classifications
      4. Explain how the divulging of any of the more confidential assets can harm the company
IV. Handling of information
   A. Where it is stored
   B. Backups and recovery
   C. What to do with outdated information
   D. What they are expected to do
V. Viruses
   A. What they are
   B. Where they come from
   C. What to do about them
   D. What to watch out for
   E. Hoax vs. real
VI. E-mail
   A. What is allowed and what is not
   B. Confidentiality in e-mail
   C. Malicious attachments
   D. Taking care of your mailbox
   E. What can happen if it is misused
VII. Voice mail
   A. Weaknesses
   B. Proper usage
   C. Housekeeping
   D. Types of incursions
VIII. Verbal communications
   A. Telephones
   B. Public places
   C. Talk to friends and family
IX. Personal responsibility
   A. Review of previous
   B. What "wrong" looks like
   C. What to do
   D. Who to call

Exhibit 1   Sample Outline (continued)

   X. Important numbers and e-mail addresses
      A. Information security
      B. Security
      C. Postmaster
      D. Help desk
      E. Others
  XI. Conclusion
      A. What your contribution in learning this means to the company
      B. What your performance means to the company
      C. What the company's profitability means to you
      D. Short quiz

on whether the policy was given to them as a part of the materials they have received, was handed to them as a page in their new employee's manual, or will be given to them at a later time. Worst case, give them the URL or other address so that they can locate it as easily as possible. I consider the sharing of this policy absolutely imperative and find it intolerable that they not have it in their grasp by this time. By any means, make certain that they do *not* have to go looking for it. Without this having been an item already in their possession, the message has been delivered that information security is an afterthought. If they come in with that impression, it will be hard to change it.

Assuming that my warnings of woe are unneeded, let us assume that they can lay hands on the document easily or that you have it projected on the wall, screen, ceiling somewhere. Now, the time is ripe to go over the document from end to end. Make certain that you leave nothing out — heck, it's only a page long — and offer the opportunity for questioning. The nature of their questions will, by the way, give you guidance as to what to stress as the presentation continues.

Note: The previous statement is a perfect example of the need to examine what is said and done for the impact it is having on your audience. Consistently try to read the class, particularly in the first few sessions, as their response is a great barometer as to how the material is being accepted. If similar questions keep popping up, then there is a chance that a subject is not getting the coverage it needs. Amend the presentation to pay more attention to it. Continue to make these upgrades until questions tend to be one of a kind. There are some people who will ask questions that you could not prepare for if you had a team of scientists sitting behind you. However, if the question is unique, it is probably no reflection on the material or the way it is being presented.

Also, remember that the points of impact will change over time. People will become more sophisticated in some areas and will come in with background in place. On the other hand, brand new information that impacts what you are saying might be important to include. Keep your eyes and ears open.

The next issue to address is the concept of information as an asset. The policy will have already made the statement, but now is the time to drive it home. Use examples like "if we made chocolate chip cookies and were very successful in the marketplace, what would happen if someone else got the recipe?" Take a few answers to make sure that the concept is getting through. Go through a few other examples if you feel that the first failed to make the desired impact.

Now, move the conversation to the product line of your company. Identify the type of information that could be construed as sensitive and that the company would not want to get out. Use examples, without going into real detail: "Wouldn't the competition love to know just exactly how we build the best widget in the industry?" Pretty simple, but effective.

At this point you introduce the concept of information classification. In most companies that might range from two classes on up to several. Minimally, there should be a classified or company secret level and an unclassified or public information level.

Note: This might be a good point at which to make it clear that I believe that there should be a minimum of three classification levels in any information classification scheme. First is what I call *Company Confidential*. This is information that is known only to a limited number of people within the organization and that on a need to know basis.

The second classification is simply *Confidential*. This is anything that pertains to company business right down to how many steps there are in making a widget and how many people it takes to do it.

Finally we have *Unclassified* information. This can be anything from the company newspaper to press releases and the jobs hotline. These are all things that might be circulated in the local media. Indeed, some of them are designed for just that.

Whether or not you use these classifications is up to you, but I would be remiss if I failed to pass along my opinion on the matter.

Once you have the concept in place, use as many examples as you need to so that you can be sure that there are no gaps in knowledge. For this reason, keep a few examples in reserve, just in case you need them.

Now is the time to give a few examples of what the company has that someone else may want to get. Mix a few of them in along with superfluous information and get feedback from the general audience as to how they would classify each item. Using things like the plans for the company's main product and the cafeteria menu make perfect examples, as they are far enough apart for the dullest of your students to pick up on. Continue with examples until you are comfortable that everyone in the room is aware.

Other examples to use include customer records versus company newsletter; cost to produce a products versus advertising copy; and on in that direction.

Remember to use comparisons that can demonstrably harm the company if the information were to be compromised. Couch it in terms of "if the company fails to make money, we no longer have jobs."

Now that we have established the value of information, it is time to touch on ways to protect it. As we progress, we will touch on specifics for the other aspects of data handling as reflected in the remainder of the outline. For now, suffice it to say that we will concern ourselves with where information is and how each individual must protect it.

This is a subject best handled by asking the question: "Where would you find information in a company?" The answers will be in gross generalities, as these people do not yet know about the intricacies of your organization. If the conversation does not flow at first, make suggestions: "Can you find it on a computer disk?" "Can you find it in a file drawer?" "Can you find it in the wastebasket?" In each case, go over how you can find it and what it will look like. Point out that even the things we throw away could often be valuable to a competitor. Describe "dumpster diving" and the ways it can compromise company information.

At this point talk about backups. If the company tends to be very decentralized, the backups are often done at the server level. To introduce this concept, one must stress the need to keep sensitive information at the server, rather than the desktop. While the means may vary from company to company, the basic concept remains the same. If backups are done at the desktop, tell them how to do it. Then, describe what could happen if they do not and have a hardware failure.

Something that is often left out of classes like these is the instruction on what to do with outdated information. While no longer applicable within an organization, dated information could be very instructive to competitors that would be perfectly happy to be where you were yesterday. Now, they only have to catch up one day to pull even. Before they got that discarded disk, they were years behind.

Talk about degaussing diskettes, shredding paper info, and overwriting sensitive files on hard drives.

Above all, make sure that all members of your class are aware of the fact that they are responsible for performing these tasks (within the confines of their job descriptions) conscientiously. Even the janitor handles whatever is in the wastebasket.

Viruses are a great, but ever-changing subject. At the time you put on an individual class, the issues from two weeks ago might be gone. By the same token, two weeks hence, you may need to refer to something new. Try to maintain currency on this matter.

The news media will help you with this, as they seem to flock to any new virus outbreak. When you mention specifics in class, individuals will be aware of them. Make certain to cull out a few really famous ones and have data as to the effect they had. *Melissa*, for example, is long gone, but she was the harbinger of the address-book-attacking virus. If you have war stories about successes within your company in fighting these things, by all means trot them out. For the newbies to be impressed by your performance is a good thing. Credibility creates believability.

Talk about the forms viruses take and the cautions about opening e-mail attachments from strangers. Talk about what to do if you suspect you have a virus.

And, finally, talk about hoax viruses. No matter how much we work at it, the hoaxes seem to keep popping up. They morph from a free offer from one company, to another, and then another, or information about a hell-raising virus that is out of control and unstoppable. Teach the indicators of a hoax the way it always originated with a reputable organization (IBM and Microsoft are two of the favorite sources) and how it will wreak havoc on your computer, family, and home. It will always contain information on how no one has been able to come up with a preventive or cleansing agent and how you should warn everyone you know and as many as possible that you do not know.

Make a point of explaining that these must end with you. Do not forward it as urged and let your information security or virus response people know about it. The faces and company names change, but the recipe remains pretty much the same.

E-mail is a subject that never seems to get enough coverage. It is widely used both commercially and privately and is too easily abused. Your involvement should start with the company rules on using it.

Then, go into the ways that e-mail can be abused and the little nuances that can cause further annoyance. For instance, most junk mail usually has an "if you want to be removed from this mailing list, reply to xyz@pure.lie.net." Of course, if you reply in that manner, your e-mail address goes onto a higher priced list as now they know that someone is there. Talk also about how easy it is to fall into the trap of conversing with friends via this means and the company's stance on such abuse. Above all, talk about the ubiquitous attachment and its insidious ability to carry viruses.

Remind them in closing that e-mail can be seen by the world without too much effort. Confidential information should never be shared in this manner. Use the e-mail to notify someone of the need to transmit sensitive information and then do it in a more appropriate manner. This will only involve a small part of your class, so do not let it take too much of your time. You will have little enough, as is.

I always start the voice mail section of my presentation with a single statement: VOICE MAIL IS NOT SECURE! For whatever reason, the person calling is too often reassured by the sound of the intended contact's voice, even as a recorded message, and often says things that are not to be heard by other ears. You must make the point above and demonstrate how wide open e-mail tends to be. Ask the class to answer to themselves how many of them have continued using the default password that came on their mailbox at inception at previous employers. I will venture a guess that the number is well over half of those present. Make the security point clear by discussing how phone phreakers can steal mailboxes and read any ones they wish. From this, you can easily get to housekeeping issues, reminding them to clean up old messages, as they too will be exposed.

Again, the usual warnings about misuse of the phones in general is best placed here.

Something that is often overlooked in classes of this nature is the warning about potential eavesdropping on any kind of conversation. This about a time when you were in a restaurant and someone at another table was either talking so loudly that he or she was the only one you could hear or, the conversation at that table was so interesting that you were able to block out everything else to hear it. Do you think the comments were actually meant for your ears? Highly improbable, at best. Use a reference like this to make people aware of the dangers of speaking of company business in public, on a telephone, or with others who have no need to know the information.

Make a major issue at this point that the information being spread to the four winds in this type of setting is based pretty much on what you know. The longer you have been with the company, the more you know, the more interested third parties might be in what you have to say. Your brain is a very real repository for sensitive information.

In a review of all other materials that have preceded this point, make it clear that the responsibility for protecting company information is really in the hands of all who handle it on a daily basis. Handling, point out, could mean working at a terminal, doing manufacturing, working with vendors and customers and even taking out the trash. Caution your audience to keep the company's best interests in mind while conducting their daily life or while putting in their shift at the company.

Caution them to understand what "wrong" looks like: a stranger carrying a PC; someone not displaying a badge in a badge-only area; someone trying to "tailgate" in through a card-access door without having some means of identification; someone doing something that looks wrong. You may be surprised to find out that you will not have to define "wrong" for them. They will spout examples all afternoon, if you let them.

Remind them, too, at this time, that while challenging someone in a nice way — "Can I help you?" — is a perfectly good means to find out whether someone actually belongs there, they need not put themselves in an uncomfortable position in doing so. If an individual recognizes "wrong" behavior, he or she can easily call security, whose job it is to challenge these folks. The message is to call security. Make sure the number is on the screen, on a handout, or an overhead slide.

In fact, this is a good place to put in a series of important phone numbers and e-mail addresses. These can be presented on a screen, on a whiteboard, or verbally but should always be backed up by a printed product to be taken with the employee at the end of the class. Minimally, the contacts should include:

- The help desk
- Information security
- The e-mail postmaster
- Security
- HR
- Others you may think of.

A great thing to do is to get this information onto a quick reference card or a FAQ sheet.

In conclusion, recap everything that has been said and relate it to the new employee's job and its security. If you are a profit-sharing organization, you have the perfect hook to create the bond with the company good — the better the company does, the better we, as individual employees do. ABC Corporation makes money; Mary Jane Smith makes money.

Even if profit sharing is not a perk to be considered, talk about layoffs, bankruptcies, and other issues that can arise and cost an employee his or her job. Push the idea that our jobs are secured by the company's success. It is up to each of you to keep it successful.

The way I presented this class outline assumes that you will minimally have an overhead projector and slides that parallel the outline we just went through. In most cases, this will turn into a PowerPoint presentation and will be "facilitated" by you or a designated alternate. We will discuss who that alternate should be in future chapters.

In presenting the material, however you do it, you must come across with passion and conviction. Enthusiasm, while sometimes hard to muster when you have already done this class every week for the past four years (with updates, I hope), is contagious. Do whatever necessary to psyche yourself up for the presentation. Believe me, it will serve you well.

Another point that bears discussion at this point is the identity of the instructor for this course. While you might be writing it so as to present it yourself, you might find that it is better taught by a member of the corporate technical training staff. To that end, make certain that your write-up is complete and perhaps more detailed than you would prepare for yourself.

To ensure that your values get across to the teacher of the class, have him or her attend one or two of your presentations so as to get the flavor of what you are doing in terms of accenting issues and manner of presentation.

By all means attend the first few presentations by the trainer and make good notes so that you can discuss things that need to be changed in the delivery or just to give a few pointers on the technical aspects of the presentation. Do not concern yourself about hurting anyone's feelings (as long as you can critique in a civilized manner!) as much as making sure that your message is coming through loud and clear.

Once they have taken over the delivery of the class, make a point of attending once every six month or so to make sure that the message is still timely and getting across as you want it to. If there are material changes, either in delivery method or presenter, make sure to attend the first session incorporating the change.

Remember that it is your message. Make sure that it is getting through the way you want it to.

Summary

The entire subject of this chapter is to help you design a solid and informative experience for new employees. To do that, there must be a face-to-face, or face-to-many-faces, type of experience. The audience will learn not only from the subject matter, but from your presentation style as well. If you tend to be a little reserved, or even nervous about appearing in front of a group of people, you might well have to work on your attitude as well as presentation style. In this case attitude is simple faith in yourself. You know the material, the people sitting out in front of you do not. You are giving them the benefit of what you know. Be confident that you know it and that they want to learn.

We outlined a model class by breaking the subject down into workable and logically sequential pieces. The model here can be used to create your own class without any loss of continuity. If the subjects are covered, it is truly independent of the specific words. Be sure to review continually to make sure that no element slips away.

In the detailed "filling in" of the outline, we went over much more specific data that can be passed along as a part of this learning experience. Again, if the information here does not fit exactly into your environment, there is sufficient detail for you to be able to identify a parallel that fits your environment.

Try to get as sophisticated a means of presentation as possible for this class. If the other orientation classes are being put on by professional instructors, you may want to consider turning it over to training. If they are all using PowerPoint, try not to be the only one using overhead slides.

Once you have the material set up for presentation, I strongly recommend that you review it regularly for currency. In the field of information systems, changes take place daily and what we teach must keep pace. If someone else is teaching the course, he or she must be kept apprised of changes and be allowed to participate in updating.

Above all, make sure that you give your audience something to take with them. This might be something in their hands or something you embed in their minds. Speak in statements as direct as the Ten Commandments because this is most certainly the gospel according to you.

What they leave with might be:

■ A single phone number to report problems or issues
■ A concept of the principle of least privilege
■ A FAQ sheet
■ A trinket, such as a mouse pad as a reminder

The single thing they will best remember is their impression of you. If you are timid, they will feel that the program does not really much matter. If you make too many jokes, they may think security is a joke. If you rain hellfire and brimstone on them, they will go to work afraid to do anything for fear of making a punishable mistake. Be enthusiastic; be serious about the material you are teaching. Do not be serious about yourself.

What you are giving them will carry through most of, if not their entire, career with your company. Make sure that they know what to do and how to do it. Make sure that they remember the importance of protecting the company's information assets.

Remember when preparing the class that you might not be the one presenting it. That being a possibility, make sure that there is as much detail as possible in the presentation write-up. Spend time with the prospective teacher to work on the subject matter.

Once the class is in place, attend it on an occasional basis or when a material change is made, to make certain that the message is getting through as you want it to.

Chapter 14

Other Resources: Human Resources and Pals in General

If there were to be only one department that you could leverage for help in getting additional exposure for your program, it is human resources (what we used to call the personnel department). HR seems to be the one area immune from downturns, layoffs, and constricted budgets. By simply changing their name a few years ago, several new director-level positions emerged from thin air. What we need to do is to get them on board to run interference and support our program.

The first thing you need to do when arriving on site is, as I noted, get acquainted with IS management. Well, you can add HR management to that list as well. These are the folks that are always in charge of finding new talent for your function and all others in the company, doing background checks on new employees and generally doing what needs to be done to get the right people in the right places.

I know, I know; about now a bunch of readers are saying that if they didn't locate the people themselves, convince them to come to work here, and then dip them into the HR department long enough for sanctification, that no one would ever get hired. Still and all, they succeed far more often than they fail. For that alone, they deserve our respect.

HR often includes a lot of areas besides employment. They run the benefits areas; often run the corporate training area; and have a number of other functions that might be whittled as thin as insurance coordination, public relations, and whatever other public/staff interfaces that might exist.

HR is the publisher of the largest number of wide distribution newsletters, bulletins, want ads, training manuals (assuming that they have corporate training in their fold), announcements, and company status documents. Those that they do not have under their direct control are usually closely linked.

If, then, they are the makers of the news reporting structure, then perhaps we should ally ourselves with them as closely as possible. Actually, there can easily be a symbiotic relationship here, even though we might not be happy with our ticket into their realm.

In order to process a negative termination, cause has to be identified and documented. Today, that tracking and documentation is either totally under our control or we are the keepers of the keys to obtain it. When HR comes calling, we leap at the opportunity to be of service, even if it means clobbering someone for 97 e-mails to his ailing mother. We do not set the standard in such matters (we may identify abuse, but HR sets the threshold for termination offenses) we simply document what happened.

As with the publishers of the other newsletters, and in this case, it may be nearly the same, we must identify ourselves as an ally that can be of assistance (I handle the spam problems in HR myself) and can provide solid input for the documents that they put out and maintain. Is the need for that creative writing course I mentioned earlier starting to make more sense, yet?

Most of the "official" documentation that comes out of the company usually comes from the HR department (this is highly dependent on the size of the company; public relations handles a lot of this in larger corporations). Therefore, if you want to get something published where everyone will see it — even before his or her first day at real work — this is the place you have to go to get it.

The view of information as an asset should be part and parcel of the prescreening process; prospective employees should be aware of the importance the company places on information even before they get a look at the actual policy statement. If persons are entertaining the idea of coming to work for your organization — indeed, if they want to come to work there — they need to be aware of these viewpoints, and what better way for them to find out but to see it spelled out in the recruiting materials.

Make a point, while you are reviewing older documentation, to check the items HR is putting outside of the company. There is far less likely a chance that they are passing along information that they should not be than that they are failing to fully prepare a possible candidate for the environment they are trying to convince him to enter.

We are not talking about a "you better be careful" type narrative here, just a simple statement as to how "The ABC Company recognizes the importance of information in its business practices and puts forth all efforts to ensure its safety and protection." That statement serves notice that the company is concerned with the protection of its information.

Follow that statement up with a few sentences about how such a progressive organization continues to optimize its chances for success by making certain that no losses are suffered through mishandling of information and how all employees enthusiastically support and participate in the protective steps taken. After all, they understand the importance of such things. Sound anything like a recruiting brochure to you?

Later in the discussion there should be mention of "state of the art tools" which should create the awareness that information security tools are included in that toolbox.

HR is usually in charge of the new employee orientation for the company. We have mentioned that function in passing a number of times already, without going into detail. Let us take a few moments right now to take a look at the overall function.

Depending on the size of the company, this type of orientation might be anything from a one-hour briefing in small companies to a multiday battery of presentations and classes in other, larger organizations (or several weeks, if it happens to be the military!). We will try to go over a moderate version of it with hope of demonstrating places where you can get your message across, without even being there.

Generally, the first presentations will be by someone fairly high up in the HR chain of command. His or her presentation will be a quick and very positive overview of the company and how you have made the best choice of your life by coming here. There will be coverage of how great things are and all of the benefits you will derive from being here. Reference will be made, scant though it may be, to the information to which you will be exposed over the next several hours or several days. It will be a feel-good session, welcoming you and praising the company for all its accomplishments and the ones it will now have, thanks to your joining up.

Assuming this to be a company of relatively large size, the next presenter will be the serious minded yet fixed-smiling coordinator of such things. This person will be a manager or director of something and will give you some insight as to how the next several hours of your life will go. The speaker will talk about the different presentations, the types of classes you will take, and the things you will get. What you are expected to gain from these presentations will be outlined as well as what the company will then expect from your now indoctrinated brain. This is all relatively simple and absolutely predictable in companies of any size.

If you were paying close attention, you noticed at least two places in which you could have placed a short commercial message. First, in the overall presentation by the top person, there was most certainly mention of the state of the art means by which this company conducts business. Even in this short mention of technology (which there certainly was), you could have slipped in a word about how important protecting company assets, all of them, is. In the second speech, the one about what you will be doing for the next few hours or days, make sure that clear emphasis on the information security class (the one we built in the last chapter) is part of the schedule. The trick is to make sure that some type of overview — even a single sentence — is included in the description. Try to get a comment to the effect of "... where you will learn about ABC information assets, how we protect them and your role in that protection." In a single sentence you have already served the first notice about personal responsibility.

The next several hours will be taken up by presentations on benefits, the health services offered by the company, several perks that are available, training that is available, and the filling out of endless forms. You may or may not find a leveraging point in these presentations, but you should review them for the possibility. If there is a general form-filling-out session — and I have seen them where you spend an hour or more around tables filling out your insurance forms, your next of kin notification forms, the ubiquitous W-2, and forms for whatever else the company needs documented evidence of what you want, have learned, or have been given. You may want to get the information security statement that we crafted in the last section introduced here, or you may want to keep it until the end of the information security class, assuming that it has been adopted as a part of the orientation.

Note: The last statement was based on the tendency of some companies to have a "core curriculum" that they want all employees to take during their first six months on the payroll. This is usually based on the orientation sessions simply getting too long and their needing to get the new employees to work.

Given a choice, you want people to walk into their work areas with the knowledge you will impart already locked in their heads. This is an excellent reason to lobby for making sure that the information security class is a part of the orientation, so that no one gets a chance to handle corporate information assets without understanding their value, the potential threats to them and the knowledge of their responsibility in handling them. Present it in that manner and you have an excellent chance to get your class into the first day session.

If you cannot get your class into the original orientation session, make sure that the information security form is carefully explained during the signing process. This will include careful explanation of every item on the form and of what signing the form commits the signor to. Once you have explained this to the HR people, they will be far more likely to help you in inserting the class into the initial orientation sessions. This way, you will bear the responsibility for explaining the form.

Without going too much deeper into the orientation process, you can see opportunities to insert references to information security into the process. Best of all worlds is if you can get a few minutes to address the new hires during the presentation phase. Fifteen minutes is all you will need and you can put forth the introduction for the class and make sure that they know who you are, how to reach you, and understand the company's commitment to information security.

Your presentation should be set up so that, after the initial introduction of the concept, it roughly follows the outline that we created for the class. It need only mention the subject headers, without going into detail, for them to be at least aware of what they can expect in the class. If nothing in terms of subject matter is a surprise to them when they sit down for the class, that few moments of explanation can be eliminated. Also, having heard what the subjects are, they already feel a connection to them. In training, that is an important leg up.

A final spot in the orientation process that you might attempt to get a plug in is in the handout process. Of course, you will have some materials in there for their perusal, most notably, the policy statement. That should appear in the employee handbook that we will address a bit later in this chapter. However, there can be a single sheet describing the function and the idea of individual responsibility somewhere in the mix. You may want to just give an overview of the function or you may want to vary the message dependent upon conditions in the world at the time. If a virus, for instance, is running rampant throughout the country, this might be a good way to make sure that new employees will have had warning as to how to treat the conditions that identify the virus before they even sit down at their desk.

If you do use this medium as a bulletin type information vehicle, use some means to make it stand out from the numberless sheets of paper that they will be receiving. Bright colors and the logo or masthead we discussed earlier all make wonderful eye catchers for this type of notification device.

Of course, the HR-based new employee's handbook is the best vehicle for introducing your program to the new staff member. In it you can, or course, put the policy statement that we have discussed right smack into the beginning, ending, or middle of the book. If there's a place, put it there.

Along with the policy, there should be a brief explanation of the overall program and what the new person will find when they get on the job. It should talk about the standards and procedures and should make clear, concise statements about what the program is about and what is expected of them. Let us take a look at the makeup of a typical presentation in the new employee's manual. In preparing (outlining) it, we will make a number of assumptions:

- There is a section for information security. This is not a given, many companies have not yet realized the importance of the function, much less that people should actually be informed of it before starting out on the job.
- We will assume, for purposes of this exercise, that you have been given a 500-word maximum to put into the book. Actually, that is pretty generous, as most will not have any provision for your type of contribution in their book.
- In your 500 words, you have to welcome the new staff members, reference the policy, make specific and directed comments about what will be expected of each of them, and reference the other tools that they will come into contact with once they start on the job.
- Word it in a manner that sounds serious without sounding threatening. This can often be a fine line, but is worth working at. If you can get others to read it, try to get a feeling for how they took the tenor of the writing. This one is worth the extra effort. The last thing you need is someone coming to work fearful of doing anything lest they violate a standard along the way.
- Make sure that your writing comes in at that ninth grade reading level we discussed. You have no means to know what is coming through the door nor even what nationality they might be. I might be impressed by your vocabulary, but an émigré from Thailand might very well be totally confused.

- Read the rest of the book first. Make sure that what you provide can stand on its own, yet does not stand away from the set tone of the book. Your structure, tone, and word usage should reflect what the rest of the book does. Do not be surprised if HR does not want to release control of the book to the extent of having copy in it that was received from elsewhere. However, if they agree to allow you to put information security information into it, but with the caveat that they write it, by all means get good copy to them. You might be surprised as to how much of the "edited" piece looks like what you wrote. By all means ask to get a look at the finished copy before the book goes to press to make sure that they did not edit any of your ideas into something else. As you are the content authority, you can request that courtesy.
- Once you have the information in the book, keep a sharp eye on it and on the company and industry as a whole. We live in a rapidly changing world and what makes sense today might not tomorrow. What is gospel now might be heresy two years from now.
- Keep the materials updated through whatever mechanism the department has for updating their manual. Most will have the presence of mind to publish such manuals in loose-leaf form (information security information is not the only type that can grow stale) so they can be updated as needed. If you meet their scheduled updates, your section will be updated with the rest. One more time, we are talking about keeping "in good" with the publishers of a company document by getting them input on time, accurately and in keeping with all of their standards.

Human resources also publishes a lot of other manuals, brochures, and fliers. Keep close track of all of those to make sure that you place informative copy wherever possible.

The other advantage of this type of work with HR is that it creates a business bond that can be most useful in the future. In many cases, HR will have to come to you in instances of potential misdeeds on the parts of employees. You have control of the Internet logs, mail folders, and other records that can demonstrate or corroborate an employee's misuse of one or more of these resources as well as reflect other malfeasance or misfeasance. This is never much fun, but once you have identified yourself as being cooperative and responsible in your dealings with the department, the easier it will be to leverage their resources to further your concerns. And, while doing that, make sure that they realize that your concerns are the company's concerns.

Somewhere down the road, there will be occasions when matters of concern to the company become your concern first and foremost. When that time comes, it is good to have a working relationship in place at the outset. Such issues might be virus outbreaks, e-mail harassment, or simple misuse of company resources.

An interesting thought on this particular symbiosis between human resources and information security:

Over the number of years I have been involved in this discipline, I have often been called upon to assist HR in what I consider one of the less enjoyable parts of the job and that is to gather information leading to the dismissal of an employee. As information security officer, it falls upon me to secure logs and other records that make the case for abuse of privilege by the staff member in question. To be sure, gathering this type of information is no more difficult than making a few calls or running a few reports, but the impact on one's moral sense is often far greater. While each of us is called upon to do this from time to time, it can never become totally comfortable in anything but cases that border on or reach the definition of a criminal act.

Hopefully, it will never become comfortable, as that would indicate a loss of something I hold dearer than being good at my profession.

Still, this type of negative feeling activity does forge a strong bond with the human resources department. They must not only count on your technical capabilities, but your character and discretion. Such tasks build the credibility that makes your use of their facilities much easier when the time comes to seek their cooperation in furthering your needs.

Perhaps this is a good indication that out of bad things, good things often come.

Summary

The human resources department is responsible for the recruiting, hiring, orienting, and often, removing of staff from the company. They control a number of documents and presentation sets that can be of important use in furthering your employee information security awareness program. This can be done in a number of ways:

- The company employee handbook is a collection of rules, regulations, and familiarization materials that make the new staff member's life a bit easier at the beginning of his or her career with your company. One of your first acts, after getting your feet on the ground and meeting the management of this and other departments, is to locate the hand-book preparation folks — be it a team or an individual — and work out a means to get information into the book. The first concern will, of course, be the information security policy statement. This is a single page document, that we have spent a good deal of time going over in previous chapters, that fully states the company's position on informa-tion security. This is information that needs to appear in print where it can be easily accessed. This handbook is marketed as the single source answer to whatever questions are likely to come up in the new employees first several weeks on the job. What better place to put the policy that governs exactly how information is viewed and treated at your company.
- A second addition to the handbook is a brief description of the functions the information security department and the expectations of the com-pany with regards to this subject by each individual on the payroll. Again, this is the best possible place to put that information.

- While it has not been specifically stated in the past, having the information we discussed in the last two points available and pointed out in a manual that all new employees get, serves another purpose, as well. In the uncomfortable situation where there is a performance issue around the information handling or usage sphere, this bit of publicly available regulation statement can often be the difference between disciplinary action and simple red faces on the parts of management. The defense of "Nobody told me I couldn't!" will not hold water with this segment of the book in place and in use.

- The new employee orientation program is generally at least a few hours long on the new employee's first day at work. It may, in many cases, last for a few days. While we discussed the information security class that we want to make a part of the overall program, we do also want to try to get a bit of time during the presentation aspect of the orientation to introduce ourselves, our department, and the company's viewpoint on information security.

- Human resource often controls other publications, Web pages, or other means of mass communication within the company. For this reason, we want to leverage our relationship to make certain that we are represented in their publication. A good example is the flyer system that a lot of companies use. In those cases, a single sheet or newsletter type format is used to communicate an idea or general news to the staff. Much like the newsletters we talked about earlier, we want to get our contributions into these publications as well. Of course, this applies to Web pages, e-mail newsletters, and other electronically delivered messages as well.

- As with any activity in a regulatory field, ours is often the vehicle by which malfeasance or misfeasance is discovered or proven. With the relationship we are building with the human resources function, we can expect to be brought in as expert witnesses or to gather incriminating evidence in such cases. While we may personally not be comfortable with performing such functions, it is important that they be done and done well. As with any relationship, this is a two-way street and we have to provide our half of it.

All in all, it is worth whatever time it takes to become known in human resources as a source of information and for the work we do in the prevention of compromise of company information assets. By leveraging that relationship and providing input to all of the vehicles by which HR communicates with new and current employees, we enhance our ability to convey information to large groups of people in a timely and effective manner.

Chapter 15

Finding and Leveraging Other Resources

As mentioned time and time again, you will never have enough budget or enough resources to do the job you want to. To that end, it is imperative that you learn the other areas within the company that control resources that can be leveraged to perform tasks or produce products that can be used in the spreading of the information security gospel. In this chapter we will try to find them and to exploit them to serve our needs.

We are not talking about taking advantage of anyone here — using something that they provide while garnering no benefit for them — but about using things that others control for the common good.

Let us take a look at some of them here:

1. Public Relations and Human Resources

Of course we have made much of the public relation and human resources areas, those functional departments that control most of what gets published around the company through paper channels. We know that we need to cultivate the management of each area, find vehicles within which to plant our message, and then deliver that message to them in the correct form and at the correct time and date.

Public relations will also play an important part in your contingency planning effort, as they will be the voice of the company to the media and to the customers and vendors involved with your company. More about the contingency planning or business resumption planning later.

2. Applications Development

Applications development groups are the folks that put new systems up in your environment. Any new system requires security measures to be attached, or better yet, built-in. To make sure about the built in aspect, why not make certain that you or a member of your staff is a part of the development team. That way, the programmers and analysts are constantly aware of the security concerns that must be built in.

3. Help Desk

The help desk talks to anyone that has a problem of any kind while working within your corporate systems. In many instances, the issues are around gaining access, forgetting a password, or not having the correct access. In the latter case, not having enough access might involve going around gaining entry in the wrong way. If you were to provide the help desk agents with cheat sheets on resolving security issues, would their responses to their callers not be illuminating and at the same time, educational? The cheat sheets also give the help desk agent a learning medium in itself. With a step-by-step means to handle specific inquiries, the routine soon becomes embedded, and the agent can spot the actual problem more quickly and respond in an appropriate manner.

4. Operations or Administration

Operations or administration, the folks charged with doing server backup and recoveries are the ones who are most interested in making certain that everything that needs to be backed up is and that the backups are complete and timely and are stored as they must be. By weaving them into the contingency planning cycle, their interests in backups can be leveraged into their own bulletins to staff with regards to storage and archiving, and backup schedules can be used to remind people of their responsibilities in making certain that all of the right things are getting backed up. You can take advantage of the same bulletins by adding in statements regarding local backup and storage and the use of the corporate retention areas for keeping vital records backed up from standalone units.

5. Records Retention

Records retention is charged with maintaining not only server backups, but also paper records and other media (microforms, etc.) for the time required by law or business needs. By the same token, they are responsible for returning tapes as required and destroying outdated media as the schedule from which they work demands. In many instances, those schedules are defined by government or other regulatory agencies. If your knowledge of those retention schedules is up to par, you can be of great service to both the retention folks and the IS people you represent. Make sure that proper notification goes out before records are destroyed and make certain that older tape records are reviewed and even copied, if time dictates (tapes have a finite life span, too). By documenting each of these things, you make certain that all involved employees have a reminder system in place with regards to backed up or saved records.

6. Corporate Security

Corporate security is the group responsible for seeing to the safety of the staff and the control of access to corporate facilities. They issue the badges, patrol the grounds, and make certain that access to the grounds and building are controlled in a manner that puts the company's interests first.

They also are the ones that have contacts in local law enforcement, city, county, and state's attorneys, and other policing agencies. There are many times when leveraging those connections can be to your advantage. In many cases, those law enforcement entities might well need you to assist them in resolution of cases with technological overtones. You may well have the software and other tracking tools (more often in the network or operations areas, but available to you (You have been building bridges to those areas too, haven't you?) that they need to locate individuals who might be sending threatening e-mails. While there are a number of shareware and "cheapware" tools out there to perform these tasks, they rarely have the sophistication of the multitask packages that you might have available. Besides, if you come with it, they have additional technical support, as well.

These security folks are the ones who maintain the card-access system that controls access to company facilities and creates records as to who went where, when, and how often. When doing investigative work, these logs are invaluable.

On the other hand, being able to create effective access groups that grant access to a number of facilities that someone in a specific job description might use, makes their work a lot easier in adding new users to the access system.

When getting information out to the troops in the most rapid fashion is necessary, corporate security is a wonderful asset. Let us say, for instance, that a virus gets into your mail system overnight. Corporate security has the manpower and access to make sure that warnings are posted at every entry on the campus, no matter how big it is. They have the ability to circulate where only a large number of people could access in a reasonable time.

Working closely with security offers another means to keep security at the forefront of everyone's mind — your main interest in these cases. As they make their nightly rounds, they are responsible for making reports on any untoward occurrences or situations. If you have a good working relationship with these people, these reports can go to you where IS concerns are present.

For instance, a door to a computer room or communications closet is left open. That information goes into the guard's log. If a laptop PC is left out during unattended periods (nights, off shifts, etc.) that goes into the log. In addition — assuming that this bridge is well in place — other things can be added to the log. If a network attached terminal or PC is left logged on, it can go into the report. If someone leaves cash on his or her desk, it can be entered. If a desk or cabinet that contains sensitive information or other assets is left open, it can also go into the log.

What, then, is done with these logs? Why, they are turned in to the shift supervisor at the end of the work shift. And what is done with these logs? Important items are acted upon and the other material is archived for future review or use as needed. If there are specific types of incidents that you and the corporate security management have agreed are important enough to be reported to you, then you can count on getting that report, daily, if need be.

When a copy of the report, along with your notes and observations is forwarded to the perpetrator of the incident — the person responsible for the cabinet or PC — and the supervisor, a definite learning experience results. A bit heavy-handed, perhaps, but most effective. Again, though, awareness is raised.

You will find that a good relationship with corporate security is a most useful tool. They have personnel and technical assets in many areas that can be of great service to your function. At the same time, you can provide assistance to them — which should be provided quickly and in full measure — that makes their work easier. Again, symbiosis (has anybody looked that word up, yet?).

In the latter case, I can recall having loaned a laptop to security for bait in an area when a few laptops had done what so many laptops tend to do: walked off. The PC was set up in a place that was sufficiently open to allow passersby to notice it, but sufficiently shielded from view so that one could pick it up without being noticed — except by the mini video camera that security had mounted nearby! Not something you would normally consider an information security function — resolving theft of property — but a good example of the assistance you can provide to your colleagues on the physical side.

7. Legal Department

The legal department is charged with defending or litigating on behalf of the company in matters that get into the legal system. However, they have a number of other functions that live much closer to home.

They are charged with negotiation of contracts on behalf of any department that is in a position to let a contract. They are also responsible for reviewing policy and procedures before they are put into place, so as to neither violate anyone's rights nor step over the bounds of legislation or regulation that might cover the incidents involved. To be sure, your policies and procedures must withstand their scrutiny before being put into place.

I know, I have put us in a place that could inspire any number of lawyer jokes, but I will try to refrain from doing so in this piece. The work these people do on our behalf is important and can make our work a lot easier.

If, for instance, there is cause to terminate someone for some act that is held unacceptable by the company, they will review the facts involved in the case and offer an opinion as to whether the case is sufficient to move forward. They will also make clear what records, logs, or other evidence must be gathered and archived to defend the termination should the terminated party choose to sue.

How is this an awareness issue? Easily defined. When any termination takes place, particularly one for cause, the informal communications network leaps into action. If the case is well prepared and bulletproof, the message sent is that it was done right. There is no cause for insurrection or other response on the part of the staff in general. That unto itself is informative to all involved. Interestingly, the reasons for the termination will become common knowledge almost immediately, once more demonstrating the technical superiority of grapevine over fiber optics. That being the case, the fact that the incursion was detected and documented demonstrates the ease with which acts of this type can be discovered and dealt with. Not positive, to be sure, but a message sent to all about how acting responsible can prolong one's career.

If you are in an organization that has provided you with the funds to secure some tools on your own, you will find yourself in contract negotiations at one time or another. In the first place, the company will not let you let a contract without legal review, and their input will ensure that you get the best possible terms. In matters like letting a contract for business resumption services, the contracts can be measured in pounds, not pages, and the work of an attorney can again put you in a much better position for obtaining value for dollars spent.

Love 'em or hate 'em, lawyers do have a place in this world and that place can be extremely important to us.

8. Facilities

Facilities wears many hats, which vary from organization to organization. They are generally responsible for the grounds and buildings and contract those that do the work that they are not equipped to. They are, or contract, the electricians, plumbers, carpenters, painters, masons, gardeners, and whatever other skilled trades might be needed to keep the building(s) running and up to speed.

The above being true, they also have any number of contacts and skills that can be useful to your program. Do they run the copy center? This is a resource you absolutely cannot live without. Do the advantages of building a relationship here seem more to your advantage?

One small item that I have found that more and more facilities operations have undertaken is to make plastic signage — you know, the little ones of laminated black or wood-tone laminate over a white substrate that can be scratched through to display the white. By using a pantograph, you can trace over an image or word while a stylus at the other end engraves through the wood tone to display the white substrate in a copy of the image you traced. By adjusting the arms of the tool, you can trace half-inch lettering and create two-inch lettering, if need be. More sophisticated units automate the tracing, and I am sure by now, computers control the whole process. My point is that this is a relatively inexpensive tool when compared to the cost of having signs made outside, and more and more companies have taken to doing this simple task in their own facility. Making up cubicle nameplates in itself justifies the expense pretty quickly.

You can, however, use the output of these machines to label cabinets and work areas or to signify restrictions or locations. While you may not order the signs or install them, you can specify such things knowing that the technology to make them is cheap and available.

In one instance, I found that people with access to the computer centers were taking guests in there without having them log in. As the visitors' badges did not have access and the visit was usually a one-shot issue, they did not bother to get temporary access badges. To make sure that we could account for traffic in the computer rooms, I designed a simple log sheet for those whose access was made through accompanying others. We placed a loose-leaf binder in a basket mounted on the wall adjacent to the door (had facilities obtain and mount the basket, too) with a sign identifying the visitors' logbook contained therein. A simple solution for a simple problem, but made much easier by having a good relationship with the facilities department.

The same type of issues crop up in a number of areas, always visible and therefore, informative to the troops. Adding badge readers to certain doors, alarming others, and putting other electrical devices in place (smoke and water detectors, etc.) all fall under the aegis of facilities.

9. Print Shop

The print shop, now a staple of many companies, is the source of much of the material you will want to get into paper form and out to the masses. These folks can not only do that type of thing, but can offer wonderful advice on what will work best and how it should look.

When it comes time to publish bulletins, design the masthead and/or create a format for any publication, these are the folks to come to. Unlike the graphics folks that we will talk about in a moment, the printers are versed in what can and cannot be done and comparative costs. They have insight on ink and paper options and the ability to use less expensive alternatives for a professional appearance at far less cost.

If you are going to publish independently, these are the people to know.

10. Graphic Arts Department

I mentioned the graphic arts department a moment ago in the section on the print shop. These people are designers and often accomplished HTML practitioners as well. They tend to appear only in larger companies where their responsibilities are to create highly detailed and polished designs for the company's publications. They may design Web pages (often, the webmasters are part of this department), manage them, and be in control of the design for printed as well as electronic media.

You will discover that these people are artists (some just consider themselves so) and often can be counted on for reactions in that manner. Cater to their sensitivities and make sure that plenty of compliments accompany your response to their efforts.

11. User Management

I would be remiss if I did not bring up the subject of user management in general. These are the people involved in fighting the good battle every day with little help from senior management. They are the victims of "lean and mean" or "right-sized" operations that look a lot better on paper than in practice. These are the people who deal with the issues we are training against and issuing our posters, bulletins, and other informational documents for. They would love to comply but are often deterred by production schedules and too much work for too few people. Often, their ability to comply is limited.

This is a good place to give our own training materials a reality check. Can we actually expect compliance in a world that stresses speed and production over safeguards and step-by-step process. We cannot go "full speed ahead" while watching for the "damn torpedoes."

If we take the time to talk to these managers, we may well come up with ideas on how we might alter our program to make sure that they can comply fully. They work with the systems we are trying to protect on a day-to-day basis and know it better than we ever will. Often, then, we can get tips from them on how we can do our job better and be more effective in this work area.

Worth a thought, isn't it?

Not all of the resources you will want to capitalize on are within the company. There are numbers of vendors and educational institutions outside of the company that can be counted on for ideas and in many cases, samples that can be evaluated as a part of the program. Using commercially supplied posters, for instance, can give you a good read on whether or not they would be effective in your environment. Also, there are magazines, brochures, and newsletters that come out of user groups — usually managed by vendors of the product line being touted — that can be of use, particularly if you use any of the products mentioned. These user groups often have periodic conferences that can be of great benefit to users of the product. If your company is contracted to any of these vendors, I recommend taking a long look at their user conference as a source for idea and solid information.

Another source not to be overlooked is the professional organizations: specifically, the Computer Security Institute (CSI), the Information Systems Security Association, and the MIS Training Institute. The first two are professional membership organizations and the last is dedicated to putting on high-quality classes and conferences for those in the trade. While the ISSA tends to hook their training efforts into those of other organizations, the offerings of all three are excellent.

In addition to both a summer and winter conference, CSI also provides excellent classes throughout the year. John O'Leary, the director of training selects his instructors well and the classes, although mainly directed at beginning practitioners, are well thought out and presented. If you are new in the field, you will find their offerings extremely useful. You are certain to come away with things you can put into practice in your own company.

Another important aspect of CSI membership is the annual Buyer's Guide, sort of a Whole Earth Catalog of information security related products. Only shortcoming: they seem pretty stuck on product lines that advertise with them or attend the trade show aspects of their conferences. I may be wrong on this one, but that is the way it appears. In any case, it is an excellent source book.

MIS runs a number of subject based (network, auditing, Windows, etc.) conferences throughout the year with one- and two-day seminars associated with the start and finish of each. Again, these classes are well taught by true experts in the field. More important, they are scaled from beginner to very high level.

I bring up these training and conference organizations for the main reasons that they offer the training I referenced earlier as well as large and varied vendor displays. Add to this the chance to find out what others are doing and you have time and money well spent. To this day, I pick up ideas from networking, often hatched among several of us discussing specific problems over a few cold ones after a session. Very often, the seeds of those discussions arose in a workshop environment.

Do not overlook the value that the vendor displays can provide. Often, in their presentations for a specific product line, you will find communications methods that can be applied to your issues just from watching their pitch. Of course, there is always the opportunity to find products and services that can be of assistance in preparing your own awareness programs.

I have tended to shy away from the one of a kind, exotic sounding programs as they are usually directed at a highly technical narrow-focused audience. They are usually put on by a professional organization that I have never heard of. The locations are generally pretty exotic and the urge to go is strong. If you choose to attend, my best wishes for eliciting something of value for your program. Personally, I find the odds too long and the cost too great to make most of them worthwhile.

Over my career, I have often been closely involved with policing organizations from a number of jurisdictions from local to federal. More and more, the issues that we face daily are becoming of greater interest to the police and the FBI. The freedom of the Internet has made border-crossing crime a lot easier, too.

As short as we are on resources to put our ideas into place, law enforcement is that much more in need of both technical knowledge and the equipment to perform even some pretty basic tasks. Earlier, I referenced a situation where I was contacted to help someone track back an IP address to locate the sender of an offensive e-mail. With the shareware available to the officer involved, the methods were chancy and extremely detailed. However, with a product like HP OpenView, there was little problem tracking it back. You will find that performing these little services for law enforcement can be most rewarding (no, I don't mean fixing traffic tickets!) in that they will pitch in and assist you when needed. With a number of jurisdictions creating posters and other media about computer crime, you might find that you can obtain such materials, or at worst, ideas for your own program.

Just like we tell our kids, a cop can be your best friend.

As mentioned, the interests of law enforcement and our private sector have moved closer together over recent years. Our problems are now their problems and the inverse. Recently, an organization called the High Tech Crime Investigation Association (HTCIA) has been started to create a formal forum for interaction between industry and law enforcement. In many cases that cross state lines, easily done in today's Internet world, new legislation is being examined and enacted to give law enforcement the clout they need to prosecute such problems. This forum has put forth much information that has led to this legislation and a lot still in the formative phases.

The membership requirements for HTCIA are extremely stringent and not too many members are from the private sector. Still, this is a great start at making the communications between law and industry more open and, therefore, more effective.

Summary

We have spent a lot of time working out relationships with various aspects of the company and some with outside sources. Earlier in this chapter, I went through a number of peripheral departments whose stock in trade can be of great assistance in our work. In each case, the assistance has to go two ways; you need to be able to help when needed as well.

The departments listed will not appear in every company, but most of them will be in a significant percentage. Often, some of the responsibilities are shifted or taken over completely by other departments: Public relations may be a part of human resources. Graphics and the print shop may both be parts of facilities. The people that make or order the signs might be somewhere else within the organization. The important thing is to recognize these functions as potential resources.

The main points of this entire section are twofold:

1. Recognize an ally in a crowd of departments that can have little or no impact on what you do. They might be involved in terms of complying with the standards and procedures we have dutifully prepared, but only certain organizations can be co-opted to assist as well as to be assisted. These are the units outlined in the body of this chapter.
2. Recognize that everything is based on sharing. If you cannot provide a service that they can use directly, make certain that they are aware of your gratitude. It seems like a simple "Thank you" is in danger of slipping from the language.

We also talked about relationships outside of the company: professional organizations and policing jurisdictions. The latter may be local, state, or federal. They are wrestling with the same issues you are, only generally with less weapons to throw at it. Never forget that they are doing your work and deserve all the help you can give them as well as the inverse.

Finally we talked about professional organizations. I gave an overview of what they offer and how I saw their offerings in terms of levels of training and offerings throughout the year. There was special recognition of large and well-attended annual conferences, where you not only get the opportunity to gain training, but can review what is new in your chosen world. Finally it is a chance to rub shoulders with often hundreds of people who are fighting the same battle you are on a daily basis. The sharing of ideas and problems is as valuable as the learning you gain from the workshops.

By all means attend the "birds of a feather" sessions where they relate to something you are experiencing or working on.

In summary, there are no resources that you can afford to overlook if your program is to be effective in its details and in its communication to the staff at your company. Use any means you can to get your message across and any gimmicks — yeah, I said, "gimmicks" — to gain their attention and compliance. In earlier chapters I talked about making sure that your message was stated so as to make it clear to the attendee/reader/listener that what you said to do was in their best interests. Never drop that idea as a central theme of your program.

As your program matures and becomes outdated or even passe to your main audience, you will have to update it with contemporary information and newer means to make it interesting and compelling to learn. The resources I listed can give you the tools to do just that.

Stay on top of it, grow it, and change it as need be, but never let it become stale. Apathy is a far worse enemy than resistance to your message. Resistance at least indicates that they have given it enough thought to rebel against it. Treat the rebellion with respect, find out its source, and either fix the issue or reword the approach. And above all, find a way to present it in a palatable manner. Perhaps the tools you gain from the relationships suggested here will make that easier.

Chapter 16

Making Every Shot Count!

The entire theme of this book has been to get the biggest possible bang for every buck spent and every hour invested. In this chapter, we will go over a few things that we may or may not have spoken about earlier.

As noted, the information security function tends to be incredibly under-staffed and underfinanced, even in the most enlightened companies. We have to ride along on the resources of others; look to different departments to help us spread the word; and beg, borrow, or steal the things we need to make things happen.

Despite its brevity, this chapter will encapsulate themes that we have played upon since the very beginning. For instance, we do not have a periodical. However, the company does. For a few hours of writing and a bit of schmoozing, we can get our words out to the entire company. That is one loud bang for one small buck.

We do not own the network. However, we can use a Web site to express our concerns and get our message out to the entire online community. Again, small investment for a whopping return.

We can go on and on with things that we have already discussed, but I want to focus on a few items that we really have not touched on as yet. You may be a bit surprised at what some of them are, but do not fool yourself, they are worthy and rewarding.

For instance, I have spoken at national conventions of information security professionals, at local information security management groups, auditors groups, law enforcement gatherings, and at every school I can get into. Who listens to me? Other professionals in the field, police figures that we might well need in the future, and students. Believe it or not, there tend to be a few folks from the media there as well.

Now, the fact that you spoke on the subject of information security in front of a civic group in your community immediately clothes you in the mantle of expertise by all and sundry. I mean, if it was in the paper, it must be right, and if they wanted him to come and speak, he must be an expert of considerable renown. Is the picture starting to become clearer?

Producing articles for professional or even general interest publications is another way for not only many people to see your work, but for them again to assume your expertise. No one asks a hack to produce copy for them. Each of the people within your organization that sees the article or hears about the speech (much less, hears it in person) will tell many more, to the extent of assuming that they have a true expert among them whose words are golden, at the very least. That level of credibility does not necessarily spread your internal work farther, but it enhances its perceived value to the reader. People that believe in you tend to believe in your work and words.

A reputation is often as intimidating or as commanding of respect as is actual work. Build it on good work and efforts and take the gravy that rolls in behind it. Understand, I am in no way suggesting duplicity in anything you do, I am simply saying, take the shortest path possible to earn respect.

A second means to gain a foothold and to spread the gospel according to you is to start stacking up successes as soon as you get into your position. You may hear this called picking the low-hanging fruit, shooting the standing targets, or any of a number of colorful analogies. What it means is simply to get after the things on which you can make an immediate impact and start carving notches in your administrative pistol butt as you do so (look at that, another colorful analogy!). Turn a few heads and do not hide your lamp under a bushel when you do.

Does the company need a policy statement? Write one your first day on the job (you now have a great sample to work from). Is there some disagreement on how something is to be done? Put together a process, run it by the necessary authorities (policy committee, executive committee — remember?), and get it into place. Has someone been dying to express concern about security to someone who will listen? Listen. If you can either take care of the issue or allay the concerns, get right to it. Start building credibility with your first act.

In a company for whom I once worked, there was a huge issue of many unrelated systems having passwords of varying length and makeup being online at the same time. As the situation existed, users often needed to remember a number of different passwords to do their jobs. Obviously, no reliable password standards existed and each system had its own standard. Some enforced password life limits, others did not. How then, to draw this all together. Enter an information security officer (ISO) who happened to have a couple of ideas on exactly how to accomplish such a thing and the project got off the ground.

Now, I have not written a line of code since about the time structured COBOL was coming into its own, so you know I did not do any of the programming. However, from talking to people and looking at a number of schematics, I became aware what a single password solution had to look like.

By presenting my ideas to my current superior, I was able to get names of people who could lend a technical hand to what I had conceived. They agreed that a third-party solution was never going to give us everything we wanted, so we began building it ourselves.

By using some of the tools available today, we were able to create a system that talked to all platforms and "knew" what the password standard was for each. By building an aging criterion into the system, we bypassed any lack that might exist in the respective platform. By "learning" the password length and makeup for each system, we were able to have a password length equal to the length of the longest allowed and simply truncate what was needed to talk to platforms that accepted shorter passwords only.

Without going into further detail, we were able to create a password coordinating tool that made it possible to change all of your passwords at once with only a single password required. We built all of the safety precautions that some of the platforms lacked, into the system. It controlled password life and makeup, stored previously used words, and compared previously used words to an extensive list of forbidden terms.

My point is that although I am not a programmer, we got a system put together. Although I did not yet know any of the systems involved intimately, I was able to enlist the assistance of people who did. Although I could not create the APIs needed to communicate, someone on the team did.

The reason that this project succeeded is that something that was concerning everyone got addressed. All it took was for someone to come up with a concept, gather the right people to make up the team, and coordinate their efforts. Getting those people was made possible because they knew the result was something they wanted.

Ideas to make any part of your efforts more memorable might come from almost anywhere. I can recall a relatively new practitioner in the field of information security who did put together a class and added in whatever bells and whistles he could think of to get the word out. Thomas R. Walsh, currently with Health Care Computing Strategies in Kansas City, MO., was at that time responsible for information security at a midwestern health organization. His addition to the classroom experience was a regular quiz show scenario, where he passed out trinkets for correct answers. He asked the questions and, for correct answers, gave out prizes such as mouse pads, pencils, and pens, all with the company logo on them. It was innovative and kept people's attention. I suspect that the cost of his extensive prize inventory was pretty meager and that the items were common stock around the company. Still, the effect was as desired.

Tom took an idea and ran with it, as each of us is capable of doing. It really is not much of a stretch to make the prizes for an exercise of this type a bit more tailored to information security by having them imprinted with a logo pertaining directly to that issue. Let your imagination run wild. Tom is a bright guy and came up with a gimmick to hold people's attention. What could you do, just starting with his idea?

Another way to gain the attention of the greatest number of people outside of information systems is to address an issue that everyone knows and is concerned about. Let us take something like viruses.

Now, everyone and his dog's flea collection have a knowledge of viruses. They have been damned, feared, reviled, and revered by press at every level and in every field. The only way to avoid having heard about computer viruses is to live on a desert island, cut off from every aspect of civilization.

How then, do you leverage viruses to get your message across? First, everyone is thinking about them. Second, anyone with a PC is concerned about them, and all employees and their management want to make sure that they are never victimized.

How then, do we make a splash out of something that more likely resembles a "thud?"

First, let us find a way to prevent virus infection. What are the best tools for that? A good antivirus product and education are the answer. How do we spread the word about the new software and what you can do to prevent viruses?

Does anybody recall an awful lot of time we spent in getting space in anything that is printed within our company? Does anybody recall how hard we worked to get into contact with the corporate webmaster? How about our classes in HTML and the subject experts we have cultivated?

All of the efforts we have outlined in previous chapters now come into play. We need to get the word out as quickly as possible, and if you cannot sell the importance of the subject to management, somewhere in the last 15 chapters you must have missed something.

Now is the time to trot out the creative writing skills and put together a bang-up column. Talk about the dangers of viruses to the company. Use the events caused by previous viruses that have made national news and talk about the efforts we are taking to keep them from getting in here.

At this point, I would like to introduce another concept, that of the Virus Response Team. This is a concept that works better than the name of that group that chased ghosts in New York in a couple of movies. A team, built of information security people, programmers, systems managers, e-mail management people, and anyone else who might help, need to be pressed into service for this one. True, for the most part, their actions will be responsive rather than preventive. But if they do their work well once or twice, think of the clout messages from this team can have. The team has the people that manage the antivirus product, the security experts, and the mail people. Among them they should recognize the biggest problems and the cures that need to be put in place. Now, here's the kicker.

Why not make them available by e-mail? What if you had a situation where you suspected that an attachment to an e -mail might contain a virus? Suppose that you could attach it to an e-mail, explain your concerns in the body of the mail note, and send it to "VIRUS," at your mail domain? It would make it easier, wouldn't it?

I can assure you from experience that this ready availability at an intuitively known e-mail address is one of the best awareness tools you can have. Most certainly, more than one person in the group that make up the virus team is going to respond, even if only to tell the user that they have received a hoax or nothing. By copying VIRUS on the reply, the rest of the team knows to

INFORMATION

ABC Company information, tangible and non-tangible, are assets.

Non-Tangible
- Ideas
- Thoughts
- Techniques

Information Security Online Course

Page 2 of 3

Exhibit 1 Self-Paced Video Training Package

stand down, that the issue has been resolved. All the user knows is there is a place to go and the place responds.

Make no mistake: the idea of an easy e-mail address that can be counted on for answers is something that most users take to like pigs do to turnips. You might even think about an InfoSec address, if you think it could help.

If you have any form of company-sponsored news source, as an attachment to the homepage of your Web presence, for instance, you might well take the time to offer them a bit of help as well. You, no doubt, get a lot of different news sources from your own connections. Why not forward those that reference hot subjects — like the viruses we have been discussing — to the editor of that daily newssheet? More coverage is of value any way you can get it. If you can convince them to run a tech spot in their newscast, you can push items about new threats, security, and any other issue that is of interest to you as potential fill for that segment.

Another item that can be used for getting a lot of mileage out of a simple act is to put your information security class onto a self-paced video training package. By using products such as Macromedia Authorware Attain 5 (multimedia authoring software) and other tools like Adobe Photoshop 5.5, you, or more likely your graphics or multimedia department, can create slick and complete classes on line. In the example illustrated in Exhibit 1, you can see how script is running down one side of the page while an instructor is delivering the information verbally on the other side. The screen changes at the user's convenience, the instructor goes through the dialog, and then goes mute and deathly still. Hopefully, it stops on a good likeness frame, so you won't be staring at a stop motion gargoyle, should you decide to review the scripting.

This type of instruction lends itself extremely well to the self-paced, home terminal idea we put forth. As have been so many of the other tools we have discussed, this is a one-time build for a many time use.

In many cases, the company will have an educational system tied into the personnel records that keep track of what classes individual should take and what classes they do take. If instructor facilitated, a simple roll sheet is used for later data entry. In cases where the course is online, as this one would be, signing onto the system and into the course would indicate that it had been taken.

Most of the time, a simple quiz at the end of the video course is used to verify knowledge transfer. The system can grade the test, notify you whether you passed or failed, and so record the information.

Let us depart from this specific course for just a moment. If the training system is set up to record what classes individuals must take and what courses they have taken, then it must record when the courses were taken and passed. What if, in this instance, a trigger was set to notify you after one or two years that your accreditation had expired and prompted you to retake the test? Would this not meet the criteria for keeping information fresh in the minds of employees? Knowing that they will have to retake the test (it need only be a few very basic questions that need not change to be effective) annually or biennially, would they not be a bit more caring about remembering the provisions of the class in the future?

In a more sophisticated mode, one might have a pool of 40 or 50 questions from which the system would randomly pick, say ten, to administer to any given applicant. Mind you, this is a one shot deal again. Kind of like the TV ad says, "Set it and forget it!" It's the gift that keeps on giving.

By all means check with your training people and your graphics and multimedia folks to see if they have expertise in the field. A class can be taped and superimposed on a paging script to make exactly what appears in the example appear on the screen at the user's workstation. It is server based, so no local or repetitive resources are used, and the system itself keeps the calendar and pings the users at the appropriate time.

I suspect that there are independent contractors out there that can produce something very similar at reasonable cost. Check your local Yellow Pages under "Video" for candidates. You might also check under "Training" for similar services with a training bent. Often the latter will either have the equipment to do what is described or a contractor that can do it. If you can give them the name of the software (check back a few paragraphs) and outline what I have stated to this point, they should, assuming familiarity with the packages, be able to put together a good approximation of what we have discussed. The video cameras will likely be in the classroom only once, so disruption is kept to a minimum.

Everything that I have stated in the last few pages does make some assumption as to the capacity and direction of your training department. If they do not feel that this something they are currently equipped to handle, by all means offer to help them justify getting it. It should not be lost on them that you are preparing to use technology to present a class on every screen in the company, verify that it is being taken, and evaluate the level of information passed. Unless I am very mistaken, the ability to leverage a single instructor and a few thousand dollars worth of equipment is a bargain at any price.

Of course, this assumes that you are in or near a municipality of significant size. No, it does not have to be Los Angeles, but it is probably better if it's not Smalltown, USA, either. You might recall the training tape that my colleague and I wrote, directed, performed, filmed, and distributed a few years back. Welcome to the 21st Century version of much the same thing.

Streaming video can do a lot of things as can the simpler scripted Power-Point online presentation that I referenced earlier.

Today's desktop and laptop computers are coming with more and more memory and greater disk capacity everyday. Where once we talked in mega-bytes of storage, we are now talking about gigabytes, and not just one or two. With that capacity being available to us, a training class either disk resident or on a CD-ROM becomes a much more usable tool. I have one particular application that I have been working on that I think may well be the wave of the future.

I currently work in a rather large and worldwide company. The size and geographic dispersion of locations and staff often make it necessary for staff to travel among these locations. To facilitate their keeping in contact and performing some useful work while away, a pool of laptop computers is made available to those travelers.

Today, when a traveler calls to reserve a laptop for a trip that is coming up, they are invited to sit with a staff member for an approximately 30-minute demonstration as to how to use the computer, the dial up technology that accompanies it (wouldn't want to miss our e-mail, would we?), and any other software- or hardware-related issues. Of course, security is stressed, based on the perambulatory tendencies of laptops left unattended in trafficked areas.

What if, instead of having a staff member go over these instructions with the dozens of travelers to be trained over the next several months, it was done similarly to the class we just discussed. Now, changing to a video or PowerPoint format will not train the training staff member nearly as well as having to repeat the same information ten times a week, but I believe that you will find them willing to live without that additional training.

If one were to put that class on the hard drive of each of the loaner laptops and script it to run as a part of the sign-on, the traveler would see it before anything else came up. It could certainly repeat all of the things a trainer did and probably would never forget anything. If questions came up, they could be answered by the help desk with a simple phone call.

At the end of the program, a simple: "Do you wish to see this instructional video the next time you log on?" with a Yes/No choice of buttons could disable (or keep enabled) this aspect of the script for next log-on. By putting an icon on the menu page, the user could select it for viewing at another time, if need be.

All of these "high tech" answers are really simple aspects of known technology, most of which you probably already have. In its simplest form — a PowerPoint demonstration — scripted into a data set, it can be prepared by someone not terribly technically savvy.

Of course, in a network environment, a message of this nature could be pushed to every terminal on the net at a predetermined time. Remember, though, that the more complex the message and format, the more bandwidth it will gobble up. That can be pretty disruptive on a large network. Work with your network people if you feel that something like this would be of benefit. They can decide what level of degradation it will cause and whether or not it is tolerable. They can also pass it to a given set of ports at one time and space the delivery out in that manner. Never leave them out of the loop when large amounts of information — and video is large beyond comprehension — is involved.

Summary

You are one, they are many. You have to spread yourself thin enough to read through, they have staff and resources far beyond any you could hope for. Your job? Work smart and take advantage of every advantage available!

Try to make each of your actions as far-reaching as possible. Use internal media in any way possible. Let no newsletter, departmental sheet, or periodical of any type go out without your words of wisdom contained therein. You write once, it is read many times. One article, hundreds or thousands of readers. Advantage: information security.

Get involved in applications development and review current issues for potential issues that will benefit security if implemented. Use the persuasive tactics we talked about earlier in this book to convince those involved how your idea will enhance security and function at the same time. Recall the example of the single sign-on product I described earlier. We helped in the design so that our interests were represented even where they exceeded those of the development community. By working closely with those that did the actual coding, we were able to get many additional features into the end product.

E-mail, the ubiquitous carrier of information throughout and without your organization, can become a tool for awareness as well. Get a few aliases, like "InfoSec" or "Virus" set up. Users with questions about either of the subjects can simply type the one word they would relate to the issue into the address field and know that they will reach the right party. Where warranted, make each address a team name, so that many get copies of urgent information. A virus response team was described and the means of communication among its members likewise defined.

Use the resources of the training department as well. They can not only include your issues in class work, but also work with you on producing other classes. Using software tools that they, the multimedia, or graphics groups might have, try to develop a means to train online. Video is effective and available. PowerPoint can be leveraged by the simplest of computer environments. All can be displayed on local terminals.

Where a training system of sufficient sophistication is available to support certification or renewal of qualification, use it in concert with a video/slide show instructional data set to verify that information is in the hands of the correct people and, by including a short test at the end, make certain that they are taking valid information away from it.

If certain information containing security considerations is being communicated repetitively, try to get it put into a computer-based training tool. With a little scripting, it can be shown at your convenience or that of the end user.

Where something does not exist within your organization, "Let your fingers do the walking." There are contractors for training and video specialties in almost every community large enough to have a McDonald's.

Above all, do not sell yourself short. In this chapter, we listed a number of tools and techniques that would take little investigation to be put into service by anyone with the technical knowledge to make them want to read this book. If questions come up, ask the experts in-house or at the help number for the software.

Miss no chance to include or insert your message anywhere possible. Work hard with others to get the pieces together and do not forget to keep them in the loop at planning and implementation time. I know of nothing short of a skunk at a garden party that will raise the ire of folks that having someone put out a network resource gobbling message to the World. Go over every aspect of your plan, at least twice, with any parties that may be impacted.

Use the tools there; make them if you must.

Section 4

Evaluation: Does It Really Work

Like anything else that you accomplish, you never really know how well you did until you give your work an objective review and fully analyze the results of that review. A program as involved and detailed as what we have been describing is certainly no exception.

The issues around doing an objective evaluation of something like this are pretty daunting. For one, you recognized a problem but could not easily quantify it. You never went out and interviewed every person in the company and asked them just what they knew about information security; that would far exceed any sensible means of addressing the problem. You certainly did not test all of them, for the same reasons as listed above.

What you could do, however, is run down the statistics on how many break-in incidents were recorded by the network monitoring group. You could reread all of the audit reports I had you finding earlier in this book and look them over for what issues the auditors felt were of note. You already made an effort to address each of them in the early steps of building your program. You could check your systems logs for the number of times that terminals were automatically logged off due to time-outs (you do have this feature set, don't you?). You could even go to applications logs and count the number of times that access attempts were made repeatedly and failed each time.

How about looking at the uptime the company lost due to virus infections? When any of the contemporary viruses gets loose on a network, they can bring it to a complete halt. Has that happened? For how long? How often?

Is there a history of company information showing up in the media? Has it caused embarrassment, litigation? Have competitors somehow come up with trade secrets, formulae, or other information that places the company at a disadvantage? While these latter items are not necessarily quantifiable (litigation certainly is; view the losses in settlements and attorneys' fees), they are situations about which the company is not proud. Reflecting on them when showing that they have not recurred on your watch is an excellent measure of your program's success that has no real comparative figures. In this case, it is strictly black and white.

Ultimately, your review will serve two distinct purposes: one, it will demonstrate to the company that the program is, indeed, successful and that the company is better for it; two, this type of review allows you to compare conditions as they are today against what they were and against the ideal that you had originally designed against. Does it do everything that you had hoped? Where has it come up short? What can you do to make it better?

The first issue is a given and will rear its ugly head at the time that budgets are being set up and approved. Once again, you will go through the annual exercise of justifying your existence.

In the latter situation, you will trot out the numbers we talked about in the past few paragraphs. You will show them how much smarter the staff must be, because of the things you have placed in front of then educationally and more forcefully, if needed.

The latter evaluation is another beast entirely. You must look at your program with a cold and calculating eye. If you implemented a measure that has proved to only address, say, 60 percent of the problem, you must identify means to address the other 40 percent. If you addressed an auditor's comment and the comment came up again in a subsequent audit, you must take another look at how you responded and what steps you took to mitigate the situation. If other steps are warranted, they must be identified and justified, assuming that they cost money.

In this section we are going to explore means to better evaluate and continue upgrading our program. We will, of course, go to all of the usual places: statistics on accesses, errors, and break-in attempts. However, we will go a few other places for help, as well. We will use the customary, but we will also be a bit innovative.

As mentioned, we need to justify what we do for the simple sake of the money that we need to make the program exist and work on behalf of the company. Second, the work we are doing on behalf of the company and the steady improvement in it is what justifies those expenditures.

Still, most of what we do is preventive, so success is actually proven by the absence, rather than the presence, of untoward events. If we keep things from going wrong, how do we demonstrate that the chances exist for them to go very wrong? Worse, after having convinced them that we are, indeed, the obstacle to things going wrong, how do we demonstrate we need to improve the program — at recognizable cost — so that we can live in a world with even less bad events taking place?

As we go through this section, we will talk about using what it as at hand and what is available elsewhere to demonstrate the effectiveness of what we are doing and the reasons to add even greater precautions into our overall program for even greater effect. We will talk about gathering statistics from within our organization to demonstrate where improvements have taken place.

We will put year-against-year numbers up so that it can be demonstrated that errors have been reduced as a result of our program.

However, if the environment is facing a threat that we have been lucky enough to avoid up until this time (virus infection, hack by a known method, etc.), we may have to go outside to find factual material that can be presented as a threat that we might well be facing in a very short time. Our objective is to get funding to allow us to put safeguards in place to protect us from those threats and to use that implementation to demonstrate to staff the steps we are taking to do so.

We will also go to an unlikely ally in this fight for funding and that is the auditors. The internal auditors' function is not that far from what we do. While their charter is to document weaknesses in our systems, ours is to find and fix them. If they find a problem, we are responsible for making sure that it is not there the next time they review that area.

Now, auditors' reports go right to the top. Senior management and the board of directors are the recipients of reports. What if those reports also indicated that the weaknesses noted could be mitigated by specific actions and that the actions should be funded as good business practice? Adds a lot of weight, doesn't it? In this section, we will explore ways to work in concert with those auditors to get just that type of information in front of management.

Once again, we will go out and do some interviewing to find other places where we could have an impact. By this time, we should be familiar enough with our end users that a carefully crafted questionnaire can do the interviewing for us. We will talk about building that questionnaire and utilizing the learned outcome in the chapters to follow.

We will also take advantage of what is going on around the industry to point out weaknesses that need to be addressed in the near and longer-range future. The experiences of others can be powerful points to convince your own company to fund issues that could be facing the company.

Finally, we will use our statistics to assist in demonstrating success and recommending additional steps. While some may question the value of these numbers, the fact is that budget committees do look at them. Call them a necessary evil if you will, but do not overlook the value of the term *necessary*.

Chapter 17

When You Are Good, Flaunt It

Unfortunately, sometimes success will not stand on its own merits. In our case, the product delivered is protection and protection means the absence of activity. The thought pattern of management usually goes something like this: Why do we need firewalls? We have never had a break-in. Of course, you have never had a break-in, because you have firewalls. Does the insanity seem a bit clearer?

As was mentioned in the introduction, the only way to keep your program healthy and growing is to convince management of its effectiveness. In this chapter, we will introduce the concept of building a reference point for your program that will make it clear to management that it must stay and must continue to grow to meet increasing needs. While you are building a better mousetrap, Nature is out there working on a better mouse. The issue is to make management — first your own, later senior — aware of what is going on out there in mouse development.

Of course, the best demonstration of your program is to show the damage being done or attacks being focused on other corporations. Usually, it does not even have to be companies in the same industry. Melissa struck anyone that had e-mail, without regard for the segment of the business world they occupied.

When a situation like that does arrive — another company is attacked by any type of newsworthy assault — take a very quick and very detailed look at what has happened. Find out how the attack was mounted — e-mail, war dialers, etc. — and investigate the safeguards you have in place against the same type of onslaught.

If you feel that sufficient precautions have not been taken, modify them to meet the need. Of course, you probably will have the cooperation of other departments with staff to address the need, but if outside assistance is needed, it will have to be presented for purchase and approved by the higher-up management. This is where the research you have been doing comes in. If you have identified the threat and the means necessary to combat it, your request for emergency funding will be well documented. Again, the preparation of the documentation might be enhanced by the technical writing course I had recommended against, but then, it might have been better served by the creative writing course I suggested as an alternative. Even capital requests are literature, and making a case for expenditure often takes the cold numeric presentation of an accountant, coupled with the sense of the dramatic that more often is identified with a lawyer.

As you move forward with building your defenses and even more so if you actually do engage the enemy, make sure that the literary skills we have mentioned work at full throttle. Let us take an example with our old friend, Melissa, to illustrate:

When Melissa first arrived, her impact was devastating to many e-mail systems. The exponentially surging number of e-mails generated clogged internal communications as effectively as if you had cut the cables. Each PC she visited became the generator for several more noxious e-mails that in turn generated that many more. The result is well known, so I will not waste space here with another replay.

However, when Melissa got into my company, our defenses were pretty well in place. We had the mail people on alert and were waiting for her arrival. To be sure, the first attacks did some damage. However, due to the makeup of the Virus Response Team that I described earlier, we were able to "trap" the virus and tear it down as to its makeup. Then, we were able to build our own filters to catch it upon arrival, even before the major antivirus vendors could get one distributed.

All of this was made possible by the cross-discipline makeup of the team: The e-mail people recognized the virus activity and trapped the malicious code in the wild, and programmers dismantled it to identify a fingerprint that could be filtered against. Then, the filter was implemented and the network group began the arduous task of cleaning up such damage as had been done.

While this very technical work was going on, the corporate security folks were getting signs up on every access to the facility, warning people about the presence of the virus, what it looked like in their mail boxes, and what to do to prevent infection.

Taking into account the flub factor of the last action, the attack was blunted in just a few hours. As mentioned, there were outbreaks from time to time, usually generated by the failure of the informative action to reach certain individuals. Despite having walked past a number of signs and having received an e-mail instructing them not to open certain types of correspondence, they still managed to unleash the old girl a number of times. Fortunately, by the time the infected mails so generated reached the mail servers, they were trapped by the filters already in place. By the way, these filters were replaced by the ones created and sent out by the antivirus product vendors as they became available. That way, updates were automatically applied.

Now, the objective of this narrative is not to pat myself on the back, but to demonstrate a very positive action that could easily slip into the background if not actively pursued. When people are not affected by something that affects many, they lose perspective as to what was involved in preventing their having gotten infected. That is your opportunity to pass along another gem of information that works in favor of your program.

First, the warning signs that were placed up indicated to all who passed that information security had detected and was working on a case involving a virus. Better yet, they became more attuned to looking for that type of information to be available to them in this manner. Signs on the doors are immediately related to some significant virus activity going on.

I mentioned earlier that the company newsletter was one of the best friends you had. By placing a large piece about the overall action, the public (your internal version) is made aware of how well the activity worked. Now, by leveraging the relationship you have been nurturing, you can get a "flash" type item in there congratulating the virus team for a job well done.

The important point in producing the article about the event is to make certain to draw attention to what occurred and what your team did to remedy it. Now, when it comes time to budget for new antivirus products or services, you have not just the event, but the widely distributed description to fall back on. There will be one difference, however, in the presentation of your budget justification.

This is the time to take comfort in the troubles that have befallen others. Make sure you find out — and the media just love to record it, so it will not be hard to find — just exactly what the impact was on other companies or organizations throughout the world. In the case of Melissa, Microsoft took a serious hit, a fact well documented in the general press, much less the technical sector. While I really take no special pleasure in Microsoft's misfortune, there are some that found it most entertaining. In your case, this is a great example of a large company, one that everyone knows, having suffered more greatly from the attack than your organization did. It speaks well of the way you and your group handled it and underlines the need for continued support.

More than anything, it is credibility. On a standard set forth for all to see, you and your program came up a winner. Work the success for all it is worth, whether for budget justification, demonstrating to the overall staff that they need to comply with your suggestions, or simply getting new projects approved.

This type of event cuts both ways, however, and never forget that circumstances can change and you might be on the short end of the stick.

Even the latter situation can work in your favor to some extent. If you can demonstrate, in some manner, that the condition would not have occurred if you had product X available to you and can show where you took all available precautions in light of what tools you had, you can successfully argue for funding for better tools. The pivotal point here is that you did all you could with what you had. This is the arguing point around which you make a capital request for product X.

Another place one can demonstrate the effectiveness of the work getting out is to be able to quote the hits against the information security Web page and any associated links. People use what they know and trust and if you can show a trend, you have stated that your system is being used. The user community has found it useful and are accessing it of their own volition.

I mentioned once before about the surprising effectiveness of a simple bulletin form, either printed or on a Web page, an e-mail, or posted in some manner for individual consumption. The end user has the ability to read it, ignore it, discard it, or copy it for reference. Check the walls of the cubicles and next to terminals in public areas. People who find something useful try to keep it around for future use. It can be most gratifying to see the masthead that you have carefully crafted hanging on walls throughout the company.

Another important way to provide evaluating feedback is through the use of revalidation of knowledge and the verification thereof. Up until this point, we have discussed how to get information to people, how to get them to behave in a certain manner and to think in a certain way. We know what we have given them, but do we know what they have retained? Let us look at a few ways to track that and, subsequently, use that information toward growing the program.

That is assuming that you have built the very important program components that we have been discussing: a short presentation during the new employee orientation overview, a class for new hires to communicate the company's views on the value of information assets, the ways to identify them, the ways to protect them, and each employee's responsibility in doing so.

You have, of course, made sure that the information security policy statement is in the new employee handbook, along with a few explanatory paragraphs and that they have been exposed to posters, bulletins, periodical articles, e-mails, door signs, and whatever other gimmicks you have been able to come up with over the span of their employment. You may have even used Tom Walsh's version of an afternoon TV quiz show format. Now, it is time to see if they retained any of it.

One of the simplest ways to reinforce learning of a given set of subject materials is to remind people on a regular basis that their performance in the specific field about which you are concerned is something they will be held accountable for. They signed a security agreement form when they came onboard and, now, must be reminded of it again. As you might recall, there was a date field along with the signature field on the information security agreement sample that we saw several chapters back. Why not renew that agreement every two years? That is sufficient time to believe that many have forgotten what they had agreed to earlier. At that time, they were signing a lot of papers and probably reading them only perfunctorily and had yet to see the environment where they were expected to protect all corporate information assets. By the time they got out onto the production floor, most of what they had heard merged into a hazy whole, with little actual definition as to the discrete parts of that whole. However, were they to see the information security agreement again, they would most certainly recognize it.

Now, there are a number of ways to get a fresh copy of the form out to the troops for signature and return. For one, it will probably be done only about once every two years. That seems to be a pretty good figure as to reasonable expectation of memory making them aware of the fact that they did, indeed, promise to protect the company's information assets. I can assure you that they will remember this second copy of the form a lot better than they remembered the first one. For one, this is being presented alone and not as a part of an overall presentation. For another, there is now a frame of reference. They have worked in the environment and have a much better feel for what constitutes what they had promised to protect two years ago.

Even a relatively small company's human resources department has a pretty good means to track anniversary dates. Normally, they use it for defining when service awards are due, when an employee becomes eligible for certain benefits like the 401(k) or other pension program, or simply to maintain service records. By tapping into that system — usually by asking someone in the HR area — you can get those figures for anniversaries in multiples of two years and make sure that each celebrant gets the opportunity to look over the form again, sign it again, and get it back to you to file.

Again, the size of the company will have a lot to do with how you go about delivering the new copy to the employee and how you go about getting it back. In its simplest form, assuming a population of under a thousand employees, you can simply mail out the forms to the parties involved with instructions to sign and return them to a predetermined place. Even in the most primitive of environments, you should be able to get a set of labels printed by the calendar system and simply mail them out by internal mail. Then, just check them off as they come in. If there are laggards — there always are — you can ping them again, using the same list and hitting the ones for which you have no record of returned forms.

Not exactly space age, but effective.

A second means for doing the same thing, but assuming a bit more sophistication and probably size of your company, is to use e-mail to perform the same task. You will still get your mailing list from the HR department responsible for tracking anniversaries, you will still mail it out to a mailing list that, in this case, will be a mail list rather than labels, and you will still send out the forms with the instructions to fill it out online and to return it via the "Reply" command. The replies with contain an electronic signature in terms of the user ID that returns it. While it is not the same as one might send through a secure signature routine, it is sufficient for this type of application. If someone else was in the mailbox being used, there would be some explaining to do in terms of why that was so. With this particular document, it is unlikely that would happen and even less likely that someone would admit to it.

Once the replies are received, they can be archived online or strictly as an offline data set. Pinging the nonresponders is as simple as running the sent list against the responses received.

In an even more sophisticated environment, one that has a recertification system or a training system resident on the corporate network, you can send out the agreement form in that manner and have the training system record the return of the document and automatically send reminders until it is returned.

However, this type of system has a lot of other capabilities that might be even more effective as a reminder and renewal system. For instance:

A short test, involving some simple questions about the expectations listed in the policy or other aspects of the awareness program as it has been consistently put forth to the overall staff, can be given by the system. All of the questions will be multiple choice, due to the nature of automated systems on this level and can be completely tendered, graded, and returned to the user. A record of pass/no pass is kept and recorded. A failure to pass it can be followed up with a tutorial, an advisory as to where information might be found to increase the odds of passing when the test is retaken, and a schedule for retaking it. There will be a finite number of times the quiz may be attempted before some form of intercession should be instituted. Usually the best way to do that is to have the person attend the new employee class again. Depending on the number and frequency of nonpassings, there might be a special session of this class monthly to offer current employees the chance to take the test in the company of peers, rather than new hires.

Depending on how you structure it, this system can be used in a number of different ways. First you can prenotify the individual that the test is forthcoming and requires passing as a term of continued employment. It can offer some advice on what the test will cover and what reading might help the taker before taking the test. The test can then follow in a few days or the instructions for going into the training system and requesting the test can be included. This gives the user an opportunity to study if so inclined and makes the taking of the quiz somewhat easier in that the user can schedule it as desired.

One final, and to my mind, most sophisticated means for the periodic recertification that we have been talking about is using the video version of the new employee class that we discussed in the last chapter. This is one of the most versatile means for reviewing information and testing those reviewers for knowledge gained and knowledge maintained. The medium can be used in a number of ways:

- Upon receipt of information as to anniversary dates, this medium generates the class via the network to the individuals that fall into the category determined (one-, two-, or three-year anniversary).
- As a precursor to the actual class work (see example page in Chapter 16), an opportunity is offered to view the class materials before taking the quiz. The program performs as requested.
- Assuming success with the quiz, the grade is passed to the training system to update the individual's record. Normally, that record would include a listing of all courses required for the person and all taken to that point in time.
- If the quiz is not passed, the option to retake the class and try again may be offered. This can be immediate, after a predetermined passage of time — 24 hours 48 hours, etc. — or at a time set by he user.
- Once the quiz is passed, the record is updated and archived.

Obviously, the last option gives the most flexibility and has the greatest opportunity for reinforcing training. Still, each of the others is functional and can be used where more technologically involved methods are unavailable.

Summary

When the time comes to see how well you are really doing, there are a lot of means to measure it. Obviously, the first measure is acceptance by the audience and a close second is acceptance by management. Our major concern in this chapter is to make certain that our successes are known and our failures are matched up to the solutions that will make them successes.

One of the battles we will constantly fight is that of our work being so effective as to give the illusion that no threats exist. To counter that, we must often match up a bad experience by another to a good experience that our company has had in the same arena.

Take advantage of those successes by demonstrating to your main audience, the staff of your company, that you have, indeed, responded to a threat to the company and done so in a manner that best protects the source of all of their incomes.

In our particular example in this chapter, we discussed a company's success in responding to a threat from the e-mail-borne virus, Melissa. While other companies' e-mail systems were brought to their knees, ours suffered only a short-term slow down. In the main part of this chapter, we discussed how applying the talents and skills of a varying group of players enabled us to find, understand, and stop Melissa's onslaught.

The upshot of this very high-profile success was leveraged (there's that word again) in two directions: first, to demonstrate to the staff in general how hard we work to protect the company and how good the people are that are working on it. The second facet on this diamond is to use it to demonstrate to management that eternal vigilance (read that somewhere) is the only way to continually protect the company. As we are putting newer and better protective measures in place, the guys in the black hats are out there trying to find a way to break through them. These successes help us to find and fund the means to stay one step ahead where possible and less than one step behind when learning about new risks and dangers.

Keeping the company's staff aware of what they need to do to protect company assets requires education and later verification that the education hit the mark and is remembered. There are a number of ways to do that, and it must be done on a regular basis.

We can ask people to come in and review the information security agreement they signed — along with a number of other documents on the day they first came to work with the company — and that can be a means of reinforcement for the message. It simply says that after a year or two here, I am still aware that protecting the company's information assets is still my job and I am willing to take on the task. Does it tell us that the individual is equipped to do that effectively? It emphatically does not. To be truly effective, there must be a means to continually upgrade the knowledge held by these people and a second means to verify that it is getting across.

In larger companies, those with training software and a relatively up-to-date network, there are a number of means to not only contact people at certain mileposts in their careers with the company, but to provide short testing to verify that their knowledge is not only up to date, but demonstrable. We can deliver a class in a number of ways, from having special sessions of the standard new employees' introduction class — updated on a regular basis, of course — to sophisticated, online course materials that can be experienced on a convenient and self-paced schedule.

Once the online course has been taken, a short quiz can be used to evaluate the level of information retained by the employee. We can even go so far as to give them a choice as to whether they need to view the online course or not before taking the test.

Successes must be kept high profile for as long as it takes to get employee buy-in for your program and its flexibility and currency. By the same token, these successes help pave the way for even further increases in risk-mitigating tools, using them to justify additional tools and necessary staff to continue growing to meet new risks. Successes create credibility and credibility reassures management that you are going about it the right way.

Make sure that when you go into the budget process for the coming year, you can cite accurately the threats that are likely to be experienced in the coming year and that you have a track record of being able to foresee some of these threats and plan accordingly. A budget aimed at real issues and the reflected light of successes in the past are the best ticket to having such budgets approved and, therefore, allowing your department to continue to grow.

Chapter 18

Statistics: The Old Numbers Game

Mark Twain was a philosopher without peer. He looked at humanity and saw right through it. As it was, he did not much care for what he saw. He always said that there were three types of lies; lies, damn lies, and statistics.

Unfortunately he was right, as usual. Statistics can be a boon or a bane, depending upon how they are applied. They can be stated verbally, numerically, graphically, and probably be set to music, as well. In whatever form they appear, they may spell out the truth or hide it beyond recognition. In demonstration of his observation that there were three kinds of lies, note that in order of magnitude, he listed statistics as the greatest. They can most certainly be the most egregious of lies, based not only on how they are used, but how they are stated. As an example, let us examine the simple factor of "average," in all of its forms.

First there is the mean average. This is simple mathematics. Take the total of all of the values in a set of examples — like the number of wheels on vehicles that pass a certain point — add them together and divide by the number of occurrences. Sounds pretty simple, doesn't it? However, these figures are capable of being so skewed as to be valueless. The larger the sample, the more likely the outcome is to be significant, but with a small sample, it is virtually impossible to come up with a meaningful conclusion. To illustrate this point, I use a mathematical average between myself, checking in at six feet even, and the floor, at an altitude of zero feet. Add the two numbers together, divide by the occurrences, and what resultant mean average do you have? Why three, of course. Now applying that example, which of us — the floor or myself — does it describe? Of course, by all of the rules of mathematics, it is accurate. Go figure.

The second way that average can be expressed is by median. A median on the road divides the roadway in half. So does the median example in a set. If you have, say, a measured population of 45 occurrences, the median is that point where there are as many occurrences above it as there are below. In this instance, that would be 22 occurrence above and 22 occurrences below that point.

In this instance, no matter how high the number of examples, the median could be a single iteration. Can you truthfully say that of 500 different items measured that any single one of them is representative if its only claim to fame is that it is exactly in the middle? The only guarantee from this type of average is that you could get as many hits shooting left as you could shooting right. Hardly a significant mathematical event.

The final method of calculating average is the modal method. Whereas the first two systems used mathematics to come up with a numerical dividend and a middle occurrence, respectively, the mode is that point at which the greatest concentration of examples occurs. For example, sat 500 units are being measured, and they represent heights between three feet tall and six feet five inches tall. If 12 examples are exactly six feet tall, one is taller — six feet five inches — and the others are all shorter, but no more than five are at exactly the same height, then the mode is six feet, even though 87 of your examples are less than six feet and only one is taller.

This last means could be used to demonstrate that the general heights of these people, tree stumps, bushes, or whatever tend toward the taller end of the overall range of heights. That is assuming that the overall trend is toward the six-foot height, which is likely. But truly, it is not a significant statistic if they are spread relatively evenly with the range of three to six feet.

I use this detailed explanation of something I have already told you is of limited value for a number of reasons, not the least of which is to warn you not to get taken in by skewed "averages" nor to use them without paying strict attention to the value of what they represent

Somewhere along the way, you are going to have to use pure numbers to represent what you have accomplished and how it is better than it was before. These cautionary tales are to help make sure that you validate your findings before setting out to prove a point without fully understanding what your figures mean and what they do not mean.

Mind you I am not saying to never use these versions of "average." There are times when expressing average in any of the ways described will be to your advantage. Just review the situation and see which expression best suits your needs. We do not refer to this as "lying with statistics," just using them in a manner that delivers your message best.

For instance, if you are trying to relate trends, the modal version of average might be your best descriptor. By showing the propensity of occurrences to move in the desired direction in terms of numbers of occurrences, this might be the way to go. In month over month or year over year, if you can show the largest number of occurrences to gather around a smaller and smaller representation of an untoward event — for the sake of discussion, let us use automated log-offs: time-outs — then your objective will be served. If the modal number of time-outs goes from, say, an average of 11 to an average of 7, you have demonstrated that the number of occurrences by user has gone down. If the actual number has not changed and the number of time-outs by users has moved downward, which is the best way to express it — as having not changed or people with the greatest number of forgetful experiences having moved downward?

Conversely, if the total number of occurrences has dropped substantially, you might want to express it in terms of average number of time-outs per user; using mean averaging. Of course, if the actual numbers are significant and will sell your program — say 100 time-outs last month has been reduced to 55 this month — the numbers stand on their own and really do not need to be massaged to reflect positively.

This last exercise, while lengthy, did provide some really important information about how to use statistics to your best advantage. The term *average* now means something entirely different to you and to your presentations.

Of course, there are a lot of statistics that you can use that are pure numbers — firewall logs, network monitors, and so on — but they are not the focus of this book. What we need to do is isolate some numbers that are meaningful and will assist you in selling the continued expansion of what you are doing.

Our major function is to pass information on to the staff of our parent organization in a manner that makes them aware of the threats to corporate information assets, gives them tools to go about protecting them, and instills an understanding of their responsibility to actively protect them. How, then, do we measure our effectiveness.

Actually, there are a number of ways to review activities and note measurable changes. For instance, we used the information security awareness class as our major vehicle to produce the three characteristics listed above. We know whom we teach the class to — the people coming through the door on their first day or two with the organization.

Given infinite time, that would ultimately force the numbers in that everyone with the organization would have attended on their first day of work. Taking into account that there are careers that span several decades, using that as the sole tool to ensure attendance would be foolhardy, to say the least. In fact, I personally would not want to wait around any company long enough to make sure that was true.

We discussed the idea of an automated training system that keeps track of the classes every employee must take and their record of attendance. This is most easily done using a computer-based system in a company of any size, but we must recognize that some organizations are still pretty paper bound on records of this nature. Still, if the inception of the class was on a given date, then anyone who had been hired after that date would have necessarily attended. Somewhere, in a file or on a database, there is a record of that.

By simple deduction, we know that people that started before that date have not attended. Again, utilizing personnel records, we can identify those that were hired previous to that significant date. We can, from this information, offer the class to those old timers and simply keep records of their attendance. Even in the most primitive of paper-based systems, there is a way to sort them by characteristics such as credit for a given class. Using this tool, we can continue weeding through the staff until we have a good sense that most, if not all, employees have been exposed to your educational masterpiece.

Of course, with training systems being written and sold throughout the world and the cost-effective nature of their functionality, most companies of any size track required courses using the provisions of the computer-based system. In this case, credit for a class is a recorded value and is sortable by either its presence or absence. That being the case, special sessions can be set up to retro teach the class to those who have not taken it. Or, in its most sophisticated iteration, the video class I described earlier can be taken online, a quiz given, and the results recorded. Reminders for those who have not taken it can be automatically generated until such time as all have been granted the opportunity to enjoy it.

On the unlikely chance that someone has still not availed themselves of the opportunity, second and third reminders can be oh, so much more personal and can communicate a true sense of urgency.

Being able to present numbers as to the number of persons who have experienced the class as versus the number of a year ago is a true boon to supporting its effectiveness. Remember that the people reviewing the numbers are the same ones that approved the class in the first place. Its value is a given; only the percentage of staff members taking it will change and grow. Even when the number of those still absent the credit approaches 0, the statistic is still valid, demonstrating that even taking turnover into account, all employees are being presented with these important materials. Coming up with the second valid statistic in this set — the exact number of persons who were presented the class during the past measured time period — and we have a wonderful picture of effectiveness to present to management.

Education is a grand indicator of our ability to keep up with an easily recognized changing of technology and the business environment. Now that you have the orientation class in place, you will likely be called upon to do presentations to internal groups throughout the year. Sometimes it will be about a specific issue facing a particular segment of the company; sometimes it will be a reflection of where the business world is going. Make a point of keeping good records on how many presentations you give to the company and how many specialized classes you prepare and either present or turn over to a training department. These are excellent indicators of productive activity and are prevalidated in that your reputation has been established through the new employees' orientation offering.

When doing your budget, remember to include this type of internal presentation in the recap of activities. If you presented a special section on viruses, for instance, make sure that all iterations are included in your records.

Assuming you stay active in the community of companies in your area and that you have maintained your membership in professional organizations, you will most certainly become known in local circles. That should be as much a testimony to your efforts to join local organizations as to your position with your company. While we will talk at length later about some of the things that can be accomplished through local or regional institutions, suffice it to say that your providing of assistance to these organizations by making presentations to their membership is another statistic that can be used to add to your credibility. It stands to reason that if others want to hear what you have to say, then your own company should have some interest in it as well.

Opportunities to use statistics that are gained from other areas of the information systems function can also be applied to demonstrating the heightened awareness your program has caused. There are a number of quick hits on this that can be easily measured and demonstrated year over year. Of course, be certain of the validity of these figures before you present them and make sure they tell the story you want them to.

As an example; let us take a long look at automated log-offs.

Every operating system around has the ability to log a user off if the session remains idle for a set period of time. Under most circumstances, that acceptable idle period is parameter-driven and can be changed at the option of the system manager. For the sake of discussion, we can say that we have chosen a 15-minute time lapse as sufficient for most circumstances.

Let us say, now, that we have experienced an unacceptable number of sessions timing out rather than being logged off by the user. I know, to many of us, one time is too many, but to a realistic individual, there is a threshold of where you think you can impact the total by a program to get more people to recognize the issue and make sure to log off when they either finish work or leave their desk area.

By now, you have already guessed where I am going with this.

Begin accumulating monthly figures on the number of timed out sessions that occur. In most cases, the system will support the naming of the log-on that was in control of the session at time out. Now, you not only have a number, but a means to identify the worst violators.

Note: Due to the great variation in operating platforms and the operating systems involved, this description will be sketchy, at best. For purposes of this exercise, let us just recognize the capabilities of our systems and the relative ease with which a systems programmer can collect these figures, even in a system that does not offer a solid reporting package. While there might be some fits and starts in getting into position to do these reviews in some platforms, it most likely can be done with a mixture of cajoling, threatening, and begging, and you can get the numbers you want.

Start charting the actual numbers each month and make a list of your ten or so worst offenders. Then, launch your program to get people to log off before leaving or going on to a nonterminal-related task. I have successfully used a "Leave it? Lock it!" campaign to get people's attention and then to give reasons why they should not be leaving their log-ins active when they are not camped at their terminal.

Obviously, the first thing you want to do is put the clamps on your biggest abusers. You need not threaten anyone; just point out the number of timed out log-offs they have had in the past several weeks and the potential for problems with that situation. You might then mention company policy about logging off when not at your desk. That mild approach will quiet down most of them.

Next month, you will still have a list of the top ten offenders, but I will wager that the average numbers will have decreased and a lot of names will have been replaced on the list. Like the prescription the doctor gives you repeat as necessary.

After a few weeks, begin putting up that phrase anywhere you can. If you have a Web page, put it there. If you have a regular newsletter, put it there along with an explanation of the program. Talk about how a terminal left logged on can be used incorrectly or even criminally by a third party and whatever takes place at or from that terminal is assumed to have been done by the person logged on. I usually use an example of the night janitor finding an open terminal and doing his night school homework on it. If he happens to need data to do the homework, well he has access to everything you do.

In never hurts to let your audience know that there are extensive reports as to where the problems with this matter are. Again, you need not threaten anyone. Simply mention or intimate the fact that you can see who is doing what and the reports that carry that information, and the specter of Big Brother will be hanging over all of them. After a few months of the steady "Leave it? Lock it!" and the continued reporting, I suspect you will see rather dramatic reductions in the numbers of violations that take place.

Now, if you had started this when you walked in the door, you would have statistics from day one and could have implemented this program or one like it as a first step. Imagine, violation numbers, in any classification, going down from your arrival forward. Makes them wish they had hired you years before.

Another type of statistic that can be used to your advantage is the number of virus reports to the Virus Response Team (you did set one up, didn't you?). As you might recall, I recommended a mail group called "Virus" a few chapters ago as a good way to keep employees involved in the virus detection business and to give them an easily remembered mailbox to send them to.

That number will probably work better for you on a month-to-month basis at first and perhaps over a year to year and month over month at some later date.

This is a statistic you can advertise as an awareness tool, making sure that you list the numbers of reports in your monthly contribution to the company newsletter. Each time you state the numbers, you can reinforce the "who to call" aspect of the program.

On the other hand, there are a number of other statistics available from the study of viruses and their effects. If, by chance, a virus does get into the company mail system, and it is one of the Melissa clone e-mail generation types, there will be easily gathered statistics on how many mail messages were sent and how many were stopped at the mail server by whatever antivirus measures you have installed there. These numbers can be used, but must be treated with a bit of savvy about what kind of message you wish to send. If, for instance, 2.5 million messages are generated at another company's site and only 50,000 were generated at yours, thanks to your crackerjack team, you just might want to laud the team's performance in stopping the virus in its tracks. If, however, you lost 50,000 files to another virus, I would not be so quick to trumpet that fact.

As with everything that you publicize, pick and choose carefully. Ask yourself if there a learning experience here. Can something be gained by publicizing this particular item? Only if you come up with the right answer do you communicate it to the overall reading community.

Statistics can be used in a reverse manner as well as what we have thus far described. As you know, threats to the security of our systems evolve as fast as do the systems. As we address one exposure and the threats generated by it, another opens with new threats to be addressed. This situation is really more serious than just job security; it is a challenge to meet these new incursions on a daily basis.

Fortunately, there are statistics collected on most new threats and they are readily available. I will not even list the Internet sources for them, as you probably know sources that I do not. Let us just say that Gartner, SANS, SAFER, and the professional organizations like CSI and ISSA can always provide numerical measurements for new threats. Review the sites where you find these numbers on a regular basis and keep track of burgeoning threats that could compromise your systems. This actually serves a twofold purpose: (1) it gives you an idea of the directions that must be taken to maintain a secure environment, and (2) it gives you information to place in front of management when it comes time to ask for additional resources to meet these new threats.

Is this part of an awareness activity? Of course, making management aware of issues and having numbers to back claims allows you to embark on high-visibility programs. These programs can be shared with the company staff as well as provide support when requesting funding.

Ultimately, statistics fall under a number of categories. Most are useful, but some can trap you if you are not careful. Use the ones that demonstrate improvements made in your systems, both for training and for justifying next year's budget. Play down the ones that show the number of attempts made against your firewall, for instance; use them to attack the problem, not to draw attention to it.

Summary

As Mark Twain said, statistics can be the biggest lie of all, if used in a contrived and unbalanced way. Judging by his ability to visualize other things in a manner that many of us missed, it is probably a good idea to pay attention to the statistics we use and the way we use them.

Perhaps with an understanding of how we lie with statistics, he also said that Man is the only animal that blushes, or has need to!

We discussed the many definitions for "average," how they were arrived at, and how they could be used. A mathematical average, or mean, had to in some way represent a norm for what it purported to measure. A median acknowledges a midpoint — a point at which half of the sample is below it and half above. This would be valid if your sample had a wide and relatively even distribution, but would not be of value if the majority of your sample was in the same numerical 10 percent — for example, if 50 of your sample of 100 items fell between 90 and 100, then your median would almost dismiss the fact that the other 50 ranged from 0 to 92.

Finally we touch on the mode, or point of greatest concentration. Using the sample from above, it would paint a much better picture. It would show that the greatest concentration is near the top of your scale.

In most cases, if it is decided to use averaging, it is valuable to use more than one method to more accurately describe the nature of the averaged population.

We also discussed using statistics in measuring trends over time. In these instances we kept numbers from given time periods and compared them month to month and year to year — comparing the same period from one year to that same period in the past year — kind of like your electrical bill reflects the information that shows you how you are wasting more energy this year than you did last. If this type of statistic is prepared linearly — in a sequence that can be illustrated across a page in a chart — you can indicate when you introduced components of your program designed to demonstrate the impact your awareness program had on personal performance over that time. The example we used was automated log-offs and I strongly recommend you begin tracking this item as quickly as you can. Information on these log-offs is easy to recover and graphs well, and its potential impact can be understood by everyone. If the term *red herring* means anything to you, this one area can be recognized as the reddest of all.

We can also track the effectiveness of our introducing staff to our awareness class. All new hires after a certain date will certainly have taken it, but we must find a way to track those that have not, expose them to it, either in special sessions or via the video version I described, and record their success in having taken it. Those statistics validate your class concept, as a greater and greater percentage of the staff having attended. Now, simply giving it to new hires will raise the percentage of employees having taken it on its own. Turnover is a fact of life and your statistics will show an elevated percentage of attendance for years on end. However, it will never approach 100 percent in your lifetime unless you begin getting the old timers — those who were employees previous to the class having become a requirement — who will never leave and never take the class unless it is retro presented to them.

A constantly rising percentage of completion is a very positive justification for your annual budget.

Take advantage of your knowledge in the fields and keep records on how many additional classes you build and teach and how many internal and external presentations you give. A strong community involvement is recognized as good for the company image, so keep good records.

Using items like the Virus Response Team to generate communications about virus activity — real or imagined — is another measure of how you are reaching your audience. Keep track of how many notifications you get from the general population about virus matters. If they ask questions, so much the better. You can actually put together a virus contact report with classification for reporting previously unseen (in our environment) viruses, new reports on viruses already known, hoaxes, and people with questions. Makes a nice report and, again, helps justify next year's budget.

You can also collect statistics from the "wild," finding out what new threats are occurring outside of your organization. By making good notes and thoughtfully identifying those that might pose a threat to your company, you may well be able to justify the financial resources needed to address the new threat. Work out viable solutions to the impending problem and present them in the context of the threat — supported by numbers — and the potential curative action. Do not ask them what to do, but present them with the solution you recommend and its price tag.

Take advantage of the great statistics on new threats, viruses, and soon that are available out there. You can find information on a number of sites on the Internet and can apply the ones that count to your purposes. As described above, it demonstrates the real world and can identify when we are out of step with it. It can also support your budget presentation each year.

Statistics can be used in a number of ways that can be beneficial, and they can also be used to skew perceptions by not showing an accurate picture. We see incongruities in daily life. Take, for example, the idea of each American family having 2.4 children. How about that .4 kid. Does he get his own room? Does he have to wear hand-me-downs, or just 40 percent of them? Can he ever get 100 percent on a test, or is he stuck on 40 percent forever? How many phone books does it take to raise the .4 kid up high enough to eat at the dining room table?

This is a highly quoted number and all of us have heard or seen it somewhere. Still, on close examination, it really does not describe anything tangible in our world. It is not a person, or even .4 of a person; it is simply a number. Do not become trapped in looking at the numbers without them relating validly to factual material.

There is an old story that came out of the Cold War and demonstrates extremely well how one can be factually correct, yet not tell the story truthfully. It stems from the first track meets held between the Soviet Union and the United States. It seems as though the ruling bodies of the two countries had decided on a match race of 100 meters, pitting the fastest American against the fastest Soviet. The winner would be declared the Fastest Man in the World.

The race went off without a hitch, televised in the United States, but known to the Soviet people only by the reports that came from the state news media. Americans saw what happened, the Soviets heard later. The American sprinter took an early lead and cruised to a five-meter win. America saw their man victorious, but what the Soviets heard was: "A great victory for Socialism! The Soviet competitor finished second in the competition, but the American was next to last!"

Now, this story is fiction (for those of you that failed to recognize it), but the use of statistical data, while accurate in wording, tells a story as far from the truth as possible. Do not fall into the trap of using statistics in that manner, as it will surely come back to bite you at some time.

As for me? I guess I'll keep an eye on that three-foot "average" guy — between me and the floor — and the .4 kid and see what they do if they get a chance to play together.

Chapter 19

Go Outside of Your Walls for Affirmation

We have been talking a lot about ways to use the statistics you gather from the performance of your systems, the numbers of occurrences of specific actions, and the percentages of your personnel that you reach with the awareness classes you describe. Yet, you live in a world community of others who face the same challenges you do, day after day. Some are competitors, some are just business people just like you. Yet, there is a kinship that can be exploited — in the best possible way — for your benefit and that of your organization.

As you are no doubt aware, there are about 6,000 people in the United States and Canada that have, in a moment of weakness, accepted the position of information security officer. Some, for reasons of their own, looked for and obtained the position. Others were thrust into the position by edict or for lack of forethought, accepted the position when offered, figuring that they would be able to fake it until they learned the ropes. Or, as old pro Bob Courtney always said: "Everybody else was doing something important."

As the field began enlarging, thanks to folks like the 404 Gang who raised public awareness of the actual threats to computer systems, there became a loosely knit confederations of people that had found themselves with the responsibility and no particular budget or tools with which to do anything. John O'Mara, with true foresight as to where the industry was going, started the Computer Security Institute back in the 1970s that has grown into the largest professional organization of its kind.

The real take-off point for our little niche in the information processing arena was the release of the movie *War Games*. For some reason, that particular film caught the fancy of the public and people started asking questions about whether such things could actually be done. I have the sneaking feeling that their concerns were stimulated more by concerns about a small nuclear holocaust than whether or not particular industrial use was made of such technology. However, the fact remains that the public now knew — even if from a less than totally accurate scenario — that there was a possibility for someone to hack into someone else's computer systems and cause no end of grief.

Interestingly, Hollywood, despite never burdening themselves with being factually correct, has managed to keep aspects of computer security in the public eye with the releases of a number of films about hacking and other computer-related crimes. People watched these films with the thought in the back of their minds that "Hal" was finally going to rebel and take things over himself (itself?). Still, each time another of these things was released, there was the inevitable seeking out of those of us in the industry to ask the one question that the movies left burning in everyone's mind: Could that really happen?

Unfortunately, that damned question forced me to watch a number of films that I would have avoided at all costs so that I could give an intelligent answer to the question. It somehow does not seem fair that I should have to answer the question accurately when the makers of the film never undertook such research. Still, it afforded us a bit of notoriety of the type that used to be reserved for private detectives in the old films. Come to think of it, I never met a "Hard hitting, straight shooting, darkly handsome man who could sweep a woman off her feet just by raising one dark, bushy eyebrow" standing behind a badge, to my recollection. Well, it is our turn now, but they portray us all as nerds!

People did start thinking more about what we did and we did get the phone calls. (I have even gotten them from an area high enough in a major company so as to raise *my* less than "dark, bushy eyebrows," both of them. Seems like he and the wife attended one of the films I mentioned, and he spent the rest of the weekend ruminating over.) These calls indicated that the people around us were beginning to see us as less mysterious and more as a part of what made the company run.

Still, I often wonder how many people in the theater thought I had lost my mind when I began laughing hysterically at the computer operator/ programmer/manager, every time he came on screen. The Nedry (Nerdy?) character (*Jurassic Park*) was a caricature of every hacker profile we have seen for the past 20 years. Watching him in action on the incredibly out-of-synch systems that supposedly ran every aspect of the park that "spared no expense to do it right" had to be as comical to anyone with a nodding acquaintance with the particulars of our work. I guess it did reach its mark, as it was entertainment and I certainly found that entertaining!

Wonder what would happen if we shut down our company's systems for a couple of hours while we tested new code on the only box there?

My purpose with the detailed descriptions of the cinema that I have given over the past several paragraphs was not to provide movie critiques, but to point out that because of their often burlesqued interpretations of what we do, we have gotten a great deal more exposure and the resultant credibility. That credibility allows us to build our programs and fund them.

Help from the outside, in any form, is always appreciated.

Other people's budgets (although rarely in the multimillions of dollars as it was for *Jurassic Park*) can often supplement ours, when we are either approaching the same problem or when research by another party answers questions that have been, or should have been, raised within our own organization. The ability to pick up a phone and call a colleague to go over a particularly worrisome issue is a great advantage in problem solving.

As mentioned earlier, there are a number of professional organizations out there that have become lightening rods for our profession. CSI and ISSA lead the way as gathering points for us, while the MIS Training Institute, SANS, Vanguard Integrity Professionals, and Gartner provide a number of annual gatherings that allow information security professionals to gather from time to time. Generally, these gatherings include a number of short workshops and full day or two-day seminars that can enhance your knowledge, not just by what they present, but by the attendees. I can recall many a lively discussion that initiated at one of those workshops that carried well into the night at a convenient watering hole in the area. The conversations were doubly as interesting in that long-time practitioners were in attendance along with some who were very new to the profession. Surprisingly, while we expect the old timers (at last tally, I was one of those) to have a lot of input based on knowledge accumulated over years in the field, a lot of the newer people had actually done college coursework on the subject and brought entirely new approaches to the problem-solving arena. Certainly, they were learning more from their elders, but they had ideas and had put many into practice. All of us came away better for the knowledge gained from the others.

Note: I have mentioned just a few of the many organizations that put on this type of periodic get-togethers around the country and world. They are not, by a long shot, the only such operators of conferences that play in this workspace. Assuming that you have been to a get-together of some kind or have requested additional information from a vendor that addressed his initial inquiry to the head of information systems or to "security manager" at your particular organization, your name became available to everyone in the industry. For once, this is more good than bad as what appears to be spam is often information on new products that might address issues that you are facing in your own environment. Also, your name and company get on the lists they sell to the operators of these professional organizations or training vendors. You will receive offers to attend annual conferences of organizations that you have never heard of from all over the world. I have been invited to such events in Spanish and Swedish (last one was in Sweden, which makes me think it was Swedish — do not speak a word of it! Spanish, on the other hand, I had a shot at.) and in English that reflected its status as a second — maybe third, or worse — language of the preparer of the announcement. Most were from organizations with a high sounding name with which I had no familiarity. In addition, this was either the first or second annual conference. Now, everyone has a right to get his or her good idea off the ground, but not necessarily with my contribution. I tend to wait until they are more established.

CSI, SANS, ISSA, and MIS all have long-time track records, and I consider their events excellent chances to pick up knowledge and to share wisdom.

The first and fourth of them are for profit companies, while ISSA and SANS are more IS professional groups, run by and for practitioners. ISSA usually coordinates their annual conference with another organization.

The fact is that they all provide exemplary training, something I might not have said a few years ago. You will gain from attending any of their conferences with very little effort on your part. With a concentrated information-gathering attitude, you will gain tremendously.

Never overlook a gathering of persons that face the same issues that you do as a source of learning. Most of them include "birds of a feather" gatherings after conference hours in which people facing a given issue get together and informally exchange ideas. Many a problem is thrown on that table and gets the attention of thousands of dollars worth of consulting hours, absolutely free of charge and many attendees go home with resolutions to problems that have plagued them for months.

Most important, you come away with many business cards and contacts with others in the industry. While you may wonder at how a program far more mature and complete than yours managed to gain such funding, the ability to discuss it with the person that built it may allow you to come away with new ideas for justifying your own program. By the same token, you may well get early warnings on something coming down the road from these same contacts.

These colleagues also have experiences that they can and do document. If you can benefit from a high-level case history that took place at a company outside of yours (suitably camouflaged so as not to make the company name available) by publishing it to your overall audience as an example of both what can happen and how you want to prevent it from happening here by doing what the rest of the article states. Later, you can demonstrate an exposure that was identified by the annotated experience when justifying your own existence and the program you have synthesized.

The media is another excellent source of outside information that can be applied directly to an issue or be used for training and defining an issue for which you want your staff to keep an eye open. Usually, this is no more difficult to distribute than to put a link in an e-mail to the desired audience. This way, they can look at it in their own time and you are giving them fully prepared copy that has been edited and verified as to content. Nice to have someone do the research, writing, and editing for you while you reap the benefit.

Make no mistake, when you use this data, make sure that it fits your case and that you properly credit it. For whatever reason, management is often more willing to accept the word of a third party on an issue than they are yours. However, if you can scale it against an issue already introduced within your organization, it can be a mighty force in hastening the recognition of the issue. Relate it, where you can.

In publishing information received in that manner, make sure to credit what is good and downplay what is not. In the latter case, you might be talking about a virus infection that, somehow, you dodged but that paralyzed another installation. If the ISO there is a friend, be extremely careful how you use the information. To be sure, you want to use the body of it to crow about the success of your efforts and compare them with the less effective measures elsewhere, but do not do it at the expense of a colleague. A good idea is to let him review the piece before publication. That way, if there are issues, they can be discussed and new wording agreed upon. If there is no way the other person can come out looking anything but the fool, think twice about using it at all and, if you do, mask the actual identity of the other organization.

As mentioned in the chapter on statistics, there are always a number of Web sites and other means of disseminating information that can be of use to you in gathering either support for your program or informing your readership. Just as effective is the information available from news services and other subscription type e-mail groups.

Information Security Magazine, for one, has a news service that sends out up-to-date information weekly or even more often, as warranted. The SANS Institute that we mentioned earlier also has a newsletter — Newsbytes — and another information service called the Security Alert Consensus. These are both free subscriptions and can be obtained at the URL http://www.sans.org/sansnews/ or http://www.sans.org/sasusr1 respectively. They are open source, and you can use any part of either within your organization (no online bulletin boards). They provide news on both a technical and administrative level, and their content can be used in a number of ways.

Another news service, SAFER (Security Alert for Enterprise Resources), a subsidiary of The Relay Group, has a product known as SAFERMAG that is distributed online on a periodic basis. It, too, is in newsletter format and is filled with useful and extremely timely information. It is normally sent out in brief mode with a URL to view the magazine online and a PDF address to download it directly. The URL for signing up is http://www.safermag.com.

Another complex of e-mail newsletters is put out by BUGTRAQ. They have a number of mail groups in which they cover threats to specific operating systems or platforms, viruses, secure programming, and a number of other issues. Their main URL is BUGTRAC@SECURITYFOCUS.COM.

There are a number of other technical information channels available and were I to list them here, there would be space for nothing else. Any reader of this book is aware of the means to use the search engines available online and can use key words for the subject in which you are interested.

The important point is to take advantage of the information gained. Actually, there are a number of ways to do that, all of which enhance the awareness of at least a segment of the company population. BUGTRAQ, for instance, often publishes information on new attacks on or weaknesses in certain software packages or operating systems. As often, patches are included for fixing the problem. In many cases, the vendors themselves monitor the TRAQ and respond to announcements of weaknesses. In some instances, they may provide a patch, demonstrate that the finding was inaccurate, or explain that by configuring the product in a different manner the problem could be avoided.

This being true, forwarding the notification to the appropriate product group not only gives them the information and potential fix, but it identifies you as a contributor toward doing their job. Likewise with warnings from SANS or SAFER.

I have found it to my advantage to archive the warnings I send out as that leaves an audit trail should it need to be revisited and gives me the ability to resend, if necessary. At this writing, I am collecting information on secure programming in an attempt to make code more bulletproof before it goes online. BUGTRAQ has a separate thread that addresses this issue alone. Bear in mind that some of what you read is posted by people whose lives revolve around this type of issue (it is a bulletin board format), and they will argue ceaselessly about what appear to be pretty innocuous points. Your job is to separate the wheat from the chaff, so to speak. Only forward the issues that are truly informative and delete the rest.

Do not make the mistake of thinking that because each item is not a pearl, the board is not worth reading. You do not have to find many gold nuggets in a stream to make all of the sand and gravel you discard worthwhile.

Some of the online versions of technical journals can also be instrumental in getting information to you and, consequently, to the troops. I suggest taking a look at *WIRED* on a daily basis and the various Ziff-Davis (ZD) publications as good places to start. *WIRED* started out as sort of a left-field type publication and has moved more toward the center over the years. They have a number of articles of current interest from a number of other forums and update often during the day. Makes it much more useful and up to date than picking up the monthly printed version. Look for explorations on new technology, news articles on items such as viruses, their sources, and writers and legalese views on some of the litigation going on at the time. There seems to be little that they will not touch on if it effects the information-processing community and offers quite a number of articles of general interest (you need to be a well-rounded person).

Ziff-Davis publishes on just about every technical subject going. I would not even hazard a guess as to the total number of news sites and publications they have, but I have rarely encountered a subject that they do not have something on. Use your browser and the key words "Ziff-Davis" and the subject you wish to get information on. My bet is that you will hit more often than you will miss. I still think they are publishing something about abacuses somewhere we have not found yet! They are, by the way, the publishers of the Computer Shopper, a 600-page-plus monthly publication. And yes, it is available online.

What we have hit upon here is another means to use outside sources to enhance your own program. In the cases listed, we have approached a new, more focused approach, directing our input to specific areas of the company. That, too, is awareness, brought directly to the people that can best apply it. They get the information and look to you to continue to supply it. Guard that responsibility, as the product groups are often the hardest to get on board with any program. The pervasive viewpoint in those areas is that security is a pain, albeit they will occasionally admit it is a necessary evil. Show them that it is more necessary than evil.

A last point I would mention is to check to see what the guys in the black hats are doing. There are a number of ways to do this, many of them not without a certain amount of risk.

I strongly recommend, for instance, that you do not shop these sites from the corporate network nor with your corporate user name. A phone line is relatively inexpensive; you can use whatever name or pseudonym you wish and it cannot be traced back to the organization. I believe that I would clear my cookie file on a regular basis, as well.

Knowing what the other guys are doing is always good business and it can be used as news for your newsletter or the corporate version as you see it fitting into what you are trying to accomplish. You can find them with key words such as "hack," "warez," and "phreak." No doubt you will learn others as the time passes.

As you have probably noticed by now, a majority of the sources I have quoted do have significant presence on the Internet. I strongly suggest you bookmark each site that has useful information. Do a daily review and capture such items as might be of use now or later.

The final source I would mention is the good old daily paper. Whether it is your local or something national, like *USAToday*, you may well find articles of interest that can be applied to either your broad brush campaign or to the more targeted audience we described earlier.

Take advantage of all of these potential tools, as the gathering of information is the precursor to the communicating of it. Our need here is to make others aware of the things that are happening and the things they need to do. By collecting already prepared information or picking up important input from colleagues and other acquaintances, you can build your ability to disseminate information in a manner that supports awareness and targets areas that need attention.

Summary

If we have learned anything from this chapter it is that every source outside of our company that comments, analyzes, portrays, or in any other way discusses computer security problems has value for us. Whether watching a movie where someone hacks into a computer with no external connections or is the sole knowledgeable person in an installation worth billions, despite having a loudly trumpeted disdain for management, the job, and the world in general, we can gain from the portrayal as seen by millions. We can ride the fame or infamy of the character by paraphrasing the threats faced into an article through which readers will associate something they saw in a theater with what really has to be done.

If we fail to have enough nasty experiences within our own four walls (We should be so lucky!), we can leverage our professional connections into learning experiences that can later be applied in our own environment. This might take the form of attendance at professional conferences or even conversations with colleagues.

In the former instance, we can learn from seminars and workshops put on by a number of authorities on the various aspects of our business. Better yet is what we can learn in conversation and even birds-of-a-feather breakout sessions, held often well into the evening during these conferences.

Another dimension of these conferences is the usual vendor display held in conjunction with it. There, we can review new tools and get a firsthand look at them, as well. Very often, we can either try them out on the spot or arrange for a trial period once we return home. At the very least, we have updated our knowledge of what is currently available and have touched and felt it.

Whatever we gain at these get-togethers and whatever we take home is pretty much up to each of us. As for me, I find that a professional conference and its associated interaction charges my batteries completely. I return home energized and ready to attack issues that wore me out just a week before.

Another means to gain information is from the many Web sites and e-mail services that are dedicated to locating, isolating, and repairing issues with operating systems, software, and computer platforms in general. When one cuts through the pontificating, bickering, and outright fighting, there is much valuable information to be had. By carefully sifting through these offerings and forwarding likely input to the application groups responsible for each, we have established a much better beachhead in the technical arena. The objective is to get the techies to appreciate what we do as much as do the nontechnical masses (they do, don't they?) and to look to us to inform them of issues and, if we are reading the right media, providing them with viable patches.

Finally, we go to the media, particularly the periodic media versions found on the Internet. What we quickly see is that a monthly magazine can never be anything but a snapshot in time. By the time the issue reaches the stands or subscribers, its contents are old news. In the online versions, information is updated daily at the very least. In most cases, news is posted as it happens. There are many changes daily. When it comes time to publish the monthly version, it will mirror a snapshot again, this time closer to deadline. In the text of this chapter, I mentioned a number of sources and gave a number of URLs, so that you could review them as well. I will not repeat them here.

Finally, we get to the bulletin board types of sites. These are sites that gather postings on new issues, weaknesses, or software flaws that the writer has noted and, in many cases, e-mail them to an established mailing list. Get yourself on a bunch of those lists. Again, the URLs or keywords are listed. Often, with a burst of largesse or just plain ego, solutions to the problems listed are included, either in the form of a patch or a configuration change that will alleviate the issue.

There is a dark side, even to this good work. In many cases the hacker community talks about what they are doing and what they are planning to do, with relative abandon. Find some of the sites and just listen in. However, do not go through the company network or PBX. Use an outside line and pseudonym and make sure to mop up your cookie file on a regular basis. When you disconnect from one of these sites, stay disconnected.

As with any of life's experiences, there is always something to be gained by reviewing the experiences of others. By gaining access to them and methodically picking through what can and cannot be used, we enrich our own intellect and have materials to share and to build on.

There is, in fact, so much information out there that can enrich our individual programs that I cannot help but raise my own relatively thin and graying eyebrows.

Chapter 20

Working with the Auditors for Fun and Pleasure

As I have done a number of times before, I will begin this chapter with the viewpoint of a colleague or someone who achieved fame in one or another way. In this case, I am drawn to a description by Bob Courtney, one of the true pioneers in the field of information systems security. Bob had a way of telling stories in such an understated manner that the most outrageous events seem incredibly humorous at his telling. However, there was one point upon which he rarely attempted to be funny. That issue was the term *auditor* which, for reasons known best to himself, he could not utter without preceding it with the word *damned*. In fact, I believe that my relating this story is absent the exclamation point that I am certain followed the entire two-word phrase.

Unfortunately, and for too many years, Bob's evaluation was echoed by many in information systems in general, and when our profession came along, we took up the cry as well. Few realized that the foundation for what we do was a direct result from a lot of their work, as well. Still, the animosity continued up until well into the 1980s.

Before we go too much further into this dissertation, let us first identify all of the players. We have internal and external auditors; of that everyone is certain. However, there are some refinements to that definition that will demonstrate that we are dealing with a far wider variety of practitioners than it would appear at first glance.

Internal auditors are pretty much internal auditors. Generally, they come in two flavors: financial and information systems. The last definition is still a bit vague in some companies; it is highly refined and is staffed by highly skilled professionals in others. Fortunately, the majority falls toward the top of that scale, and they are getting even better day by day. In some organizations, IS auditor is on the career path for skilled programming and operations types on their way to management. To say the least, working with an auditor that has been on your side of the fence is much easier than working with one who is not fully aware of how your business runs.

External auditors have a number of different faces as they may be representatives of the third-party auditing team that comes in annually to make sure that you are effectively guarding the stockholders' revenue stream or they may be from a regulatory agency of one or another type. As examples:

If you are in the financial business, you have dealt with auditors — regulators, they used to call themselves — from the National Home Loan Bank (NHLB) or Federal Depositors Insurance Commission (FDIC) if you are in the Savings and Loan business. These regulators make certain that your bookkeeping is in order, that you maintain sufficient reserves against loss or default, and that you take proper precautions in your dealings with the public and corporations and that you maintain reasonable security in all operations, including information processing.

Full-service banks have pretty much the same type of regulators with whom they deal. In this case, we are talking about the Federal Reserve Board and the Comptroller of the Currency if you are federally chartered and any number of state regulators if you are state chartered. Just as the definitions of a full-service bank and a savings and loan are growing closer together, so are the responsibilities of the regulators.

I see no point in further defining the different types of reviews of state or federally regulated organizations. If you work in those industries, you are fully familiar with who comes calling once a year. It might be the Atomic Energy Commission or some state health care regulator, but you will see them.

What most of us are familiar with is the good old Big 5 accounting firm auditors and our own internal folks. No matter what other regulators show up, these folks will be there as regularly as Christmas.

Interestingly, their work often overlaps tremendously. Despite the number of different agencies and internal and external folks that I mentioned, they all start out the same way: they have a look at what the last set of auditors did and review the steps taken to comply since that report was issued. In the cases of some state regulators I have known, that is about the extent of the audit. Others will review that and follow the thread to where the finding originally arose. Their report might well contain several more findings in the same area. The quality of the audit — particularly among regulators — varies widely.

Historically, our response upon seeing the final draft (previous to this time, we were not privy to the work papers and interim findings that came up along the way) was to accept those issues that we could respond to and set about finding a resolution to the point. Management expected us to alleviate whatever condition was defined and do it without spending any money. Is there any wonder that each set of auditors checked the findings from the last audit? If there was a cash outlay of any significance, the response was usually "working on it," a resolution that usually had a life span of several audit cycles.

This response, while waffling, was not really all that bad. The auditors, of whom I spoke earlier, often did not have the knowledge level, the time, or the willingness to delve more deeply into many of the issues they brought to light. And because they usually worked in a vacuum, they did not ask questions along the way. Very often, a response would demonstrate a compensating control down the road a bit that was totally missed by an auditor that either could not or did not get that far in the review. As often as not, it was a lack of knowledge as to how the system worked, rather than any lack of diligence.

This confrontational approach — even with our internal auditors (sometimes particularly with out internal auditors) — continued into the '80s, with a shift starting at that time. The internal folks were the first to experience the shift that only over the past 10 or 15 years has begun to take root in the relationship with the external folks. Regulators, on the other hand, are still often stifled by the lack of uniformity in the regulations within the framework of which they must operate, the uneven enforcement of regulation among jurisdictions, and the differing skill levels among those active in the discipline. The tendency is for them to follow the overall direction of public employees in whatever area they operate. As we know, the variation in capability, and therefore performance, ranges from excellent to inept. At their best, these people are not only serving the community well, but can assist you as well. At their worst, they rank right up there with poison ivy.

From time immemorial, the attitude of both auditors and auditees was that the objective of the engagement was to catch someone doing something that they should not be. The auditors hung each finding up like a poster and the audited parties scrambled to come up with resolutions before the board of directors got their copy. At least, they wanted to have some time to embark on searching for a resolution. Still, with no idea of what was likely to be in the audit until they saw the preliminary findings, the time they had to take steps was pretty short. Worse yet, they might well have to respond to something that could have been explained away had they known what the finding was.

The enmity between the two groups was pretty apparent to both parties and neither held much in when corresponding over the issues. Where the auditors dealt in "gotchas," the audited parties took particular delight in preparing responses that demonstrated how poorly researched the finding was and why there is no issue because of compensating controls, a poor measurement of the probable impact, or a host of other issues.

Whose fault was this confrontational relationship? It was, at the same time nobody's and everybody's. Auditors felt that they lived with the expectation that they would reveal all that operations was hiding, and the operations people viewed them as parasites there to do nothing but make them look bad. To say that the relationship was rocky was to say that Everest is a pretty fair-sized hill.

For the external auditors, it was often a pretty easy gig to live with. They got to come in, do their work, present it to management to demonstrate everything they had caught the operation at, and be on their way, leaving the audited party with a list of to do's that might or might not be reasonably doable. Better yet, they were not there to explain their actions, once the final report had been delivered, but went on their merry way to spread ill will and dissent elsewhere. Very often, if the audit was performed by one of the big accounting houses, the same auditors would not be coming back for the next engagement a year from now. That meant that there was little or no way in which the individual caught any of the potential repercussions for the work done.

The internal auditors had a different problem altogether. They not only had to deliver the audit, but also had to live with the resultant fallout from that point forward. They were expected to know the systems they were auditing a lot better and were therefore held to be more responsible for the resultant task plans that evolved from the attempts to resolve the finding. If, indeed, the finding was deemed to be off center, it was the internal auditor who took the heat for sloppy or incomplete work.

The credibility issues with which the internal auditors had to deal is probably what led to the gradual shift in the relationship between their department and the ones they had to audit. Their choices were really pretty much between the proverbial rock and a hard place. They could hold back and "make nice" with an audit, in order to not incur the wrath of the audited party. Or, they could come down hard and live with the result while basking in the adoration of management for their "hard-hitting, devil take the hindmost" approach to getting to the bottom of things.

As the reporting structure of the company and the personalities of the individuals were mixed into the situation, both types of auditors came out of the brew. In many cases, a single information systems auditor was charged with reviewing the entire environment and was able to only skim the surface over the course of a year. The findings were rarely of any depth and the fixes were easy enough so that IS management did not mind them at all. They could repair the issue with minimal expenditure of resources and could point out how seriously they were taking the auditor's recommendations. Looked great, on the surface, even though greater problems might have been hidden just below that plane. I hasten to add that the larger problems of which I speak might not have been recognized by the operations folks and might have been noted by a more detailed audit. In short, the feel-good audits that might have gone on for years might well have left the company seriously exposed to a calamity.

Going back to the other extreme, we had the avenging angel of internal audit. This person's one direction in life was to bring to light the issues that the operations area had obviously been hiding. There was no way that any department could be clean as it was the function of management to hide as much dirty laundry as possible in order to make themselves look good. No way was that going to get by *this* auditor! Of course, the upshot of this approach was that they did, indeed, hide things from the auditor and did whatever they could to be uncooperative. If audit wanted a war, by gosh, they were going to get it.

It does not take any level of genius to see that either of these approaches misses the mark substantially.

I cannot say where it started, or with whom, but somewhere in the early 1980s, someone realized that this combative approach to auditing was doing no one any good. The big accounting houses saw the trend to where their engagements were not getting the reaction they should and began recruiting auditors with better people skills and redirected their approach to make certain that no enmity was created by their coming into a company to do a review.

Still, I believe that the credit goes to the internal auditors and, to a great extent, our own colleagues in information systems security. We were the first IS internal function actually on a search and destroy mission against weaknesses that could harm or destroy our systems or the information resident upon them. Now, with the auditors also having the charter to do at least the first part — the search — we finally had an ally. And, with our usual ready acceptance of using someone else's resources to accomplish our ends, the marriage was all but sealed.

Offhand, I cannot recall when I first established a symbiotic relationship with the auditors, but I do clearly recall that it was the internal version, the ones who lived in the same house. They found that by talking with me before an engagement, they had a better idea as to what they were getting into. I, on the other hand, discovered that by knowing where they would be looking, I could assist in making certain that they got the whole picture and could come up with in-depth findings and recommendations that were viable in the environment that they came to know so much better due to my contributions.

This type of easy communications began leading to more and more conversations during the life of the engagement and not just at the beginning and end. We were actually conversing about issues as they were being reviewed. Strangely, the auditors began asking me about things that they did not fully understand and I was more than happy to respond, rather than have to field a finding that really did not exist once the whole picture was understood.

As this type of relationship continued to grow, I found that I could take the same approach with the external auditors as well. In this case, I initiated the relationship and discovered that in this arena, too, we could come up with a product that made both of us look better and headed off the heated exchanges that so often accompanied an exit conference.

It was from these initial beginnings that I began formulating what I call the *audit interface* function, a real and working part of information security. It is worthy of including in a job description and having project level time assigned to it. I will explain in the following paragraphs.

Why, I reasoned, could we not have an integral working relationship with the auditors just as we do with the other departments and outside parties with whom we deal on a regular basis. After all, their aims are the same as ours — to make certain that corporate information and its processing are as effectively protected as possible.

To this end, I first volunteered to be the contact point for the auditors when they came into our shop on their next engagement. My plan was to demonstrate that we could, by working together, issue a better product that served the needs of both participants. Under the circumstances, I extended my hand first.

When an audit team made their first contact with the organization for which I was working at the time, I had my name placed as the contact for the audit lead. I further made certain that he was urged to contact me as early before he was to arrive as possible. I figured I ought to be a person, rather than just a name, as quickly as practical. I suspect that this was one of the first times he was afforded the opportunity to talk to someone this early in the game.

My first order of business in our first conversation was to ascertain his space needs during the engagement. How many people was he bringing in? What type of dial-out capability did he need? Did they need a conference room in which to spread out and work? Were they planning on leaving records or equipment on site that would need to be locked up after hours? What were the names of the folks he was bringing in? We wanted to have security clearance for them and made certain that badges were ready for them when they arrived.

The next issue I discussed with him was the scope of his work. What did they plan to look at? What did they need to make the work as brief and effective as possible? In what form did he need it? Who did they need to speak to during the duration of their stay? In what order did they wish to speak with them, and starting when?

Note: In most instances, an auditor can tell you the functional responsibility of the people they wish to speak with, rather than having names. I made certain to get them in touch with the right people on the schedule that they needed.

Now that I had a date for their arrival and had started making appointments for the auditor *and me*, I began reviewing my shopping list for records they had requested. Usually, there were a series of logs to be checked and some other general reports needed. Almost without fail, access lists to various areas and applications were requested.

At the time this was going on, the shift from 11" × 14" paper was just taking place. Most printing was now being done on 8½ by 11", but green stripe was still much in evidence. It made for an interesting show when the audit team arrived. I took care of getting them through security and walked them into the conference room I had reserved for their entire stay. I must admit a certain amount of amusement when I watched a few chins drop when they found the table covered with the information they had requested.

Note: Remember, this was some years ago. Today we would not have the remains of so many deceased trees out there, but would have arranged for accesses to the online areas they had to check to find this same information.

Of course, all accesses would be logged.

You will note that I made a point of stressing the words "and me" in the statement above about setting appointments with the people they needed to confer with. My aim in this instance was to be able to intercede if any misunderstandings occurred. Also, it let me be in position to ascertain whether we were, indeed, talking to the right person. In many cases, discussion demonstrated that we needed to go elsewhere to find the specific information that the auditor needed. This is not always easily spotted by someone not familiar with the organization.

Once we had the folks busily working with the materials we had provided and with continued interface with the members of the managerial and technical staff they needed to interview in order to complete their work, I was able to limit the time I spent with them. I did make a point of visiting with them once a day at minimum. Before turning them loose on their own and at each daily meeting, I made a point of stressing that I was always available to answer questions and to help them expand their knowledge of a given issue. Note that we are still doing very much the same thing as we did in the old days, only now we are doing it cooperatively.

At a number of junctures during the review, I made a point of getting together with the entire audit team, to go over their findings to date and to discuss just how accurate their reading of the situation was. Often, we were able to expand their knowledge to show the compensating controls we spoke of earlier. Soon I did not have to come to them; they were calling me if something did not look right or if they needed more information or direction.

Ultimately, we got to talking to one another as colleagues, rather than opponents. If they found something that did not look right, they often called me to verify that what they were looking at was what it seemed. When they started to synthesize their statements of findings, we went over them together. If remedial action was already in place for one of the findings, that fact was included in the write-up. In short, by the time the interim report draft was completed, I knew everything contained in it. It would be pretty hard to surprise anyone in this position with the content of the final report.

Even at this early stage of the game, I tried to get the parties involved in the interviews and the auditors together for meetings to discuss things as they were going. Generally, we were able to go over the findings that were now being formulated and, in many cases, work with them to make certain that the composition and wording clearly explained the issue in a fair and open-minded manner. If work was underway to fix the issue, it was included as a part of the finding. More interesting yet was the ability that meetings of this type gave us to demonstrate that some of what they were calling findings were risks that had been recognized and that our management had chosen to take in order to continue work in the most effective manner. There was not always agreement, but the statement that the risk was recognized and assumed was in there.

By the time we got to the draft report, all parties involved knew and had their input into what was printed. In many cases, we had assisted in word-smithing the terminology and statement to an agreed-upon level of clarity of meaning. While not everyone always agreed, all input was heard and considered. Also, they now had time to prepare a statement on their own, should the findings actually fall to them. After all, this was preliminary and there were a number of opportunities ahead in which to modify the findings and their weightings.

Once the initial draft report was complete, I set up a meeting between all of the persons on the auditing side and the individuals with whom they spoke throughout their stay. I also invited the managers of the departments that had been audited. Together, with me moderating, we went through the preliminary report finding by finding. In many instances we worked over the tenor of the finding and the issues it addressed. Often, there were wording modifications based on agreement between the two sides.

To many, this might sound like an overbearing corporate entity keeping up the pressure on the auditors to say what we felt management wanted to hear. Those of you who think that have obviously never worked with an auditor. They will say what they want, and we simply presented them with additional facts when they needed them (not when we felt they needed them). The result of this first attempt to have all parties cooperate to the benefit of the company were advantageous to all. The auditors completed their assignment with time to spare and the audited departments knew exactly what was in the final report and had the opportunity to air their concerns and opinions about the findings that were agreed upon.

I hasten to add that no effort was ever made to intimidate anyone nor to force the dropping or complete gutting of a finding. The advantage was in the tone of the statement, its factual content, the recognition of work already done or in progress, and the preparation to address it at an earlier date.

I have continued using this methodology in audit engagements for the 20 years or so that have passed since this first effort at approaching the issue together. To be sure, there have been modifications made to the process as time and the technology change, but the spirit of the process is as it was when I first used it.

Now, let us talk about the auditors, particularly the internal ones, and their role in getting your job done. As we have mentioned, the aims of the auditors and you are pretty much the same, in terms of protecting company information assets. However, big differences do exist in our relationship to the problems cited. For one, you, as the information security professional, have to resolve the issue. The auditor simply has to recognize it. Second, you go to your management in seeking funding to fix a noted issue. They go to the board of directors and the senior management committee with their findings, a place you rarely get any insight into.

What if the findings that get to the final presentation reflect some of your unfunded concerns? The circumstances would certainly raise the knowledge and interest among those senior folks of the need to fix the issue once and for all. Now, I am not for a moment suggesting that you load the auditor with your concerns to be fired off at the final findings delivery. Still, if you have been working closely, there is some chance that the auditor would notice the things that frustrate you. Never can tell what a good auditor might pick up.

The methodology I have described has proven extremely effective for me and for a number of my colleagues. Auditors, despite anything you might have heard, are people. Treat them as friends and the likelihood is that they will treat you the same way. Above all, respect what they do. To a great extent, they are well educated and often versed in our fields, as well.

I have found that this type of working relationship with internal audit has resulted in my getting their cooperation and assistance in such varying subjects as documentation and investigations. They have the interest and most want to learn your organization as well as possible. The better they know the landscape, the more effective and accurate their findings are going to be. And if they happen to run across an issue that you already have an interest in and write it up, and put it in their final findings, and senior management gets a look at it, your management just might find the funding to resolve it. What with direction coming from above, rather than below, they just might recognize the importance a bit more clearly.

Summary

Like dogs and cats, auditors and operations personnel have found themselves on opposite sides of the table on almost any issue they approach. The auditors, feeling that they are demonstrating their worth by plugging away at everything an organization does, gain the undying ill will of those they audit. Next time they come in, there is no help available, access to specific resources is impossible to get, and all answers are vague and misleading. Each reiteration of the engagement creates more stress and ultimately, the auditors find little because they are allowed little and make up for it with innuendo and attacks on the management of the department. Rarely is anything gained from this type of relationship.

The external auditor is at an extreme disadvantage in that the same people do not often do follow-up audits. So, they attempt to prove or disprove the findings of the earlier audit, only to find that the trail has grown cold, perhaps from the chilling effect of the work by the auditee to cover it. Again, little can be gained from that type of relationship.

Internal auditors, on the other hand, were, and often still are, treated as the pariahs of the management team. Despite their performing a valuable service, they are often perceived as spies or worse by operations departments.

Regulatory auditors are the least predictable of all. Most of them could be making more money in the private sector, so there is a chance that they might not be good enough to be on staff there. By the same token, state regulations differ, as do the expectations of the audit department. In one state you may have an excellent practitioner, working in a system that is strict but fair; in another, you may have little regulation and the auditors might be accountants pressed into service. Worst case of all, the position might be simple political patronage, with totally unqualified individuals being there strictly because someone owed someone else a favor.

What I have attempted to demonstrate in this chapter is that one can leverage the work of the auditors, no matter which classification, by working with them and making sure that they have full access to what they need and full cooperation in their work. By doing this, you can be certain to have input to their findings and be able to gain insight into the way that they are preparing their report. I hasten to add that when I say input, I mean wordsmithing and providing input on the larger picture as they work up their findings. I do not in any way refer to any efforts to coerce or in other ways force changes in the findings. As stated before, this relationship must be symbiotic, with each element providing value to the relationship.

Remember that if an auditor happens upon a situation that you feel requires attention, the auditor's position is likely to be similar. If that finding hits the final report, senior management will be aware of the exposure without your talking with them at all.

Internal audit has the same charter as you: do what is best for the company. Often, their review serves as an extra set of eyes with a different point of view. They just might see something that you have missed, just from being too close to it. If a weakness is found, they will be right next to you fighting to get it righted. In the language I speak, that makes them allies, not enemies.

Chapter 21

Keep Your Eye on the Industry

There is an old joke that never seems to go away: the person that has the most trouble keeping up with the Joneses is poor Old Man Jones. He works hard, but cannot seem to keep up with the material desires of his family, even though he is managing all of the necessities for life. Still, his hard work has provisioned his spouse and brood with the accoutrements that breed jealousy wherever they go. No one has noticed that Mr. Jones is the one suffering for all of the splendor.

Our objective is not necessarily to follow the Jones clan around, trying to match their expenditures and collection of riches, but to closely observe them and figure out what they have that is making them worthy of emulation. Find that component and we have matched their success without having matched their cash outlay. By the time our research is well on its way, Pop Jones just might want to abandon his brood to adopt us!

This story, hokey though it may be, demonstrates an important point: Throwing cash at a given issue or shotgunning every new potential exposure is an extremely unrewarding activity. We want to have all the advantages that the Joneses do, but we do not expect to have all of the frills, bells, and whistles that they have attached to them. And, as has been stated since the beginning of this discussion, no one has asked Mr. Jones how he feels about what is going on and if he feels benefited in any way. As usual, he is expected to pick up the tab, with little or no insight into the selection process. With luck, he will gain some benefit, but there is no guarantee. Would one not expect him to become a bit less generous as the material goods mount up — along with the bills — and he has not yet seen any benefit from the outlay?

Is corporate management so different from Daddy Jones? Probably not too much. In the beginning, he (they) accept requests for funding for pet projects on the premise that the outcome of the purchase will be of visible advantage to them. Perhaps one or two such rubber stamp approvals will be taken on faith, but it will not be long before results are demanded. And, I can assure you, management is not in love with you or your function as Mr. Jones is with his family. Their patience with you, or lack thereof, will in no way match his.

Every industry is a bit different and a bit the same. There are thousands of different lines of business out there, but there are not that many major purveyors of equipment and software. Whether you are a grocery chain or a software giant, you still have to process your orders, pay your vendors, collect from your customers, and crunch the numbers for the tax people. In your particular situation, you have to make sure that the systems are being used in a prudent manner, that the network is safe from break-in, and that all employees are aware of their responsibility in maintaining that level of security. We have spent the last 20 chapters discussing that. Your job will differ materially, if not significantly, based upon the type of company you are.

As an example of the statement above, I bring to mind the financial industry. If they are a savings and loan, they have to follow a full set of regulations set forth by the federal government or a state association. If they are a federally chartered full-service bank, they have another set of rules to follow; if a state chartered bank, yet another set. A similar situation comes into play with other corporations as well. Utilities are regulated, usually by the states they do business in. If they generate power through nuclear reactors, the Atomic Energy Commission hands them a few manuals on how they are to do that.

Without going into further examples, I think we can agree that while we all process information and concern ourselves with protecting it, the types of information and the threats to it will vary widely. What works for one industry might not work in another.

Much of this is based on the types of software designed and sold to respond to the needs of a specific industry. At the same, we are called upon to train the users of that information in how to recognize what is important, what aspect of it is likely to come under attack, and what the actual threats might look like. A financial institution, for instance, might have their concerns based on not allowing customer records to be compromised and, at the same time, keeping financial records and information from being misused. On another plane, a forest products company will find that their Web sites are particularly vulnerable to protest from one or another fringe group that has appointed themselves guardians of the trees.

So, along with consideration for the way we have to educate users, we need to familiarize ourselves with the types of systems that are likely to be employed and the specialized software tools that may be purchased for those specialized purposes.

Visualize a company that manufactures electronic parts for worldwide distribution. They are successful in an extremely competitive industry because their product line is based on proprietary designs. To say that these designs are sensitive is to say that a skunk is a bit aromatic. No words can say it quite strongly enough.

Is this electronics company concerned about eco-terrorists or industrial espionage? Certainly, the forest products organization is more concerned with the former, the design for a tree being held somewhere higher than at corporate headquarters! However, to steal, rather than destroy, information would be the aim of someone attacking the electronics company.

Most of us got into this niche in the industry through working in systems areas, and the concept of industry-specific software is no novelty. What I am attempting to point out is although we do bring a buck in the front door in much the same way — provide a product or service to an identifiable end user — we face different marketing issues when selling our information security awareness program to management and, ultimately, to our end user, the corporate staff. We can keep up with the Joneses if we must, but we had better be very certain that it is not the Smiths that we should be watching. I guarantee that the electronics concern is more paranoid about protecting formulas and drawings than in scraping demonstrators off of the walls.

I mentioned the idea of industry-specific software a few paragraphs earlier and I would like to explore that a bit now.

No matter what industry you work in, I can guarantee that you get mail daily from vendors with software and other tools that are designed to make your life better and simpler in dealing with the security of your systems. A majority of the offers will be for generic or pan-industry tools to protect communications, databases, dial-up access, or any number of other across the board concerns. However, a significant percentage of the products will be directed at your particular industry.

In either case, you have two questions to answer immediately: One, will it help? And two, can I sell the idea to my audience (total staff)?

Assuming that it does raise your interest, another set of questions is raised. Does the product offer advantages that I cannot acquire easily (or more cheaply) elsewhere? Do I really need all of the features it offers? What is the training curve to get it into use by our employees?

All of the usual product evaluation questions come into play if you are happy with the answers for a significant percentage of the baseline questions above. Is the vendor solid? Do they have references? Has the product been reviewed? By whom? When? I need not go into the rest of the details.

Just remember, if you are Smith, you might not need Jones's answer.

Every modification you make to your security environment is an opportunity to sell the overall program. If you change a process, let them know what the new way is all about and what it is going to do for them. If you add a new software product, laud it to the sky, while teaching them about it. Couch it in terms of what it is going to do for the company, rather than what it is going to require of the staff. This is diplomacy at its highest form. You sell a change in terms of what it will provide. You get buy-in by telling them how little it is going to cost in terms of behavior modifications on their parts and overhead (assuming that there is a noticeable impact).

Note: If there is an overhead challenge involved in a new process or control software, take another long look at it. In today's processing environment, there is rarely enough to be gained from any new tool to absorb a significant hit in performance. For one, there are too many products out there to settle for one that beats up your system. Two, if your security program is so lame that a reasonable step toward greater protection causes a significant change in systems response or ease of use, you have too much other work to do before adding new software. Save the purchase until your house is in order.

Every alteration of this type is a window of opportunity to add to your educational materials. Take a good look at your training materials, your periodical articles, and your bulletin schedule and find places to add in materials about the new product and why it is better than the old way. As I mentioned above, tell them what it buys them, and how low the cost is.

My suggestion is to build up a product or program well ahead of its installation. Start with an introduction based on the approval of the product/ change. Your first communications should be based on what solutions the product offers. Ask the question, "How can you secure your terminal with one finger?" Assuming that we are using some type of screen locking device/ program, this makes a good lead in. It tells people that something is coming and it intimates that whatever it is, **it's a cinch to operate and things are going to be better.** Continue along those lines as often as you can.

I had mentioned any online communications media that the company has as the best means to place these short messages. As we spoke of earlier, posters can be used in this manner. Try being pretty cryptic early on. Raise questions, without answering too many. As you give more and more infor-mation as implementation (or training) approaches, begin using the company logo of a purchased product or acronyms for a built product. Whatever means you use, have people waiting for the next blurb.

Once we are on top of the training date for a change of a magnitude that requires formal training, you can start "advertising," rather than playing mind games with your audience. Let them know exactly what is about to enter their lives and start talking about what it will do for them and for the company. Make no mention of any negatives.

Note: As mentioned earlier, there are sufficient resolutions to any given problem that making something difficult is a good way to keep it on the shelf, either in a vendor's warehouse or in your own library. Today's world has the most computer literate population of all time and hardware and software that complement one another to the extent of allowing products to be created with enough tutorial and intuitive function to allow any but the least sophis-ticated to learn and function within it quickly. Most often, the learning curve is a part of putting it to use in production.

Very often, the last and most detailed informative publications you will put out preceding implementation can have the instructions for the use of the new product included. If the vendor uses the intuitive nature of the product as a selling point, sell in the same manner. Use corporate e-mail to either reinforce those instructions or to deliver them in the first place. Toggling back and forth between windows is the easiest of all ways to learn online, so to speak.

So, do the Joneses have this newest addition to your security arsenal? Or, did you learn about it from them. The latter being true, they just might have some training materials that you could use. Better yet, they could very easily tell you what cliffs they walked off in the process of implementing. No sense both of you kissing the rocks at the bottom. By the same token, be ready and willing to share your experiences with others, should you implement before they do.

Often times, the way you contact the Joneses is through the vendor of the system in question. Now, you must understand that they are not going to give you clients that were less than satisfied, but sometimes they overestimate just how elated someone was with the product itself or support. I have, on occasion, had "references" tell me that if they had to do it over, they would not have purchased the product! Others, a bit less disillusioned, have told us of training issues and environmental impact as a part of their concerns. Under any circumstances, take advantage of any information you can pick up in this manner.

Vendors, as we all know, can be helpful or less than helpful, once a commitment to purchase their products has been made. I strongly suggest that you hold their feet to the fire to deliver everything contracted or even agreed to. If they promised training, make sure that exactly what they agreed to is delivered. If you deal with your corporate attorneys in finalizing a contract, make sure that you can give them chapter and verse about what was promised outside of the boilerplate. Believe me, they expect to get back a much-amended document because everyone knows that an auditor's ability to generate paper pales in the glare of a lawyer's impact on forestry. There used to be a Sahara forest, before lawyers started writing contracts.

The best time to work sales representatives for anything is while they are still in pursuit of the sale. Do not just work them to put additional training and propaganda materials in the contract, start working them for those things **up front**. If you can get sample copies of full-function demos into enough hands, you will have your training and publication needs covered. It sure is nice to have three or four analysts working at a terminal and deciding how best to teach the troops how to use what you are just then trying to learn to use.

Sales reps can be very helpful and almost any of them can act like they are your best friend. Indeed, they can become friends in some instances. Just make certain to understand that their first responsibility is to move product, and that does not always totally overlay your needs.

That leads us to another aspect of keeping up with the Joneses.

One of the major components of any advertising campaign is the reference section. Somehow, a products just released has a list of "satisfied users" from here to Oraibi. If it has been in the marketplace in one form or another for any length of time, the list will look like the Fortune 500.

When going over those references, do not concern yourself too much with the big names as much as the ones of companies in your workspace. I am not suggesting going to competitors, although there are times when there is enough contact between individuals with different companies to do so, but to look for some similarity in the market niche that you occupy. Rather than ask the vendor for names, do a little research and find out who tested and recommended the product. Also, find out what they think of it, of the support, and of the company.

Note: The comment made with reference to leveraging old relationships and talking to a direct competitor is not generally acceptable for all of the conflict of interest reasons. If you do go this way, I really suggest that it be off the cuff and used only for an informal opinion. Neither of you need the heartburn that more formal conversations can cause.

We have touched briefly on the value of attending industry or discipline specific conferences just a few chapters back. Such expeditions give you the opportunity to meet a thousand or more colleagues and to see what is being offered in the marketplace. I can virtually guarantee that if you stand long enough at a booth that is pushing a product in which you have an interest, someone who has it installed will come by. Now, I do not suggest picking the person's brain right there on the spot, beyond a few general questions. However, make a point of meeting later during the session and unload all of the questions you might have.

Another source of input on the viability of a given product is to attend sessions addressing some aspect of working with it. In many cases, an hour or hour and a half are dedicated strictly to that product and its application in industry. Bring your questions there and ask whatever questions you might have. Watch for "weighted" facts if the presentation is dealer offered, as it well might be — although most reputable conference organizers try to prevent that from happening with general use products (yes, Junior, Microsoft is allowed to talk about Windows) so as to prevent their becoming sales pitches to a captive audience. Look for sessions run by consulting groups or specialists from major corporations. In most cases, they will address the issue, only then making observations on the tools available to cope with it. Generally, their biases are pretty clear up front, although if you do not hear of any connections between the product lines and the speaker, ask if they resell any of the tools mentioned. Very few will utter a direct lie, even if they wish you had not asked.

Off-line discussions often yield more information yet. These same presenters all are most likely willing conversants at a relaxed moment outside of the sessions. Have your questions and ask.

I would be remiss in not mentioning the paper and conceptual items you can glean from these conferences that will help you communicate the ideas and parameters of the product and an impending installation at your own company. Use their words, if need be, to describe the product, function, and expected performance by your staff members.

Once you have decided on a product for purchase, you should renew your contacts with the individuals at other companies whose experiences with said product convinced you to add it to your arsenal. Now, your questions are about their experiences in implementation and training of staff to use it. Make no mistake: what they have to say is valuable, if only to convince you not to take the same approach they did. This can actually take two different colors: if what they did failed to work effectively and they recognized it, or if the way they implemented and trained did not work and they failed to notice it. In the former case, work with them to understand where the pitfalls were and what they did to correct the situation. Brainstorm a bit if they acknowledge that things are still not as good as they might be. Perhaps they can retrofit your ideas into their environment. Do not worry too much about doing their job, as the information you are amassing is reward enough.

In the other situation, we face something entirely different. If they are sitting in a mess and fail to realize it, continue to work through their methods until you are satisfied that you have discovered each screw up, no matter its size. As you implement, you do know some things to dodge, now, do you not?

Of course, you will have the vendor's information, as mentioned above, with which to create your publication and training materials. They are always excellent and never mislead a potential buyer, right? Obviously, your contact at the company that has already implemented was exposed to those materials — or the precedent version — as well as the product itself. That would mean that you not only have a product insight, but good insight into the training materials and their applicability. This information itself is useful in putting your own program together.

We have continually throughout this book talked about leveraging other areas to the advantage of the information security program and the need to make the general corporate populace aware of conditions and performance expectations with regard to the entire program in general and this product evaluation, purchase, and implementation in particular. Let us take a look at the roles of these other folks in terms of the entire process.

If, indeed, we have formed the bonds with these external parties as we have discussed in the past, then the only wild cards in this deck will be the vendor staff and the contacts you have made external to the company. The last mentioned of these participants are the folks in whose shoes you will walk in very short order. Perhaps we need to get them involved and familiar with some of the other players at a point before the purchase is completed.

Once the decision to pursue the product is understood, it would be most prudent to set up a few meetings with the project team involved in the evaluation and your outside connections. Assuming that the two involved companies are not raging competitors, this should be pretty low key, with the project team probing for information as to the value of the product, the validity of the advertising claims, and the issues involved in implementation. If your environments are similar, there will be a lot of compatibility issues to be ironed out. This is the best possible arena to discuss that.

Later, once negotiations are complete and assuming that the purchase is pending, is a good time to get your training people together with whoever designed and delivered the training at the other company. Trainers speak their own language and they will quickly iron out the best approach, the time needed to complete, and some ideas as to form and format.

Your job, now partially completed, as you have participated in the selection process, gets polished up during these last interchanges. You already have the product features in hand, you know what issues the product is being purchased to address, and you have now heard the opinions of your colleagues, the training people, and the implementation folks as to how each is going to do their respective jobs. This is the point at which you leverage all of that information into your awareness plan. From these beginnings, awareness programs grow.

I will not go further into whether to use posters, trinkets, special classes, or other media to introduce the end users to the product and its function.

We have covered that pretty effectively in the past 20 or so chapters. What I want to mention here is the scaled introduction of the process. As mentioned earlier, start with an "It's coming!" approach. Using just a name and a date (the go-live date), you can let people know that something is going to change and when it is going to happen. This approach also piques curiosity and your next missive should expand only a bit. By the time you have done three of these, timed to precede going live by about four weeks, they are ready for a full overview and a countdown time line until D-Day.

From this point forward, you are back in your own bailiwick: the place we have invented throughout this book.

Summary

Contrary to popular belief, all good ideas do not originate here. By the same token, they do not always originate elsewhere, either. We need to mind our knitting, but should be paying a lot of attention to what is going on elsewhere. As we have discussed, colleagues with whom we speak on a regular basis, trade publications, and even the media are constantly full of hot new ideas that have been built to respond to threats that are becoming more newsworthy every day. Viruses, for instance, are no longer our private hell, but have the star quality to merit front page coverage in many national news sources. The jury is still out as to whether that is a good thing or bad, as we do not know whether the publicity will encourage new and better efforts just for the notoriety, or if the knowledge in the user community will cause an awareness and consequently, stop the attack more quickly.

As an added potential plus, this media coverage often stirs the antivirus product vendors into quicker response and, therefore, a shorter viable life for the virus.

A mistake we must guard against is to want every new thing on the shelf. While our knowledge of the problems we face and the steps needed to neutralize them can allow us a more rational decision than someone else might make, we do have to guard against the desires of management, who learn of many of these threats through that same media we just discussed, to have that "thing" that defeats that "stuff" they just read about in the paper. Now, while this level of hysteria is often a way to bolster a budget, it can have repercussions if you purchase it on their whim and it fails to deliver as advertised. Somehow, that is when it becomes your baby instead of theirs.

Pick and choose carefully before recommending the purchase of a new product. If need be, use the media hype to justify the purchase, but make sure it is something with which you can live and not just something to spend money on.

There are a number of things you can do to make sure that a potential curative miracle is really right for you. Ask questions, such as:

- Will it live and play well in my environment?
- Does it meet with the criteria currently present in my industry, e.g., does it or its function meet with regulators' requirements?

- Does it address threats consistent with those we face in our industry?
- Can we reference its performance and promises with someone in our own industry? Is it someone known to us and whose credibility is respected?
- Is it worth the price? In every company, we find people who can build certain things; would we be able to build something that not only works as well, but is better suited to our environment?
- What does the vendor company look like? Have they been around awhile? Do they have a solid installed base on earlier products?
- Will it fit smoothly into our operating environment?
- What type of user training is required? Is the product relatively intuitive to use, or will we have to hold weeklong classes for everyone who might use the system?
- Does the company provide training tools?
- Do colleagues that have implemented have any constructive advice about the product and training?
- Do they have something that we might use? This includes negative experiences that, if not show-stoppers unto themselves, will tell us what *not* to do.
- What is it going to take to sell it to the troops?
- Can you get publicity materials to begin "early warning" messages before going live?
- What kind of program of information and training can you develop in order to make the product acceptable to all users?
- Beyond the experiences of those you know personally, what type of references can the vendor provide? Can you get the names of the beta testers? Can you find out what they learned and if the vendor responded accordingly?
- Has the product been available and does it have sufficient industry acceptance and an installed base that would make it worthwhile for training or a conference group to put on a seminar with regard to using it?
- Or, as in the preceding item, is it one of a group of products directed at a function that might be explored by such a seminar? That way, the product, in company of other, similar products, would be explored in a comparative manner with regard to its value in resolving the problem.
- At the same type of seminar, one meets a number of people with the same issues. Would that not be the perfect forum for making comparisons among peers facing the same problems?
- Is the sales rep a really great person? Funny, they all are. Watch for someone trying to substitute charm for substance.
- Finally, does it work in your industry, in your environment? Even if there are potential alternate solutions, is this the best? Will it do the job, even if it is not?

Every year, hundreds of new issues arise and thousands of software tools are created to address them. Some are good, some are great, some are a total waste of time and money. We are in the position of having to make a decision as to whether one will resolve our problems and live quietly in our neighborhood.

Also, we are often the voice of reason when someone from another organization adopts a tool and those around us are clamoring to get the same one. Again, we have to decide whether it will do for us what is needed. Needless to say, we, too, have to guard against jumping on the bandwagon just because someone else does.

Certainly, demonstrated need is the best way to gain financing to introduce new tools or processes into the company. However, we must continue to pick and choose wisely. We are not allowed too many mistakes before our credibility takes a hit large enough to keep us from getting funding for something that must be done.

Most of all, remember the plight of Old Man Jones. He had to keep up with a family that wanted and got everything. Ultimately, he, who got nothing from it, had to pay the piper.

Chapter 22

So Much for Today, On to Tomorrow

We have spent a serious amount of time talking about building a program, leveraging resources, and augmenting, as the situation demanded. Now, let us talk about how we keep our program viable and responsive.

One of the easiest things to do once you have put a program in place is to sit back and collect the plaudits for a job well done. Now, everyone takes the information security awareness class when they first come on board, you have a training system to pick up those that were here before the class was offered, and you have leveraged every piece of paper in the company to get your pearls of wisdom in front of the masses.

Among your other accomplishments has been to build a full policy, standards, and procedures document of lo, these many pages, and you have even gotten your HTML skills up to a point where you have been able to put up your own (information security) Web page on which to post all of this documentation. You have worked with the graphics people to put posters in likely locations, you have formed a virus response team, and have made certain that you have a means to get information to the masses in short order.

Now we can sit back and relax, right?

Information systems, either as a relatively imprecise science or as it pertains to the end user, is among the most rapidly changing environments. New viruses appear, new software, each with appropriate holes in it, falls out of the sky on us. And we have: complacency.

Sounds pretty scary, does it not?

When I think about the need for change and the speed at which we are forced to do it, I am reminded about an old story: It seems that a specific ship in our U. S. Navy was captained by a tyrant that came right out of the Captain Queeg mold. His idea of a happy ship was a working ship, and he brooked no loafing among the crew under his command.

On a specific warm, South Pacific afternoon, while the crews of the rest of the ships in the flotilla were relaxing and taking in the sun's warmth, a young seaman on Captain Queeg's ship was applying a new coat of paint to a specific bulkhead that had been scraped down and painted away too many times previously. As he finished his labors, he sat down for a moment to rest. As luck would have it, who should happen by at that precise moment, but the captain, himself. "Sailor," he barked, "Just what do you think you're doing!" "Sir," came the reply from the quick-thinking sailor, "I just painted this bulkhead and now I'm waiting for it to dry so I can swab it down!"

We are, at this time, in swabbing mode. As each project was completed, we embarked on other projects, sometimes forgetting to think about going back to swab down our particular past accomplishments. These things need to be refreshed, lest they become out of date and, therefore, no longer valid. Let us take a look at some of the things we have discussed throughout this document and see what we mean.

First off, of course, is the heavy documentation that we discovered, caused to be prepared, prepared on our own, or collected from outside sources. When we put it in place, it was as apropos as possible, for that day's issues. Today, however, may present a far different picture. Let us say, for instance, that you completed your standards and procedures document in 1997. That would only make it four years old (at this writing). Of course, you did have a section in there about PDAs and the more sophisticated instruments such as Palm Pilots, did you not? Simply because they were actually kind of rare in business at that time certainly does not mean that we would not have addressed them, does it? The fact is that as recently as 1997, Palm Pilots were in their infancy and few applications were available to do real business at that time. Putting a section on them into a procedure at that time was not germane and, therefore, not likely.

How about your virus section? Does it address e-mail attachments and the entire idea of address book attacking and replicating viruses? Again, we are talking about something that did not exist at that time. I can continue, but I think you have gotten the picture by now.

What, then, do we do?

First, start right at the beginning and begin reviewing your documents. Do not just do it yourself, but distribute a few copies to managers in information systems, who can have a shot at spotting things that have not been addressed due to their recent arrival in the environment or that have outlived their useful life as a part of the manual. (Anyone know what to do with a 5 1/4 inch diskette?) Section by section, go through the volume and, working in concert with your selected peers, begin identifying what has to be added, what has to change, and what ought to be dropped completely. Pay specific attention to what your help desk supervisor comes up with. Those folks hear more questions and have to give more direction than anyone else in the company. They can tell you in a heartbeat what questions they hear and what issues they cannot come up with a directive for. I am quite certain that their supervisor will use whatever statistics (not lies!) have been amassed and you will find that they have many suggestions for adds and replacement for what has become outdated.

Also, make a point of going through the standards you have created. Take the standard configuration for a desktop PC. Three years ago, a 350mHZ Pentium processor was the hottest thing out there and most of our standard configuration included a processor of that size. Today, that is a boat anchor! Three years ago, a 3-gigabyte hard drive was state of the art and nearly $400. Today, one three times that size is nearer $200.

There are a number of other steps to take in checking out the currency and validity of your documentation. As mentioned, the review should involve others, the same others at a regular interval, for the greatest chance of success. If your company does not have a policy review committee, this would be a wonderful chance to organize one.

What you can look for:

- Are there any parts of the work that are obviously no longer valid — e.g., standards for equipment no longer in place?
- Have descriptions of some standard operating procedures been forced to change because of changing conditions (new legislation, adoption of new software, etc.)?
- Are their equipment or software standards that have become outdated due to changes in technology or in the operation itself?
- Are there requirements that the company itself does not seem keen to support? You can lead a horse to water, but,,,,
- Does new technology warrant additions of sections? This might mean new to the industry or new to your organization.
- In a period of three years or so, you will have most certainly changed some aspects of your security scheme. Watch for chances to add in new processes (dial-up direction, smart cards, etc.) as they come to market or are adopted by your company. These items, under usual circumstances, are added or modified as the change takes place.
- Does your committee have advice on any issues they feel should change? If not at first, then certainly by the second iteration of the review, their input on such matters should be extremely valuable.

Make certain that if the fallout from these changes invalidates anything you have printed elsewhere — e.g. the new employee handbook — you make changes there by the very next addition to maintain your continuum.

Another thing to be careful to watch for is each issue of the company paper or another medium with which you communicate with the troops. Things will change, often replacing what was considered conventional wisdom with an entirely new viewpoint. A great example of that was the idea that you could stop spam by responding to the "Please remove my name from this mailing list" statement. Now, we know that the offer is almost always a gimmick for the senders to find out whether they are reaching someone out there. Then, a list can be built of the guaranteed e-mail addresses that will sell for a much higher price than did the original prospecting one.

As with anything else you do, examine the content of the article for changes that need to be made to current documentation.

The first real look new employees have of your program is what is presented in the information security awareness class during orientation. Every care must be taken to keep this up to date, as the first impression tends to last through a number of issues presented later.

By the time the class is well established, it will no doubt be handled by a trainer, rather than by you or a member of your staff. To prevent getting too far away from your original meaning, I strongly suggest that you attend the class at least once every six months. Take careful notes as to what is outdated and what needs more emphasis. If something is left out that you think is important, remember to note that, as well.

Later, consolidate your findings in an e-mail to the current teacher of the class and to the person who is maintaining the content. The majority of time, it will be the same person. Make sure to list all of your concerns and recommendations and await a response as to what will be done and when it can be expected.

If you do suggest changes, sit in again once they are in place, to make sure they do what you wanted.

As has been mentioned many times in the past, make sure to keep your knowledge of the industry on the cutting edge. Often, we sight new threats and cures for old ones in the media. The knowledge that comes from this constant check on what is going on in our world, as well as the general one, can be applied in many ways. Most important, the reaction to the news can easily change the way we do business and, consequently, the ways we go about protecting it. Try to stay a step ahead and begin the groundwork on taking the steps needed to effect an environmental change. You look really good when management brings a problem to you and you can demonstrate the steps you have already taken to address it. As the credibility of your program grows, so will the ability to get new tools in a timely manner.

This is another place where conference attendance is vital to gaining new ideas and new ways to handle issues. No matter what else you do while in attendance, you will be in contact with a variety of other practitioners in the field. What with the cross section of industry, government, and utilities that you will encounter, you may well find new ways to deal with issues that are already of concern. I have yet to return from a cross-cultural conference of this type without valuable new ideas and new contacts that will become of value in the future.

In such conference situations make sure to collect cards and information. If you go with certain goals in mind — research tools to address certain concerns, etc. — make sure to grab all of the knowledge and product information you can get. Once you get home, keep that data on file in some manner so that it is easily retrievable if the need is present. You will have taken a long step ahead by having product and vendor contacts and information at the time the subject first comes up within your own company.

As mentioned earlier, there are few better ways to keep up with what is occurring within the technical side of the industry than subscriptions to mailing services like BUGTRAQ and its various faces (NTBUGTRAQ, etc.), SANS, SAFER, and the newsletters published no less than weekly by the various other publications — *Information Security Magazine* and others of that ilk. More often than not, these are in *listbot* formats and postings go out as e-mail to all subscribers. Unfortunately, with only moderation by the board owners, some subject matter turns into arguments that can get pretty heated and lose track of their original subject in the heat of pawing up the ground and staking out their territory. While it can be quite amusing at times, it really is not particularly instructive. Still, the posters to these boards are hard-core techno nuts and geeks and they are, at the very least, tireless in their efforts to find holes in products we all use on a regular basis. If the poster does not list a fix in the original post (they usually do, as that is the best way to demonstrate one's ability), several others are posted in short order.

Never devalue these boards based on the sometimes flakiness of the participants. Many of them are as good as anyone in industry and the weaker ones are usually weeded out by the scorn heaped on them by the elite. To give you an idea of the position these boards hold in the industry: Often, vendors will respond to posts about their products. They will explain in detail why the post is wrong, or will post a fix, freely admitting that the fix was built in response to the original finding of the exposure. I am not talking about seeing those vendor responses six months after the fact, either. They often appear the same day! I am quite certain that a lot of products are enhanced over time through the evaluation and inclusion of items posted on one or more of these boards.

For our purposes, being able to spot potential exposures in such a timely manner can work wonders for our ability to get fixes in place. Under normal circumstances, the area of the weakness is not under our direct control. For this reason it is important to know exactly who to forward the items to facilitate fixes. By the same token, you must forward any fix that is posted as well or at least provide the link. Keep track (TRAQ?) of what you send out and to whom, for purposes of monitoring progress on eliminating the exposure.

The latter practice serves the double purpose of recognizing and fixing holes in products or configurations, but it also provides you with a window to applications groups within your own company. You become the sentinel that warns them of potential danger and they in turn see you as an ally. Not a bad relationship to foster.

Another excellent application for the news you pick up in this manner is fodder for your bulletin or news articles. If the issue has an end user component, you can quote the article in your articles. Again, you are forging and strengthening the bond with that community as well.

Finally, warnings of this nature, coupled with the need to research and purchase a resolving tool can be of great use in funding the purchase of such resolutions. At the very least, it can justify the project should extensive time and effort be involved in securing your environment.

By the time you have been in your position for any length of time, you will have become familiar with many of these informative sources. The "miracle of the Internet" allows rapid dissemination of warnings and upgrades of this nature to the advantage of all. Interestingly, the worst violators of corporate network sanctity tend to be the virus writers. Because of the ability to rapidly deploy information of a threat of this nature, the active life (before a fix is available) of a virus is quite limited. To be sure, it will continue cropping up in isolated cases for the next 40 or so years, but there are certain users out there that are absolutely immune to any warnings you might send out.

The subject of viruses brings up another handy and effective means to keep abreast of new threats. All of the major antivirus vendors have some type of bulletin system by which they notify customers of new viruses found in the wild. Most often, they will include the pattern as an attachment to the e-mail or provide a link from which it can be downloaded. That's the good news. The bad, or at least not so good, news is that someone has to report the virus to them before this can occur. There have been a number of occasions when, they get warning of the new infection only after a high-profile company has been attacked. I can recall times when a really crackerjack virus response team was able to build filters to keep specific viruses out hours before the antivirus vendor had a fix available. This mention is not to denigrate the efforts or performance of the vendor, but to simply state that someone has to report it before a fix can be developed. If you are unlucky enough to be the one, you might suffer greatly in making your contribution to the rest of the world! I have been fortunate enough to have technical staff available to counter these attacks; not everyone is so fortunate.

So, we have spent a good deal of time talking about ad hoc warnings that appear through less than formal sources and their role in helping us keep our awareness program up to date. How can we apply this information to producing some form of positive impact on that program?

I began this chapter with a discussion of the various components of the program and the means necessary to update them. We talked a bit about reviewing documentation against the changes to the environment since the last update and altering our awareness class(es) as needed to reflect shifts in areas of concern. Now, we have this huge input from almost uncontrolled (by conventional means) sources that can place urgent warnings on our doorstep on a daily, possibly hourly, basis. How do we apply this ever-changing, dynamic input to our program?

I have discussed at length how to use your written media to communicate new concerns and new directions that the company must take to protect itself from new threats. We take a single point or direction, expand on it, put it into non-tech format, and publish to our world. Fairly straightforward and effective.

In terms of classroom activity, similar changes in subject matter are made. In this case, a little tweaking, rather than wholesale change, is the usual means of modification.

Now, how do we communicate the other, grand scale and urgent warnings?

Again, going back a number of chapters, I remind you of two particular items. First, there was the interaction with the corporate security folks, to get signs up at every entry of high traffic point with the facility or facilities to warn about current or impending virus activity. By the information security staff writing the copy, there can be an explanation of what the infection will look like and what to do should you see it. Of course, there is that small percentage of the staff that will walk by 10 or 15 of these signs which will, for reasons best known to them, totally escape notice. That phenomenon will protract the situation for several more days. Still, although labor intensive, this is an excellent way to disburse urgent information. The signs are informative and their appearance sends a message of urgency.

Why not use that format to distribute other information as well? If, for instance, a threat against the Internet browser currently installed at the company can cause havoc, if left unchecked, why not use this means to inform the internal public. We do, in this situation, take advantage of both characteristics of the tool — we pass along information, we pass along the sense of urgency.

Of course, as with any emergency activity, we must guard against overuse. An emergency message seen daily becomes daily life, rather than an emergency.

The other tool I mentioned is the information security bulletin. This forum is a great way to get news out, particularly if you have the medium of e-mail to do so. Going back in time, you might remember that I cautioned against having a bulletin type tool become too predictable. I said that you can make some assumptions as to how often you wanted to publish — say, an average of one a month — but not to make it a scheduled event. Well, warnings of this type are the exact material for such bulletin warnings. In these cases, however, you have more time and word space to give a deeper understanding of what is happening and what the reader must do to blunt the attack or seal the hole. Later, in one of your regularly scheduled outlets, you can give even greater detail and discuss the results of your addressing of the issue.

Note: This later, scheduled item is the perfect place to shower kudos on all that were instrumental in resolving the issue. (I do not want to even address the possibility that you failed to address it effectively. Were that the case, someone else might be writing the article!) Make sure that the general audience knows about the folks in programming who built the patch, the people on the mail team that stopped the attached virus, or whoever assisted in stopping whatever. Everyone likes to be appreciated and likes even more that someone acknowledges that appreciation "out loud," as in the printed media. Should a similar problem arise at a later date, you have just ensured the enthusiastic involvement of all mentioned.

By the way, if the performance of the rank and file aided in solving the problem, or if they had to undergo some inconvenience or suffering due to it, thank them, too. As I said, everyone likes to know that they are appreciated.

Save that bulletin for this type of emergency and I believe that you will find it an outstanding tool of alarm.

I have gone quite a distance into this chapter without mentioning one of the top means to keep in touch with how your program is addressing the issues facing the company. This is a means that will not have you searching the Internet for information. It will not have you scouring your vendor lists for contacts and will not require any subscription services. Furthermore, it will not place you in debt to any vendor rep nor force you to canvas your connections for information.

I am, if you have not figured it out by now, talking about the dreaded auditors — the people with whom I showed you how to work just a few chapters ago. I can recall a gentleman I once worked for who hated auditors beyond reason. It was not that he did not like the individuals or their choice in vocations. What he hated was the definition of the audit function, as he saw it. In his mind, the only way an auditor could justify his position was to find something wrong. If there was no material problem in the audited area, then the auditor magnified the importance of smaller findings.

As I also mentioned earlier, I had another colleague who could not even utter the word *auditor,* without preceding it with the acidic adjective "Damned."

Now, are these the people we will voluntarily work with? I respond with a resounding "Yes!"

Auditing must be a wonderful profession. You get to walk into someone else's place of business, set about snooping, and consider pointing out everything they are doing wrong. No one is reviewing your work and you can write up the most innocuous finding as though it put the company at dire risk. You write up the issues, defend them — usually in a most lukewarm fashion — and be on your way to your next victim's digs.

At least, that is the picture that is painted.

I have seen an entirely different protagonist and have identified the good those people can do for me. All it requires on my part is a willingness to work with, rather than against, them.

There is no reason to revisit the definition I gave for the audit interface function that I described earlier as it is well covered in Chapter 20. If you have forgotten, please reread it. What is contained there is important to what we will cover from here onward.

Let us build a scenario in which I will demonstrate how much the auditor can help you in making certain that your awareness program does not lag behind the advancements of technology and the criminal (please excuse the editorializing) element.

First, the auditors send an introductory letter informing you of their intent to audit within your area and defining the specific segments they will be reviewing. Then, if they have not indicated that they will call and when, it is up to you to call them before the engagement begins. In either case, your responsibility is to clearly define the parameters of what they are checking and what they feel that they will need to do the job. Then, upon their arrival and during the entire engagement, you are to stay closer to them than their pet hamsters.

As interim findings are unearthed, there are actions that can be taken to assuage the difficulties potentially caused by the circumstances involved in the respective findings. It is your responsibility to begin formulating means to address each of them while the engagement is still under way. Then, when interim meetings are held with the auditees, you must assist the auditor in weaving those steps into the finding. In short, you will begin addressing the issues before the report is issued and make certain that those steps are included in the final write-up.

How, you may ask, does this help to update the awareness program? Simply, I state, in that the department being audited is involved in putting the remedial action in place and you are discovering the weaknesses noted by the auditor. Their function is to methodically ferret out issues that you really do not have the time or the resources to. Still you benefit, and in more ways than one:

- Through their investigations, you find out the problems involved.
- By getting this early warning, you can begin addressing the issues.
- By the time the report is published, you have a head start on remedial action.
- Your responsiveness is documented, through your much closer working relationship with the auditor.
- The management of the audited area is relieved of some of the pressure of the audit, due to your work with the auditor.
- Your stock goes up with the auditee due to your assistance with the problems noted. This is absolute awareness of what you are doing on behalf of the company, and is as fresh as tomorrow morning's newspaper.
- For those items that need to be addressed, but you do not have the resources to fully resolve, the report will reflect both issues. Remember that this report goes to the board of directors and officers of the company.
- Due to your involvement in the wording of the finding and the identification of the remedial action needed, all of the above noted individuals are aware of what must be done and your involvement in identifying those actions. When you come looking for funding, they will already be aware of the issues.
- Any actions that grow out of the audit findings become fodder for your informative articles, bulletins, Web page, and any other means of communication to which you have access.

I have outlined this relationship pretty simply and have identified how the auditor's work and yours can make the environment better and more secure for the company. What remains unstated, but very important, is that the auditors, particularly of the internal variety, have a sunk interest in getting their comments noted and acted upon. Your work has made that much more feasible than it might have been in a more confrontational contact. Remember that they — particularly the internal auditors — have the same end goals as you. A relationship of this kind helps both of your credibility, allows the company to address and fix issues of importance, and both your and the auditors' brains will be far less damaged from the experience.

Repeated annually, this type of activity ensures a steady stream of looking ahead and communicating needed changes to the troops.

No matter where you learn of new threats and solutions and no matter whether or not they result in action on your part, the communication of this change in the working world to your constituency is important. Whether you need to tweak your orientation class, change policies and procedures, or simply make the general populace aware of an issue, it reinforces your relationship to them and makes them more aware of the issues that are a large part of their work day. It keeps the concept of security in front of them at all times, coming from several directions at varying times. So much so, in fact, that it can appear that your issues are a preoccupation of the company and, therefore, should be theirs. This, my friend, is a good thing.

No matter what steps you take, reflect them against the status quo and verify whether or not that status quo needs to be changed. If so, do it and make certain that the company hears about it, from the executive offices down to the janitor.

Summary

We work in one of the most dynamic professional environments in industry. What with the capability of hardware increasing so fast that you cannot get a new home PC to your house — barring you driving a very fast car — without its being obsolete, staying a step ahead is a daunting task. What was truth yesterday is history tomorrow.

Applications have become larger too, causing what amounts to a race between their becoming more feature filled (and, I might add sloppier in their coding) and hardware becoming faster and demanding of more memory and greater storage to keep up. In essence, we are seeing the expansion that struck the mainframe environment in the early 1970s transposed to the desktop arena. In 1971, 6 meg of "core memory" made a state of the art mainframe computer and a room full of peripherals. Today, that amount of memory would be insignificant in a desktop unit. At this writing, a business computer is usually fitted with 128 meg of memory and that might be changed by the time you are reading these words. The storage that used to take a floor-mounted disk pack now fits inside of the box that is on or next to your desk. Today is way cooler than was yesterday.

As these changes slam into our world, the ways we do business change as well. The bad guys get the new gear as quickly as we do and can build their programs of destruction in as short a time as we build the responses to them. Their directions and means of attack vary and we must not only be watching on all fronts, but also enlisting the assistance of the other employees of the company to do likewise. They are smart and they are interested in doing their part. Our part is to let them know of the risk and how they can help address the resolution.

Our environment is changing in good ways as well. Old equipment is retired — now junked, rather than recycled — and newer machines with far different features and capabilities are brought in to replace them. In that time between their introduction and ultimate demise and trip down the conveyer and out the back door, we have to change our behavior to accommodate these new machines and the applications that will accompany them.

The applications, of course, are being pumped out to meet the demands of the business world that are accelerating at a dizzying rate. New applications hit the streets with huge quantities of code and minimal testing, in order to be first to the marketplace. The other side is aware of the flimsy testing that took place and rips these products apart, seeking out the weaknesses that are certainly there. As they are discovered and, too often, exploited, we are left with the problem of blocking the attacks launched at those weaknesses. By any means possible, we have to find out what is coming — more so than what is here — and take appropriate steps to stop them. All of the bulletin boards, e-mail warnings, and whatever other means we can use to discover these new threats must be put into play and quickly.

In order to do this, we must retest and rethink the measures we have in place daily. We must evaluate our documentation frequently to make sure that it still applies. If modifications are required, they must be made and the public informed as expediently as possible. The things we teach and the way we teach have to be examined and adjusted so that what is important *now* is firmly in place and being communicated.

We are involved in this race on a daily basis and it is up to us to use every means available to make sure that we are doing it as well as it can be done. Whether it is going through a few hundred e-mails daily, making sure to touch base with colleagues, either individually or in groups, or reading all of the trades to gain important input as to the pulse of the environment, it is and will continue to be our problem about how to counteract the attacks from outside and how to make sure that our own employees continue to be allies, rather than the uniformed dupes of the other side.

All through this book we have identified means to inform our user community of whatever items were necessary at any given time. We began training them as they came in the door, so that they would have a foundation of knowledge upon which we could build full awareness in each of their minds. We documented the corporation's expectations of behavior, introduced them to it, made it readily available, and even had them acknowledge that they were aware of these things and understood their own responsibilities.

We made sure that they could find us with phone numbers, e-mail addresses, and a Web page that reflected all of what was going on right now. We continued to reinforce this knowledge through the use of every company news medium that we could locate. Whether it was teaching a class, speaking at new employee orientation, or simply being available to talk to someone with concerns, we made it as easy as possible to learn about information security.

There were special means of communications developed as well. From posters to signs on the door at all entries to warn of urgent issues that we were experiencing at the moment. In the matter of viruses or other high-profile attacks, we provided a response unit that not only helped us solve the problem quickly, but was by itself an advertisement for the concerns of the company and its willingness to throw whatever resources were necessary behind the effort to protect company information assets. In addition, there was the bulletin, brought out in a manner that demonstrated a sense of urgency where one was dictated.

There were always the major components of the program, each designed to perform a function that was under constant scrutiny to make sure that it maintained its desired effect of making the staff aware of the current situation and how they could help and were expected to help. Their roles, although changing as conditions dictated, were always a matter of priority. No one can be expected to know intuitively exactly what they were expected to do and our program made a point of spelling it out in not one, but several ways.

We explored means to take advantage of resources that we could neither afford nor be certain to locate if we could. Special skills in graphics, video, publishing, and even in auditing were cooperatively enlisted to add to the depth and effectiveness of what we are attempting to do. By working hard at these relationships, by offering help as we could, and demonstrating the effectiveness of their contributions to our success, we were able to leverage their specific skills. By remembering to honor their assistance and remembering to say "Thank you," we enlisted their continued help in the foreseeable future.

Most of all, we watched to see what the situations called for. We asked questions, we answered them. We built measures, we measured their effectiveness. We respected the intelligence of average employees and drew their cooperation and assistance in the task of protecting corporate information assets. Most of all, we handed them the tools to do their best. And, if a question arose we were there.

Information security was, in its infancy, the job that was added to someone else's plate. For the first several years of its existence, it was "we have someone working on it" as a response to auditors' questioning. Later, as the need became more apparent and tools were developed to aid in user identification, actual duties were assigned to the position and full-time staffing became a necessity. Later, and only when the rest of information systems became aware that these practitioners were information processing professionals and not "cops," did the profession begin to take on an identity.

Proudly, we can say that we were among the first to acknowledge the need for all employees to be involved in the important practices around securing data and started speaking in language that the rank and file could understand. We were among the first to drop the acronym-filled jargon so often associated with the "computer gurus" and went about enlisting the assistance of those in whose hands the asset we were trying to protect was most often found. To do that, we had to speak the same language they did, while maintaining our ability with "computerese" in order to communicate with our colleagues.

All of what has been written here is in response to the need to communicate with the user community and the need to "sell" the idea of information security to them.

Whether or not you choose to use the measures described here, you must find a way to communicate with those people and to let them know what they are expected to do and what you are doing to help them. What I have prepared here is based on my experience of 23 years and the things that I have learned along the way. My hope is that you will find among them things that you can leverage to make your work easier and more efficient.

Best of luck in all of your future endeavors.

Epilogue

Once I had completed the text of this book, I looked over what I had written and realized the years of training and trial and error that went into putting it together. As one of the old guard of this peculiar section of the industry, I realized that I had experiences that will probably never be duplicated by the practitioners of today. If they are, then we have done a poor job of communicating what we have learned over a few decades. The ground we trod need not be revisited, as we have covered it, stumbled on it and hopefully, found out where most of the potholes are. In retrospect, I certainly did not miss very many of them!

I would certainly be remiss if I did not mention a few colleagues, some of whom I have had the pleasure of working with a great deal, some only once or twice. I am pleased to be able to call Hal Tipton, Donn Parker, and Alan Krull friends and hope they feel the same way. Bob Courtney, a pioneer in the field for so long one would expect him to be wearing a coonskin cap, was a cohort to some extent some years ago. Tom Peltier, I know you're not sitting down, but you certainly have proven that you measure a man from the eyebrows up. I learned from Bill Murray, Rich Koenig, Jerry Lobel, and more than I could ever record here. If I missed someone whose feelings are hurt, you have every right to call and castigate me and I will offer my humblest apologies.

The point is that these are the folks that first broke the trail for what we do now. Much of what I have written here is based on what I learned from them and what we learned together. We were there first and we did, I hope, leave tracks marking the trail.

In the last chapter, I spoke of our group — the information security professionals — being among the first to realize that we had to talk with the user community on their level, in order to accomplish what needed to be done. We never had enough staff — still do not — to do everything that needed to be done and no one will ever have enough staff to watch over every member of the company payroll. Therefore, we are left with finding a means to get that group of people around to our way of thinking and to get them to practice safe computing.

I have often said that for someone to do what we do, you have to have a masochist's taste for stress and disappointment. For those of you who have heard me speak (and enjoyed it, I hope), you know that I have a little story about the role of information security professionals. They are to the information processing industry what proctologists are to the medical field. I say this for three reasons:

1. No one wants to come to see you in the first place.
2. Although when you are doing your best work, and they definitely know you are there, they cannot see you.
3. Even though they know you are helping them, you are still a large pain where sunburn is rarely an issue!

All of us can identify readily with that definition and probably as well with the lighthearted spirit in which it is rendered. We know what our lot in life is, but feel strongly that the work we do needs to be done. And, to all of our credit, we have taken the discipline out of the shadow world and inserted it directly in the spotlight. Even the mainstream media now pay attention to our activities and those of our antagonists. They have identified with us as the last bastion of hope to keep some sense of order in the information processing world.

As certainly as we have gained a degree of notice among our peers, vendors have rushed in with new tools and completely new releases of old ones. We are not just a blip at the periphery of the radar screen anymore, but a solid presence that needs to be accommodated and dealt with. Of course, "dealing with" usually represents products and services that might be of some assistance and some that are no more than frosting. Still, as with other such offerings, the good ones stand the test of time and are improved at a rate of growth almost equivalent to that of the tools the bad guys use.

I had occasion a few years ago to sit in the lobby of a popular resort within which a major professional conference was taking place. With me, and enjoying a morning cup as was I, was Hal Tipton. It was interesting that the two of us, in the time-honored tradition of the professional, were both wearing slacks and sport coats. In deference to the climate and the relatively informal surroundings, we were both wearing sport shirts, rather than a dress shirt and tie. Still, we were, by a substantial amount, the most formally attired individuals wearing the credential of the event. We watched and commented (and if you know Hal, his comments were both astute and hilarious) on the changing scene, not just here, but in the professions as well.

Back around 1990, I wrote a piece for a periodical on the changing images of the industry and of the ISO that I expected to see in the coming decade. Luck was with me in terms of guessing where the industry was going, but I seem to have missed on the image of the ISO. Certainly, the chance was there and a number of people rose to the occasion. Still, many more did not.

My premise was that far too many of us were identifying too strongly with our backgrounds as techies and were still viewed as bit-fiddling geeks by too many in senior management. The exact phrase I used in describing what we should be doing was to "take our leads more from the board room than the computer room." It was a direct statement that what we were doing required a professional manager, someone with a knowledge of the business, with the support of the aforementioned geeks. Rather than being one of the bit heads, we needed to be recognized as managers.

Those that heeded those words (or came up with the idea on their own) have gone right where it was predicted; the others are still insulated from management.

I think that both of us were impressed by the sheer weight of numbers of those attending as compared to the few hundred that attended the scant number of such events that typified our early years in the industry. I suspect that some of those we saw were more worried about crayons than computers when we were attending those get-togethers.

Still, despite the longevity in the field, Hal and many of the others I mentioned earlier have kept up with the technology and its exponential growth, not just to stay employed, but because it was so exciting to have these new ways to do what we did with little or nothing so many years back. Heck, to us, this was fun, not work!

While this might be a bit rambling, I feel that this closing forum is mine to discuss what I have written and the background from which it came. Believe me, a lot of what you have (I hope) read, comes from these relationships and the experiences of the years in the business.

One of the interesting things about breaking new ground is that you really can only estimate what you might find or find out. If no one has been there before, there is no history to fall back on. When I first started in this field, that was pretty much the conditions we found. There were a few of us around. John O'Mara up in Northborough, Massachusetts, saw a need for some means for the few professionals in the field as well as those charged with the responsibility as a part-time undertaking to get together to mull over common problems and potential means to alleviate them. That was nearly 30 years ago and as anyone around the discipline knows, the Computer Security Institute is the bellwether organization in the field.

Of course, there are a number of other organizations in the field today, many excellent, many pretty good, many too new to really evaluate. The simple fact is that that are enough of us now to create a valid marketplace for many of the items I discussed throughout the text. Old line companies like Commonwealth Films out of Boston are making slick videos on many aspects of our field today. They started out with 16mm. films a very long time ago. Like us, they have grown with the trade.

I can recall my first awareness efforts at a large credit card company many years ago. The first few steps were to write articles for the company newspapers. At that time, the employee newsletter was hungry enough for copy that it pretty much printed whatever I had to offer. That was when I first made the observation that people had to find what you wrote entertaining, or they simply skimmed over it. As a long time Mark Twain fan, I found that his writing style of outrageous overstatement fit me just fine and I use it to this day. If you think you recognize his style in any point in this book, I am humbly proud.

Later on, when we started up our own bulletin, something I covered in detail earlier, I made my first logo from a batch of clip art of unknown origin. As I recall, we used the old style skeleton key, an ornate padlock and a line drawing of an old style dumb terminal, along with gothic lettering to build our first masthead. It was gratifying when I started seeing them around the company, pinned to cubicle walls, as a reminder about the content. We were definitely reaching someone.

Later, when the realization that security was enough of an issue on its own that it could not be fully covered in normal departmental documentation, we started writing these things from the floor up. The first efforts were using whatever format other company procedures were in and simply preparing rules and regulations in that manner. Usually, they were added into general manuals and were no doubt left to molder as many of the paper versions are today.

As time passed, the importance of policies, standards, and procedures became apparent to most and we began producing far more detailed and inclusive manuals. Tom Peltier, whom I mentioned earlier, wrote two fine books on the subject, on each of which I was privileged to be involved. Charles Cresson Wood also prepared an excellent manual, with the added electronic tools that by now had become available.

If you got no other ideas from this book, remember this one thing: **Policy, standards, and procedures are the absolute baseline for the success of any program.** Build on sand and a collapse is guaranteed.

The one thing that no one ever wrote a decent book on was how to get the news out to the rank and file. For some strange reason, it was assumed that a manual, tucked away on a shelf and coupled with some type of log-on ID qualification and distribution, a violation-tracking software package and someone to use them were the only things needed. People would pick these things up by osmosis, wouldn't they? I think the result of that thinking is obvious.

Today, what with trying to protect an environment that might spread worldwide over several networks and jump among platforms like a frog touring lily pads, the need for awareness on all levels is greater than ever.

By the same token, that ability to spread information far and wide over closely connected but totally dissimilar platforms, to bridge between different networks, and to talk to virtually anyone in the world can be used for our purposes, as well as the less righteous purposes of the guys in the black hats. Why not leverage the same technology for our training? It has to be better than the stand-alone manual as it could not be any worse. That thing was a waste of paper, printing costs, and space without really giving you any payback at all.

Note: We have spoken about the isolated information security manual a number of times and I really do not think I have been particularly positive about it. To prove my point, I will offer you this challenge:

- First, find out if there is such a manual. If you stop at less than ten different people when asking around, you are making a half-hearted effort and we won't count it as really trying. If you ask 20 or more, in different areas, and make sure that they have been around awhile, I will consider it a good effort. You may be surprised that something will surface. If you fail to find it, the game is over and I win.
- Second, if you find a manual, check the last date of the update — most likely initial publication — and see if it is three years ago or less.
- Third, see if you can find out who wrote and issued it. If they are still around, locate that person and go to the fourth item.
- Four, ask them if they know who has the most current issue of the volume. This should be the final stopper in the scheme of things.

Thus is the plight of printed manuals that are not a part of an overall program.

I know the above note is a bit harsh, but, unfortunately, it is right about 95 percent of the time. No manual, old manual, lost at sea manual.

My point is that we can use the same tools as industry and the bad guys use, and use it to our advantage. Still, as with the book, it has to be an intrinsic component of the overall program. That is what we have been trying to sell here.

Another point I have tried to make throughout the book is that it is necessary to become an expert on experts. Learn where the knowledge and skills lie and recruit their efforts into your program. As with the parable of one hand washing the other, you need to be a good partner as well, but doing so is to your advantage. There is nothing wrong with accumulating owed favors for the future. Just don't let your stack get too big without paying off in return.

Ultimately, the goal is to be nice to people. We, in this discipline, have been viewed as the cops since we first became separated from the regular line programmers. That has stuck with us, no matter the professional accolades we have earned.

Perhaps one of my favorite stories is about a lady I dated for a bit a few years back. Of course, we had discussed what both of us did for a living (I was at that time information security manager for a multistate bank holding company), and she had apparently communicated that to her 13-year-old, computer whiz son. When he and I met for the first time, the conversation went quickly to computers. He wondered why I knew so much about them. You see, based on her explanation, and his interpretation of that description, he figured that I was a security guard in a bank! I assured him that the difference in my paycheck and the security guard's was how I could afford to take his mom out.

Now, to be sure, we spend an ample amount of our time tracking down careless — if not evil — folks every day, but our tools and our training are pretty technical. But, if we are to dispel the image of the cop, we need to become faces and responsibilities to the troops at large. They need to know what we do and why we do it and, most important, what they must do and why. This is the central theme of any information security awareness program.

What I have attempted to do in the 22 chapters that preceded this was to put forth a methodology for building a program. That methodology was something that I have contrived over nearly 23 years in this business. The components of it have grown from trial and error and the efforts to take advantage of everything available to me. It was the old "run out of ammunition, use the bayonet. Lose the bayonet, start throwing rocks!" syndrome. Whatever it took, whatever was available.

Needless to say that by the time contemporary tools, such as the Web and e-mail common to every desktop, became available, we knew very well the type of applications we would have for them. Heck, these were ideas that had matured over years and now we had a chance to broadcast them as never before. We were kind of like the streetcar diner, waiting for someone to invent tracks!

As mentioned, these ideas came from trial and error and were the best ways to approach the problems we faced at the time. Are they the only answers? Of course not. Are they the best answers for the particular circumstances? Boy, I sure hope so!

The point is that they are a jumping-off point. Were you to emulate what I have described exactly, you would have an effective and operable information security awareness program. Would the program be the best it could be? Therein lies a real question. My gut feeling is to say "No." No out-of-the-box solution can possibly fit every situation perfectly. What I expect you to do with what you learned here is to use each point as a place to start. If it fits, go ahead and use it. If it seems to fit, take another look and see if you can make adjustments for a more perfect fit. My instincts tell me that you might well be able to do just that.

What we have is a sturdy skeleton, not a filled-out body. Or, in the examples cited, the body might have been quite robust. Your task is to apply new musculature where it is needed or replace parts that are not equal to your needs.

If there is one byword that fits what we are trying to do it is *flexibility*. Consistently, throughout this book, I have tried to demonstrate how to leverage conditions that exist in the *now* time frame to drive home a point. If a specific virus is virulent enough to make the papers and newscasts, there is probably a bulletin or some form of attention-grabber that can be synthesized from it. Never allow your classes to become so rigid as not to be able to adjust to stressing different aspects of the overall program or absorb a point about a risk that is facing us at the moment. When you can bracket a virus warning around something people have read in the papers or seen on TV, you have entered their world of reality. With this addition, you have drawn them into the news stories they have seen. And if you think about it, you have leveraged the newscasts and stories to use in your program, just as we have stressed throughout. All you have to add is the link between the abstract of national news and your audience. It is for this reason that I strongly recommend maintaining a good review of the national and international news. You should be looking at two or three national papers daily, a not too difficult thing with online editions, as well as subject-based technical media.

This book is not the Gospel According to Mark; it is a framework for building and a catalyst for your own contributions to the overall knowledge database of our entire faction of the industry. Perhaps, in a few years, you will be relating your experiences in this same media, relating what you have done in expanding what you have read. That being the case, I have succeeded in my mission.

You may well decide that what you have read is of little use to you and that is not altogether negative. What we have done in that instance is defined a delimiter, a place where you now know that you do not wish to go. That being the case, you have the knowledge as to what directions you do not wish to explore, a success in its own right.

Rather than continue this segment until it starts sounding like a diatribe, I want to end with a few thoughts about what we have done and what we hope to do. Consistently, I have directed the attention of this volume to the people, rather than the burgeoning technical aspects, of the business. I do this for a single reason, something that you must never forget if you are to be successful in your undertakings: Information security is a people issue, not a technical one. While we apply technical tools to its resolutions, we cannot lose sight of the fact that what we do and say must be directed toward getting the staff on board. They must understand what the threat is, they must understand the threat's potential impact on the company, and they must understand their role in protecting those information assets. We must relate the success of the company to the success of each of its employees, and we must do it in a manner that fosters loyalty and effort on the parts of our listeners.

Ultimately, our role in informing is not that different from that of the teachers we had back in school. They informed, they coddled, and they identified what the knowledge they were imparting would do for us in later life. What we are doing is not that much different, albeit on a much narrower and higher plane.

Way back in the earlier portions of this book I identified the concept of corporate culture as a grossly overworked and overstated aspect of the way a business runs. I have not changed that viewpoint. However, if we can foster a culture of all personnel looking out for the best interests of the company, even in our little corner of the world, then we have created an informal culture of teamwork and common goals. While this will never be a stated goal of the spinners that crow about corporate culture, this will be an integral component of assisting the growth of the company and making it more successful.

Those of us who have chosen to get into the information security business have not, as a general rule, striven for recognition or the conditional "Attaboys" that are so often the stuff of which departmental meetings are built. To be sure, we like to be recognized for doing our jobs well, but seeing something work correctly is often reward unto itself.

In the final analysis, what we want to do is create an environment where all parties to the function are working in concert for the common good. What we can do is to create an environment where that is possible and where no one is prevented from doing their job — the level of responsibility that we have described — by a lack of tools or a lack of knowledge. Our biggest single concern is to provide that knowledge and to make sure that the tools are available. In reality, we are linking the end user to management by our ability to, first, demonstrate to management that specific tools and attitudes are necessary to provide reasonable security and, second, to provide the employee base with an understandable view of the problem and their roles in resolving it. When we are able to tell them and then put the tools in their hands, performance is the only logical result.

I hope that I have provided you with the tools to perform this function as well as it can be done.

About the Author

Mark B. Desman (the "B" included for a more formal mien and represents an abomination of a middle name thrust upon an unwary child by doting parents) has worked in the fields of information systems security and business resumption planning for more than 25 years. In that time, the entire field of IS has evolved from a glass room, mainframe-oriented industry into the networked, server-based, desktop phenomenon we see today. As a practitioner in the field during that metamorphosis, he has had a strong role in building, rebuilding, and refining an overall information security program for each of a number of major corporations, including American Express, Del Monte Foods, Financial Corporation of American, Tandem (now HP) Computer, The Banknorth Group, and Micron Technology. In addition, he has consulted in both fields and, due to his approach of believing that information has to be presented in an interesting format to be accepted, has had innumerable speaking and teaching engagements.

Throughout his career, Mr. Desman has found himself "breaking trail" finding answers to challenges that perhaps never existed before — for the industry in general. Many of the techniques he has developed, particularly in the business continuation and communications fields, are now part and parcel of generally accepted practices in both disciplines. As he is quick to add, many of the main merits in his contributions is in their being the original answer to the question, rather than the result of high impact technology.

Among other things, Mr. Desman discovered early on that the basis for any program is in a complete set of policies and procedures. Where his approach diverged from the mainstream was with the notion that the populace in general ought to be made aware of this body of irrefutable knowledge, and once they have found themselves knee deep in it, they should be able to understand it. These two characteristics, and the explanations as to how to put documentation in this form, are the main thrust of this book. Perhaps most important is the notion he holds that information security is a people issue, rather than a technical one. To be sure, we use technical tools to resolve the problem areas, but we must rely on the knowledge and cooperation of the people involved for any program to be successful.

Mr. Desman also co-authored the manual, *Business Resumption Planning* (Auerbach Publications) and has published articles in numerous periodicals and journals. From all indications, his muse is still active and will no doubt present the world with additional publications as time goes by.

Index